THE ART OF
COOKING

PREPARING AND PRESENTING FINE FOOD

HPBooks

THE ART OF
COOKING

PREPARING AND PRESENTING FINE FOOD

Publisher	Rick Bailey
Executive Editor	Randy Summerlin
Editorial Director	Elaine R. Woodard
Editor	Retha M. Davis
Art Director	Don Burton
Book Assembly	Leslie Sinclair
Production Coordinator	Cindy Coatsworth
Typography	Michelle Carter
Director of Manufacturing	Anthony B. Narducci
Photography	Arnold Zabert
Recipe Testing & Copy prepared by International Cookbook Services	Barbara Bloch, President Rita Barrett, Director of Testing

ANOTHER BEST-SELLING VOLUME FROM HPBooks®

Published by HPBooks
A Division of HPBooks, Inc.
P.O. Box 5367, Tucson AZ 85703 602/888-2150
ISBN 0-89586-376-6
Library of Congress Catalog Card Number 86-81350
© 1986 HPBooks, Inc. Printed in the U.S.A.
1st Printing

Originally published as Kochen: Die neue grobe Schule
© 1984 Verlag
Zabert Sandmann GmbH
Hamburg

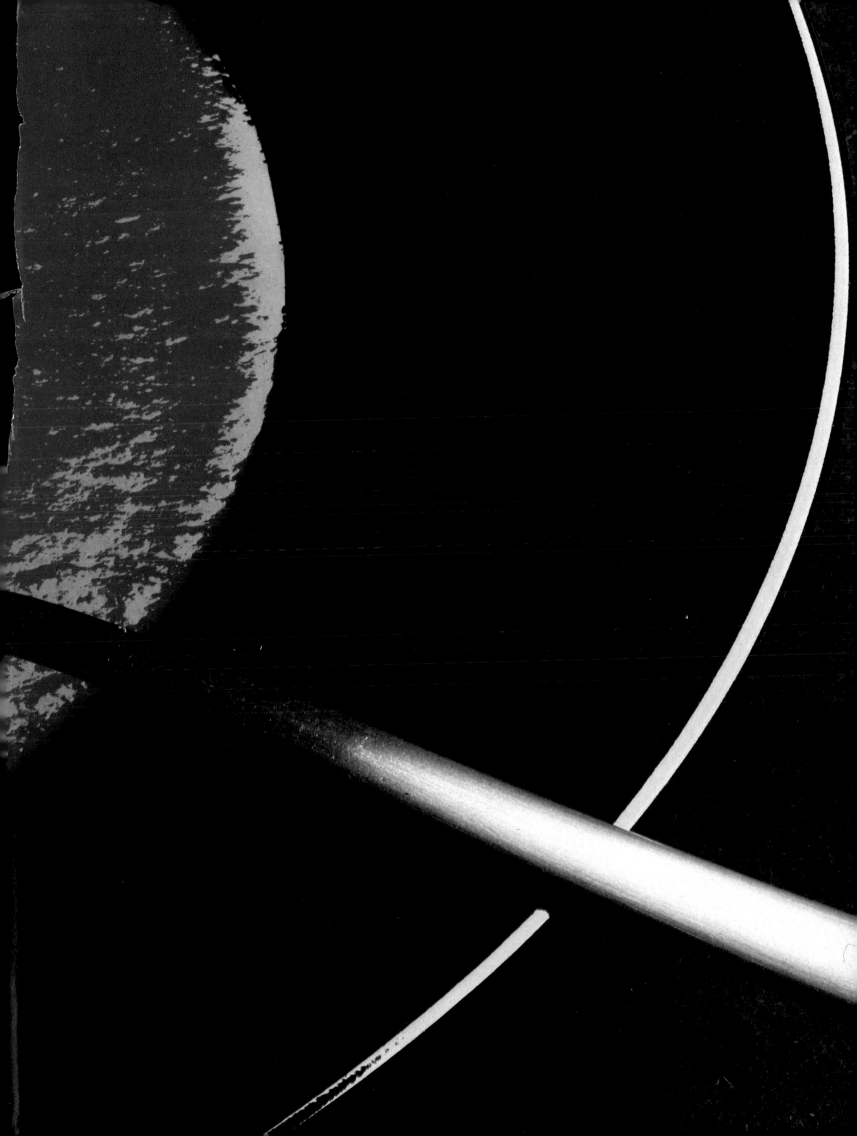

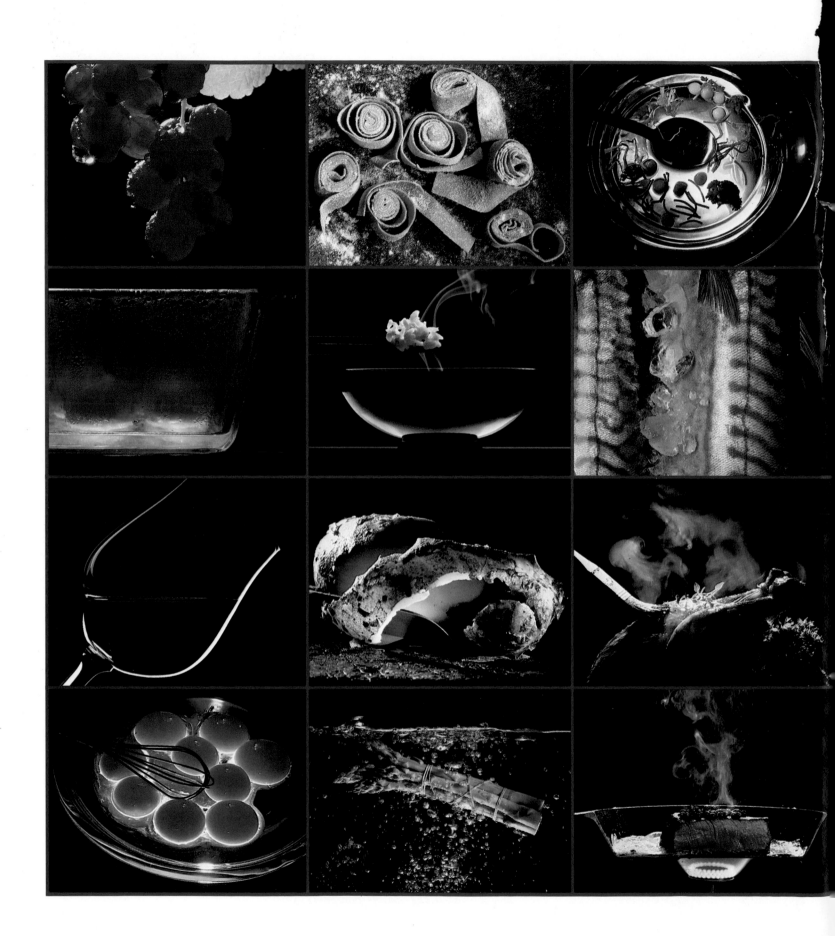

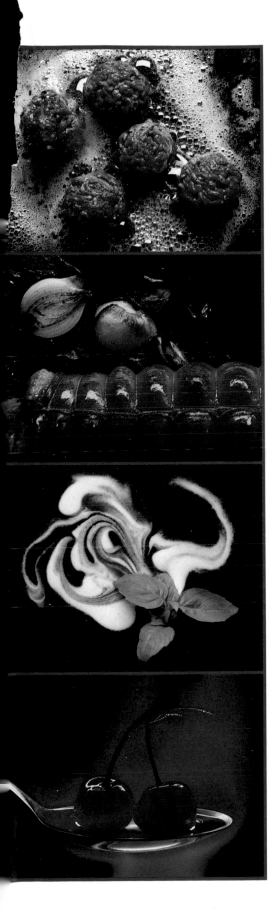

CONTENTS

Why This
Book Was Written

An interesting change in cooking has gradually been taking place in recent years. New awareness of nutritional requirements, concern for health and diet, foreign travel, increasing affluence, a zest for living—all have contributed to the development of a new school of cooking. As a result, many cooks have begun to adopt new attitudes toward food and drink and to the way in which they prepare food.

This new cuisine has grown in popularity as its basic principle of fresh food, cooked quickly and served attractively, has become better understood. Increased availability of all fruits and vegetables, the ever-widening variety of frozen food, together with the growth of ethnic food sections in supermarkets and specialty food stores around the country, all point to changes in taste as well as a growing familiarity with food from all corners of the world.

It is our hope that this book will provide a modern, useful, and innovative guide for a new generation of cooking enthusiasts, as well as for those who have been cooking for many years.

How This Book Works

Our purpose in writing this book is to provide basic cooking information; show ways to build on these basics; and encourage new cooks, interest experienced cooks and persuade everyone to experiment in the kitchen.

Our approach is to provide a well-illustrated book with a wealth of color photographs. Photographs are accompanied by precise text for basic recipes and filled with ideas for an endless number of new recipes, all geared to help you cook systematically and easily.

Each chapter, from eggs to dessert, begins with basic recipes. We build, in gradual stages, from the basic recipes. Every important cooking method is illustrated by photo-graphs, every variation is explained. And best of all, you can start cooking at every stage! This is our systematic cooking method, a building-block technique. You can combine the information in each chapter with the recipes in other chapters to create an endless variety of dishes—the very essence of creative cooking.

In addition to basic cooking information and recipes, there are hints about food preparation, suggestions about drinks and advice on table settings. There is even information on how to equip a new kitchen and how to plan a menu. Our goal is to provide all the basic information necessary to simplify cooking and make it a pleasure.

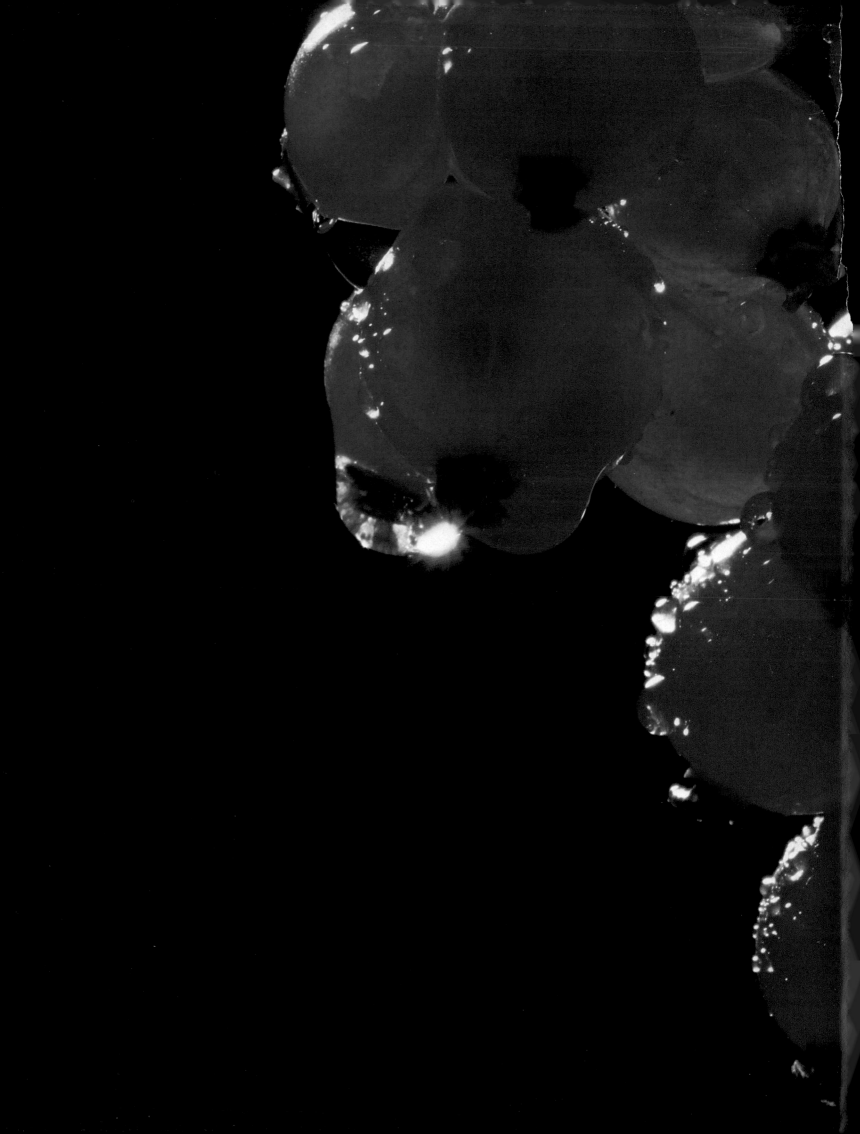

Marketing: The First Step, Made Easy

Compared to 50 years ago, or even 10, today's shoppers have an almost unbelievable selection of foods to choose from. Supermarkets have added whole sections of imported and exotic foods. There are also specialty food sections in department stores and small stores that sell an ever-widening variety of foods. Gourmet food stores, health food stores and ethnic food stores can be found in many parts of the country. Food shopping, as we know it today, would have seemed like a fairy tale to our great-grandparents. Airplanes along with modern freezing and refrigeration techniques have made it possible to buy almost anything you want—at almost any time of year. But availability is not the only issue. It is important to learn how to buy top-quality food at reasonable prices so good cooking is an affordable pleasure.

A Whole World of Spices

The history of spices reads like a story from the Arabian Nights. Efforts to obtain spices caused wars, made countries and merchants wealthy, and supported smugglers and dishonest customs officials in grand style. However, this unfortunate state of affairs was not confined to the Far East where these new scents and flavors originated. Even in 19th century Austria, salt mines were forbidden territory, accessible only to those who had a "salt pass" because this white mineral was so valuable to the Kaiser.

Tips:

● Store spices in tightly covered containers in a cool, dark, easily accessible place.
● The flavors of spices are reduced through long storage. Buy small quantities and use within about six months.
● When possible, buy whole spices; then grind just before using. Freshly ground spices have the best flavor.
● Use spices sparingly. Spices should never overpower the natural flavor of food; they should enhance it. You can always add additional seasoning.
● When adding whole spices to a recipe, tie them in a cheesecloth bag for easy removal before serving.
● Be careful not to burn, scorch or overcook spices. Some of them become bitter when subjected to high heat or overcooking.
● When a recipe is increased, do not automatically increase spices in the same proportion you increase other ingredients. Instead, season to taste to avoid overseasoning.

Paprika
Made from pods of dried sweet red capsicums or peppers. Sold ground. Flavor ranges from mild to very hot. Imported and domestic available. Used on fish, meat, poultry, eggs, in sauces and as a garnish or coloring.

Juniper Berries
Aromatic berries from an evergreen tree. Bitter, slightly resinous flavor. Used in stuffing and with game and gin.

Cinnamon
Dried bark of cinnamon tree. Sold ground or in sticks. Used in baking, pickling, puddings, drinks and with cooked fruit, vegetables and meat.

Cloves
Unopened, dried bud of an evergreen tree. Available whole and ground. Whole cloves used to stud ham, beef and onions. Ground cloves used in baking, casseroles, vegetables, desserts and sauces.

Ginger
Root of a perennial plant. Often used in Oriental cooking. Fresh root available whole or candied. Dried ginger available whole or ground. Whole ginger used in syrup, pickling, marinades and drinks. Ground ginger used in baking, main dishes, vegetables and desserts. Candied or crystallized ginger used in baking and desserts.

Bay Leaf
Dried leaf of laurel bush. Must be removed after cooking. *Poisonous if eaten!* Used in stock, pickling, poaching, marinades, boiled main dishes and stews.

Saffron
Dried stigma of saffron crocus. Slightly bitter. Available as threads or ground. Crush or dissolve in hot water. Used in risotto, paella, bouillabaisse, sauces, bread and some desserts.

Curry Powder
A blend of spices which can include allspice, cardamom, fennel, mace, chili powder, cinnamon, cloves, coriander, cumin, fenugreek, ginger, nutmeg, cayenne pepper and turmeric. This Indian seasoning ranges from mild to hot. Used with meat, fish, poultry, rice, vegetables and in sauces.

Nutmeg
Aromatic dried seed of an evergreen tree from which the spice mace also comes. Available whole or ground. Used in main dishes, vegetables, soup, sauces and desserts.

Caraway Seed
Brown seeds of biennial plant Carum carvi. Crushed to make oil or liqueur. Used in bread, pastry, cheese, with potatoes and in main dishes.

Pepper
Berries of a climbing tropical vine. Black, white, red and green available whole, ground or pickled (green). Used in savory dishes.

Cayenne
Ground from small dried capsicums or chili peppers. Sometimes called *red pepper*. Very hot. Used in Mexican and Creole dishes and in casseroles, rice, sauces and with seafood.

Using Wine in Cooking

One of the easiest and nicest ways to add that "special touch" to almost any dish is to add wine. Many rather ordinary dishes, such as Cheese Fondue, Coq au Vin or Boeuf Bourguignonne, have become classics as a result of the addition of wine. For many cooks, a touch of wine is as important as any other ingredient used for seasoning.

Probably the most important rule to follow when using wine as a seasoning agent is to remember that wine that is not good enough to drink will do nothing to enhance the flavor of any dish. This means you should not use the cooking wine sold in most supermarkets because salt has been added and there is nothing to recommend its flavor. On the other hand, it is not necessary to use expensive wine in cooking because, when combined with other ingredients, some of the subtlety of its flavor is lost.

Since the flavor of red wine is stronger than white, it should not be used with food that has a delicate flavor. It will overpower the dish. Red wine is used in dark sauces and with food that has a strong flavor. It will add color as well as flavor to the dish. White wine is used in light sauces and with delicately flavored food. All wine used in cooking should be dry rather than sweet, unless it is going to be used in a sweet dish.

Tips:
● The alcohol in wine will evaporate at about 40 degrees below the boiling point of water, leaving behind flavor and aroma, but none of the alcohol.
● Wine has a tenderizing effect on meat and can be used very effectively in a marinade.
● When a strong flavor of wine is desirable, add it just before serving.
● Recork leftover wine, then store on its side in the refrigerator. It will keep about one week.
● Keep a bottle of dry vermouth on hand in the pantry. It will keep almost indefinitely after it has been opened. Vermouth can be substituted for white wine in almost any recipe.
● Sherry and brandy can be kept on hand after opening and used to dress up a dish at any time.

Seasoning with Herbs

If you have a nose for it, sometimes it is possible to identify certain areas, or even countries, by the special aroma of the herbs used. While some elegant Parisian cooking has the delightful smell of tarragon, Provence is famous for the combined aromas of thyme, lavender and garlic. Roman cooks use lots of sage and Northern Italian cooks use basil. Many English foods have the sweet smell of mint. Scandinavia is dill country. And in Germany, parsley is treated almost as a national plant. All these wonderful aromas can be found throughout America, the great melting pot. You will find some fresh herbs and most herbs dried in your supermarket. If you are adventurous, you can grow herbs in the garden or on a window sill and be assured of a good supply whenever you want them.

Tips:
- Use fresh herbs whenever possible. The flavor and aroma of fresh herbs are superior to dried herbs.
- To store fresh herbs, wrap in a damp cloth or paper towel or place stems in fresh water and store in refrigerator.
- Fresh herbs can be preserved by drying or freezing at home. Some can be preserved in vinegar. A few herbs are sold frozen.
- To substitute dried herbs for fresh, reduce amount to one-third.
- Store dried herbs in airtight containers, away from heat. Buy in small quantities and use within about six months.
- Reconstitute dried herbs by a brief soaking in a small amount of liquid or heating in butter over low heat.
- As with spices, when a recipe is increased, do not automatically increase herbs in the same proportion as other ingredients. Season to taste.
- Use herbs to enhance the flavor of food, not to overpower it.
- Fresh parsley is a beautiful and almost universal garnish. But other fresh herbs can be used just as successfully. Use the same herb to garnish that you have used to season a dish.

Chervil
Slightly licorice flavor. Relative of parsley. Often included in fines herbes combination. Used frequently in French cooking, egg dishes, creamed soup and sauces, and with meat and fish.

Rosemary
Strong resinous flavor. Use sparingly. Member of mint family. Used in marinades, in combination with wine, and with pork, lamb and poultry.

Thyme
Several varieties available, all with delicate flavor. Used in stuffing, with meat, poultry, fish, rabbit and in sauces.

Tarragon
Licorice flavor. Can be preserved in vinegar. Essential ingredient of Béarnaise Sauce. Also used with poultry, fish, meat, eggs and vegetable dishes.

Marjoram
Sweet, spicy, Mediterranean flavor. Perennial herb of mint family. Frequently found in Italian dishes. Often used with tomatoes and in stews, eggs, meat, fish, poultry, casseroles and marinades.

Parsley
The all time favorite herb for seasoning and garnishing. Member of celery family. Flavorful stems used in stocks and bouquet garni. Leaves used to flavor any savory dish.

Dill

Another relative of parsley with delicate but spicy flavor. Use as seeds or dry leaves. Turns bitter when subjected to high heat. Used with dairy sour cream, fish and vegetables. Also used in pickling.

Lovage

Bitter-sweet, celery-like flavor. Use sparingly with meat and in soups, stews, casseroles and salads.

Basil

Member of mint family, available in several varieties. Popular in Italy. Has special affinity for tomatoes and is essential ingredient in Pesto Sauce.

Sage

Sharp, slightly bitter herb related to mint. Available whole, rubbed or ground. Should be used sparingly. Used in stuffing, sausages and with vegetables, meat, fish and poultry. Also in some breads.

Chives

Most delicate flavor in onion family. Rarely cooked. Used raw with dairy sour cream, cheese, eggs, salad, soup and vegetables.

Winter Savory

Spicy, peppery flavor, less delicate than Summer Savory. Used with dried and fresh beans, rice, meat, fish and in stuffing and salad.

Seasoning with the Onion Family

Members of the onion family are unquestionably a primary seasoning in every kind of dish except desserts. These popular relatives of the lily include onions, garlic, shallots, green onions or scallions, chives and leeks. They are included in the cuisine of every country.

Onions, yellow, red and white, come in various strengths from mild and sweet to strong and pungent. They range in size from tiny to very large. Buying onions by name can be very confusing because there are yellow Bermuda onions, also called Spanish onions; large red Spanish onions, also called Bermudas; and smaller red Italian onions, often called Bermudas. Every food encyclopedia has a different set of names for onions, and incorrect signs in supermarkets simply add to the confusion.

The strongest member of the onion family is garlic, which is not only excellent for flavoring, but something of a philosophy of life. Friends and enemies of this highly flavored bulb remain irreconcilable. But those who dislike garlic are surely to be pitied because they are missing an exceptional culinary experience.

To remove the smell of either onion or garlic from your hands, rub them with lemon juice, vinegar or salt. Use a very sharp, non-carbon knife for cutting onion or garlic. Also cook them over medium heat to prevent burning. Both onions and garlic have a very bitter flavor when burned.

The most noble member of the onion family is the shallot. It is often used instead of onions in elegant French cooking. Shallots have a very subtle flavor that goes well with wine, butter or cream.

Green onions, also known as scallions or spring onions, are small and delicate in flavor. Both the bulb and green portion are used raw or cooked.

Chives are a popular herb. Leeks, often used in soups and stews, are growing in popularity in America as a vegetable.

The Ancient Art of Preserving & Storing Food

In the so called "good old days," it was absolutely vital for cooks to master the art of food preservation. Although we still use some of the old methods to preserve food, we also have modern methods to help us preserve and store food so it will be fresh and safe to eat.

Drying Herbs
Tie fresh herbs in bunches and hang them in a cool, well-ventilated place. When they are thoroughly dried, remove the stems, if desired. Then store them in airtight containers.

Freezing
Place food in airtight containers, leaving room for expansion, or wrap food in moisture-proof, vapor-proof freezer paper. Seal, label and date packages.

Vacuum Packaging
If you have the proper equipment, you can vacuum pack food at home. Store the food in the pantry, refrigerator or freezer, depending on the type of food and how soon you plan to use it.

Tins or Cans
Baked products, such as cookies and fruit cakes, keep well in tins or cans. These tins also make fine gift containers. When properly packed, they can be used to mail baked products. Add a piece of white bread to absorb excess moisture and keep cookies and crackers fresh. Replace bread every few days.

Preserving in Oil
Herbs and garlic can be preserved in an oil-filled airtight container. Use a

neutral-flavored vegetable oil. Store in a cool place.

Plastic Wrap
Wrap food with plastic wrap before placing in the refrigerator. This will keep food from drying out and from absorbing odors of other food.

Damp Cloth
Some herbs and vegetables can be wrapped in a damp cloth or paper towel and placed in the refrigerator to keep them fresh. Place the wrapped food in a plastic bag to help keep the cloth damp.

Growing Herbs
When possible, buy herbs growing in flower pots. Place the pots in the sun and water them regularly. Herbs will continue to grow and be available to use.

Cheese Bell
Unwrap cheese and place it under a cheese bell about one hour before you are ready to serve the cheese. This will allow the cheese to come to room temperature, but will prevent the cheese from drying out.

Foil
Foil can be used to wrap or cover almost any food. Use a drug-store wrap whenever possible to keep out moisture. Foil will help retain the temperature of wrapped food for a short period of time and therefore is excellent to use when food must be transported.

Jars
A tall thin jar can be used to store spaghetti. Jars in other shapes can be used to store various kinds of pasta and cereal. The cork makes an airtight seal that keeps out moisture and unwelcome bugs.

Cooking
Basics

The purpose of this chapter is to provide information about cooking equipment, preparation of food for cooking and basic cooking technique. Although experienced cooks may own a wide variety of specialized cooking equipment, it is not necessary to invest a fortune in special tools to become an accomplished cook. What is necessary is to have good-quality basic equipment to prepare food properly. It is also necessary to learn how to prepare food properly for cooking and to understand the basic techniques of cooking, from heating delicate food in a double boiler to cooking a roast to the desired degree of doneness. Once you have assembled the correct tools and understand the basics of cooking, there is almost no limit to what you can accomplish in the kitchen. add a good recipe, a little bit of practice, some imagination and the courage to experiment. You will be amazed at how soon you'll be cooking with confidence!

Equipment

The most important rule for buying cooking equipment is to buy the best. Equipment such as measuring cups and spoons, vital to a properly functioning kitchen, are inexpensive to begin with. But other equipment, if bought cheaply, will ultimately prove to be a poor investment. Lightweight pans that do not sit evenly on a burner will cause food to cook unevenly and burn. Inexpensive knives that cannot be kept sharp will tear rather than cut food. They can also be dangerous to use. On the other hand, heavy, well-made pans and properly tempered knives will last a lifetime and longer. Because they will never have to be replaced, they will prove less costly in the long run than poorly made equipment that must be replaced constantly. Some of the basic equipment necessary to get started is shown here.

Equipment Shown in Photo

1. Skillets: Available in many sizes, made of stainless steel, cast iron, aluminum, lined copper and with non-stick coated interiors. Skillets should be thick and heavy, have flat bottoms and heatproof handles, and conduct heat evenly. Covers are available for most skillets and should be tight fitting. A well-equipped kitchen should have skillets in at least two sizes.

2. Skimmers: Use to skim fat from surface of cooking liquid.

3. Ladles: Use to serve soup and transfer liquid from one container to another.

4. Double boiler: Bottom of double boiler can also be used as a saucepan. When insert is added, pan becomes double boiler. Water is placed in bottom pan and food is placed in insert or upper pan.

5. Liquid measuring cup: Use to measure volume of liquid. Available in many cup sizes. DO NOT USE to measure dry ingredients. Dry measuring cups, #19, provide a more accurate measurement.

6. Rubber spatula: Use to scrape food from sides of bowls or to scrape food out of bowls or pans. Also used to fold ingredients together. Available in many sizes with wooden or plastic handles.

7. Pastry brush: Use to glaze pie crusts and bread, for basting, to spread glazes and grease pans. Available in many sizes. Avoid inexpensive brushes that tend to lose hair easily.

8. Wooden spoons: Available in many sizes. Use spoons with long handles to stir hot liquid in large pots.

9. Whisk or wire whip: Use to beat egg whites and whipping cream, to make egg-based sauces, to combine liquid ingredients and to blend roux.

10. Mesh strainer or sieve: Use as a colander to drain food or for such chores as sifting powdered sugar. Available in many sizes from fine to coarse mesh.

11. Dish towel: Use to dry dishes, cover food, wrap food and as a very large pot holder.

12. Paring or decorator's knife: Use to peel vegetables and fruit and to make tomato or radish roses and other garnishes.

13. Chopping or chef's knife: Use to chop all types of food. Chop in a rocking motion without lifting knife from wooden chopping board.

14. Utility or carving knife: Use to slice food and carve meat and poultry.

15. Long flexible spatula: Use to spread frostings and to lift or turn food.

16. Meat thermometer: Use to check internal temperature of meat or poultry to determine if food is cooked to desired doneness. Insert into center or thickest part of meat away from bone or fat.

17. Chopping board: Wood is the best and most serviceable surface for chopping, however it requires special care for cleaning. Hard plastics will damage knives. Some softer plastics are available which minimize knife damage and provide a very sanitary cutting surface.

18. Measuring spoons: Use to measure dry and liquid ingredients. A standard set contains 4 spoons: 1/4 teaspoon, 1/2 teaspoon, 1 teaspoon and 1 tablespoon.

19. Dry measuring cups: Use to measure dry ingredients by spooning ingredient into cup and leveling off top with blunt side of a knife. A standard set contains 4 cups: 1/4 cup, 1/3 cup, 1/2 cup and 1 cup. Also available in 1/8 cup and 2 cup sizes.

20. Sauté pan: Available in many sizes. Should have wide flat bottom with sloping sides and be made of heavy gauge metal that will conduct heat evenly. Some pans are available with covers.

21. Glass mixing bowls: Use to mix or store food. Can be used to cook food in microwave oven. Available in many sizes and in sets.

22. Dutch oven or large covered saucepan: Use to cook food, such as stew, pot roast, soup and pasta. Can be used in oven only if it has heatproof handles.

Helpful Cooking Tools

A fully automatic kitchen with everything controlled by a computer is still a thing of the future—thank goodness! It is doubtful if cooking will still be a creative adventure if this ever really happens. Nevertheless, we already have many wonderful, efficient, modern appliances that simplify a wide range of cooking chores and make it possible to prepare dishes at home that used to be too time-consuming. In addition, there are some old-fashioned kitchen tools, perfected over the centuries, that are still available and are a welcome and helpful addition in any kitchen.

1. Small adjustable slicer from Italy, designed to slice truffles, but can also be used to shave chocolate, or slice cheese or mushrooms.
2. Flat combination grater, shredder and slicer
3. Egg slicer for hard-cooked eggs
4. Nut cracker
5. Garlic press
6. Mortar and pestle, one of the earliest implements designed to crush food. Use it to crush nuts, spices or garlic.
7. Pepper mill
8. Star-shaped rosette form from rosette iron. Used with handle to deep-fry pastry batter.
9. Mezzaluna for fine chopping in a wooden bowl or on a chopping board.
10. Cherry and plum pitter, lightweight and easy to use. Will also pit olives.
11. Citrus juicer
12. Fine strainer
13. Ice-cream scoop
14. Meat grinder
15. Fluted biscuit cutters in three sizes.
16. Egg sectioner for hard-cooked eggs.
17. Fluted pastry wheel
18. Small fine grater
19. Kitchen shears
20. Cheese scraper or gouger for use with hard cheese.

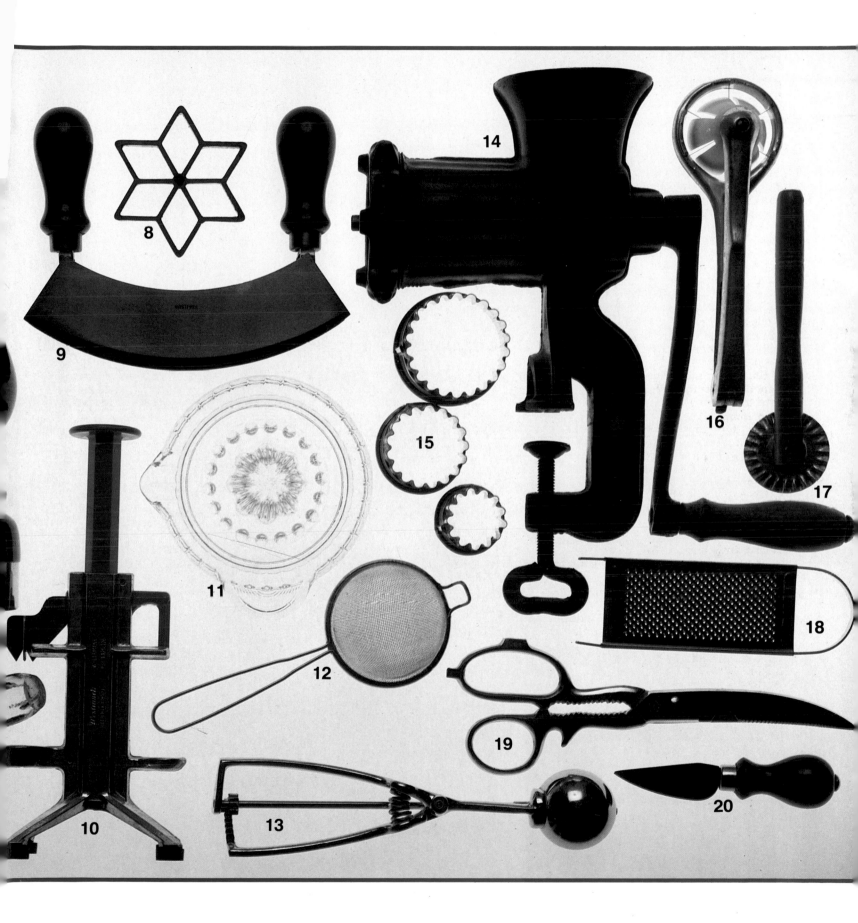

Special Cutting Tools

Some cutting tools used by professionals are familiar to everyone. But some of them are designed for very specific tasks and are less familiar. Every indentation, every curve and every hole in a specialized tool has a particular function. By using these special tools, you can cut food quickly and easily in many different and attractive ways; everyone will think you spent hours in the kitchen, even though you didn't. With the exception of knives, these tools are very inexpensive and take up little space.

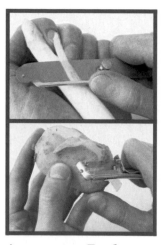

Asparagus Peeler

Not everyone feels it is necessary to peel asparagus. It depends on how tender the stalks are. If you want to peel asparagus, this tool will do the job very well.

Vegetable Peeler

European model with a short blade to remove eyes of a potato.

Paring Knife & Peeling Knife

Use a paring knife or chef's knife to chop onions. Cut onion in half through root, leaving root attached. Place onion, cut-side down, on a work surface; cut onion in three directions without cutting through root, as shown above.

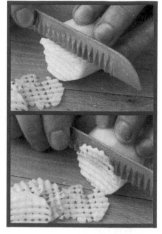

Decorator's Knife

Works best with firm, raw vegetables. Can also be used to make a decorative edge or waffle-cut on uncooked homemade pasta or dough. Place peeled vegetable, such as a potato, on a work surface; make a 1/4-inch slice crosswise. Discard first slice, if desired. Turn potato half way and make a 1/4-inch slice. Turn again and make next slice.

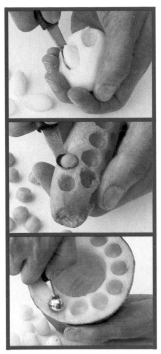

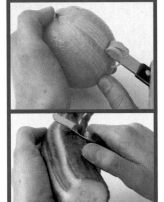

Apple Corer

Push through center of apple from top to within about 1/4 inch of bottom. Pull back out with core. Apple will retain shape and can be filled for baking.

Melon Baller

Available in several sizes. Use to make attractive shapes with fruit or vegetables; to scoop out centers of food, such as cherry tomatoes or small potatoes; or to make small balls of ground meat or other mixtures, such as nougat.

Zester

Used to remove zest or peel from citrus fruit. Zest can be used in strips or finely chopped.

Combination Zester & Peeler

Use to peel citrus fruit or decoratively peel vegetables, such as cucumbers.

How to Buy & Care for Knives

1. Knives must be well made, which means they will be expensive. Poorly made knives cannot be sharpened properly and will not do the job they are designed for.

2. Buy carbon-steel or stainless-steel knives that are perfectly balanced, have a comfortable handle and a finger guard. They should have either several rivets to attach the top end of the blade or tang to the handle or a molded polypropylene handle.

3. Choose the proper knife for a specific function: small knives for paring; larger knives for chopping, cubing and dicing; serrated knives for cutting bread or tomatoes; thin-bladed knives for boning; long knives to slice meat.

4. Store knives in a well-designed knife holder. Don't store knives loose in a drawer because they will become damaged. Don't hang knives on a small magnetic knife holder because they will fall off if even slightly greasy or if they are large and heavy.

5. Sharpen knives regularly. A dull knife will tear rather than cut food.

6. Wash and dry knives promptly. Carbon-steel knives will rust if not dried immediately. Don't put knives in a sink of soapy water because you may cut yourself when you reach into the water. Don't put wooden-handled knives in a dishwasher. The heat in the dishwasher will adversely affect the tempering of the blade and the soaking cycle will destroy the handle.

7. The best cutting surfaces will not damage the blade of a knife. Two excellent choices are a wooden board or a polyethylene board used by many professionals. Hard surfaces, such as laminate countertops, marble, tile or ceramic will chip and dull blades.

Helpful Cooking Techniques

Many simple, easy, but necessary techniques used to prepare food for cooking are second nature to experienced cooks. However, these procedures are often unfamiliar to new cooks. The tips given on these pages will save time in the kitchen and simplify many cooking chores.

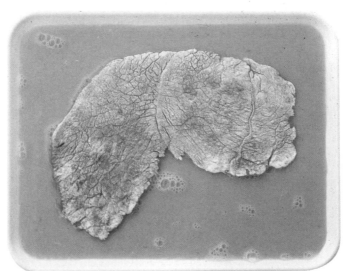

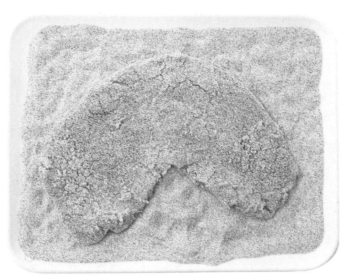

Breading

1. Dip thinly pounded veal cutlets, chicken cutlets or fish fillets in flour. Shake off excess.
2. Dip in beaten egg to which a few drops of vegetable oil have been added. Lift with tongs to drain off excess egg.
3. Press gently into seasoned dry bread crumbs. Place on waxed paper; refrigerate 30 minutes to set coating.

Tying

Kitchen string has many unexpected uses. Tie asparagus in bundles before cooking. It will make it easy to remove asparagus from pan when cooked.
Tie a slice of lemon to the bottom of an artichoke to prevent discoloration.

Preparing Tomatoes

1. Make an X with a sharp knife in skin on bottom of a tomato.
2. Plunge tomato into a saucepan of boiling water about 30 seconds.
3. Remove from saucepan; rinse under cold running water.
4. Peel off skin.
5. Cut tomato in half; remove seeds if desired.
6. Cut tomato into strips or dice.

Seeding a Cucumber

Cut cucumber in half lengthwise; scrape out seeds with a teaspoon or grapefruit spoon.

Mincing Garlic

Peel garlic; place on a lightly salted cutting surface. Cut into small pieces; then mince with a very sharp knife. Salt will prevent garlic from sliding around.

Pounding Meat

Cover thin slices of boned meat with plastic wrap; pound with the flat side of a heavy knife or meat mallet.

Spiked Onion

To season soup or stock, insert a bay leaf and whole cloves in a peeled onion. This will make it easy to remove bay leaf and cloves when cooking is finished.

Trimming Meat

Use a sharp boning knife to trim excess fat from meat.

Crushed Ice

To prepare a base of crushed ice or make crushed ice for drinks, wrap ice cubes in a dish towel; then crush ice with hammer.

Straining

Press fruit or vegetable purees through a fine strainer to remove seeds.

The Art of Cutting Fruits & Vegetables

The way food looks is almost as important as the way food tastes. To the Japanese, the look of food is of paramount importance. They have perfected the art of food presentation well beyond that of most cultures. But even without striving for the same degree of perfection as the Japanese, you can enhance the look of the food you serve by learning the many ways in which food can be cut. Use some of the tools shown on the preceding pages, make sure your knives are very sharp and use photographs of food and your imagination as a guide. But remember, the way in which food is cut can affect the cooking method because small pieces of food cook more quickly than large pieces of food.

Cutting in Strips

Cut potatoes into thick slices; then cut into thick strips ready to French-fry. Vegetables such as red peppers, beets, leeks, celery, green peppers or carrots can be cut into even, matchstick strips and cooked or used raw in salads. Cut lettuce into ribbons; then make a base of lettuce to arrange other foods on.

Cubing & Dicing

Food can be cut into cubes or diamonds of various sizes or it can also be finely diced. Shown above are cubes of eggplant, zucchini, kohlrabi and beets; potatoes cut into diamonds; and diced carrots. Foods cut this way can be used in soups, stews, salads or as a garnish.

Slicing

Slicing is the simplest way to cut food. But, as you can see above, not all slices look the same. Food can be thinly or thickly sliced before or after cooking. The shape of sliced food can be changed by the direction in which it is sliced. The cooking method or the way you plan to serve food should determine the way you slice it. Cucumber, potatoes, mushrooms, carrots and eggplant are shown above.

Paring

Use a small, sharp paring knife to cut vegetables into even, attractive shapes. Cut in desired lengths, then make about six lengthwise cuts around vegetables to shape. Ends can be pointed, rounded or flat. Vegetables cut into even sizes will cook evenly, particularly in a microwave oven. Shown above are cucumbers, carrots, potatoes and kohlrabi.

Balls

Use different size or shape melon ballers to cut fruit and vegetables. Use fruit balls in fruit salads or fruit cups, punches or desserts. Cook vegetable balls in soup or stew, or serve raw as a salad or garnish. Shown above are melon, zucchini, potato, carrot and apple balls. To make carrot balls, use thick carrots and a sharp cutter. Sprinkle apple balls with lemon juice to prevent discoloration.

Grating or Shredding

Graters are made with different size holes. Small holes are used for fine grating and large holes for coarse grating. Coarsely grate potatoes to make potato pancakes. Finely grate carrots, apples or radishes for salad.

Waffle Cutting

Use a decorator's knife to slice or cut vegetables in thick strips, large cubes or diamond shapes. To make Potato Gaufrettes, page 117, deep-fry slices in hot oil until golden brown; then drain on paper towels. Add salt, if desired. Serve hot.

Garnishing: The Final Touch

A touch of paprika or a sprinkle of freshly chopped parsley can go a long way toward making food look elegant and appetizing. Many cooks automatically add this kind of simple garnish to their everyday cooking. When time permits or company is coming, there are many other ways to decorate a finished dish. And, you don't have to take a course in food decorating to learn how. You can use simple ingredients, like lemons, onions or radishes, and add special eye-appeal to almost any dish.

25 Garnishing Ideas

1. Peel, halve and thinly slice cucumber. Arrange slices overlapping around platter.

2. Use twists of lime to garnish fish or poultry. Lemons and oranges can also be cut into twists.

3. Cut a cherry tomato in half and scoop out center. Pipe herb butter into tomato half; garnish with parsley. Serve with broiled meat, fish or poultry.

4. Use a spiral cutter to cut small white turnips into spirals. Open spirals to make garland.

5. Slice red onion down from top through root; use as a garnish with a flowering herb.

6. Thinly slice carrots; then use miniature aspic cutters to make carrot flowers.

7. Slice leeks; then pull apart into rings for an attractive garnish.

8. Use a paring knife or zigzag cutter to make four cuts through center of lemon in spoke fashion. Cut lemon in half. Decorate with radish sprouts.

9. Cut lemon in half. Use lemon peeler to make a strip of lemon peel, but leave peel attached to lemon at one end. Curl or knot peel on side of lemon.

10. To make a tomato rose, start at top of a medium tomato and thinly peel off skin in one continuous strip. Coil strip; place on a platter with a leaf of Italian parsley.

11. Thinly slice lemon; then cut slices into triangles.

12. Using a small sharp knife, cut small petals around outside of radish. Cut a second series of petals inside first set. Place radish in iced water to open.

13. Red peppers and celery can be cut into diamond shapes; then arrange on a platter to look like a flower.

14. Finely grate carrot; then arrange on a plate with green herbs.

15. Use mint leaves or red peppercorns to add color to many dishes.

16. Cut vegetables, such as carrots or kohlrabi, with a melon baller. Cook briefly in lightly salted water until fork-tender. Season with butter and salt. Serve as a side dish in hollowed out kohlrabi half with a sprig of chervil.

17. Pipe mashed potatoes around a platter of sliced meat.

18. Cut thin slices of carrot into unusual designs with aspic cutters.

19. Use onion rings and sprigs of lemon balm to dress up a main dish.

20. Pipe herb butter onto thin slices of lemon; garnish with parsley.

21. Use butter paddles to shape butter into balls; then roll balls in paprika or finely chopped parsley.

22. Thinly slice cucumber; cut slices with a scalloped-edged cutter. Sprinkle slices with finely chopped parsley.

23. To flute a mushroom, hold mushroom firmly in left hand, if you are right handed. Place tip of sharp paring knife at center on top of mushroom. Draw knife down toward edge of mushroom while gently rotating mushroom counterclockwise. Point of knife will make a curved, shallow groove. Make a new groove 1/8 inch behind first groove and remove sliver. Repeat at regular intervals around mushroom. If mushrooms will not be cooked, immerse in water with a little lemon juice to keep them from discoloring.

24. Cut lemons into wedges; use to garnish fish, veal, or poultry.

25. Slice small gherkins lengthwise, leaving gherkin attached at one end. Spread in a fan shape.

Cooking with Liquid

All food is cooked by either dry or moist heat. When a liquid is used to cook food, the method is moist-heat cooking. There are many ways a liquid can be used to heat food, directly or indirectly. The liquid used most often is water, particularly when the heat generated by the liquid provides indirect heat, such as when food is steamed or cooked in a double boiler. When food is placed directly in a liquid, the liquid can be water, plain or flavored, or it might be stock or wine or a combination of liquids. It is important to remember that liquid evaporates as it boils and is therefore reduced or, if cooked long enough, eliminated entirely. Therefore, most of the time, food should be covered when cooked by moist heat in order to retain as much moisture as possible inside the pan. When food is cooked in a liquid for a long period of time, it is important to check periodically to determine if it is necessary to add additional liquid to replace liquid that will have evaporated during cooking. Depending on the method used, food cooked by moist heat can be cooked gently or rapidly by high heat. Different foods require different cooking methods.

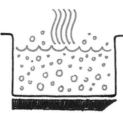

Boil

Liquid is heated until large bubbles rise and break on the surface. Boiling point of water at sea level is 212F (100C). Once liquid reaches the boiling point, it never gets any hotter, no matter how hard the liquid boils. When a recipe calls for a fast rolling boil, it is not to increase heat, but rather to make certain the liquid has reached 212F (100C). When a fast rolling boil is maintained, the liquid will evaporate and be reduced. Liquid is usually brought to a full boil over high heat, then the heat is reduced just enough to maintain the boiling point. It is important to use a pan large enough to accommodate boiling water because it can boil over, particularly when the pan is covered. Food that should be cooked gently or slowly should not be cooked in fast boiling liquid.

Blanch

To blanch or parboil, plunge food briefly into boiling water. Use to
● loosen skin on fruit.
● set color and flavor in fruit or vegetables before preserving.
● retard enzyme action before preserving.
● remove excess salt from foods, such as salt pork or bacon.

Simmer

Liquid is heated until tiny bubbles break gently on the surface between 135F (55C) and 160F (70C). Medium heat is used to maintain a simmer. Simmering is a gentle cooking method used to cook delicate food as well as to tenderize some kinds of food. Food that is simmered many be cooked covered or uncovered. When food is covered, it is important to adjust heat carefully in order to maintain a simmer and not allow liquid to come to a full boil.

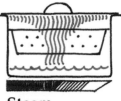

Steam

Food is cooked in a perforated container placed in a deep, tightly covered pan over, not in, boiling water. Steam circulates gently around the food to cook it. This cooking method minimizes color and nutrient loss.

Pressure Cooker

To cook food with a small amount of liquid in a special strong, heavy, airtight pot called a *pressure cooker*. The cover of the pot has a valve over which a weight is placed. Pressure is built up in the pot when it is placed over high heat. The pressure produces steam that cooks food very quickly.

Stew

To simmer food slowly in a heavy covered pot in liquid for a long period of time until food is tender. Some recipes call for a small amount of liquid, some require that food be covered with liquid. Frequent stirring is often recommended in order to prevent food from sticking to the bottom of the pot during cooking, and care must be taken to be sure the required amount of liquid is maintained during cooking. Liquid will be reduced and will thicken as the food cooks and, in some recipes, the reduced liquid can be used as a sauce or gravy for the finished dish.

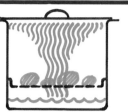

Double Boiler

A special cooking utensil that consists of two saucepans or a saucepan and special bowl, with one saucepan or the bowl fitting into the bottom pan. The bottom pan is partially filled with simmering water and the top pan or bowl is placed over, not in, the simmering water. Food is placed in the top utensil. This provides a method to cook food gently by indirect heat. Food can also be kept warm, covered or uncovered, in the top part of a double boiler.

Steep

To cover food with a hot or cold liquid and let it stand to soften food, intensify flavor or reconstitute dried food.

Poach.

To cook gently in a small amount of simmering liquid.

Reduce

To cook liquid, uncovered, over high heat, boiling, to reduce and thicken the liquid and intensify flavor.

Bain-marie

Similar to a double boiler, left. Main difference is that the top pan sits in, not over, simmering water, providing a water jacket for the top pan or bowl.

Water Bath

A term used primarily in canning. Jars of food are placed in a rack inside a large pan. Enough boiling water is poured into the large pan to cover the jars. The pan is covered and the filled jars are cooked the recommended amount of time with the water boiling.

Cooking in Fat or Oil and Braising, Flambéing and Smoking

When food is not cooked in liquid, broiled or cooked in the oven, it often is cooked in fat or oil over relatively high heat. The amount of fat or oil used can be anything from the relatively small amount necessary to sauté food to the larger amount necessary to deep-fry food. Both the temperature of the fat or oil and the type used are important. When the cooking temperature is too low, food will not brown. If the cooking temperature is too hot, the fat or oil will smoke and the food will burn. Fats do not all reach their smoking point at the same temperature. Unclarified butter burns easily but vegetable oils and olive oil have a high smoking point and can be used alone or combined with butter for frying at high temperatures.

Fry
Whole pieces of food, such as steak, chops or eggs, are cooked uncovered in a skillet in a small amount of fat or oil. This is a direct-heat method of cooking over high or medium-high heat. Food is cooked until browned and usually turned over and cooked until browned on the second side. This method of cooking is sometimes called *pan-broiling* or *pan-frying* and the effect is similar to that achieved when food is broiled in the oven or cooked over an open grill.

Sauté
Similar to frying. Food is usually cut into small pieces and cooked uncovered over high heat in a small amount of fat or oil. Food is tossed lightly or stirred frequently during cooking and sometimes must be drained on paper towels after cooking to remove excess fat.

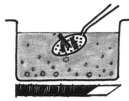

Deep-fry
A large amount of oil is heated to a specific temperature in a deep, heavy saucepan or deep-fryer. Small pieces of food are lowered directly into hot oil or placed in a basket that is lowered into the oil. Food is cooked until browned, then drained on paper towels. The important things to remember when deep-frying are to cook food in small batches and to make sure oil is kept at the correct temperature. A deep-fat thermometer and electric pan are helpful in controlling the temperature of the oil. If the food that has been cooked does not have a strong odor or flavor, it is possible to strain the oil and store it in the refrigerator for use at another time. Sometimes mild odor or flavor can be removed from oil by frying raw-potato slices in the used oil. If the oil develops even a slightly rancid odor, discard it immediately.

Braise

This cooking method is a combination of cooking in fat or oil and then cooking in liquid. Food, usually meat, is browned in a small amount of fat or oil to seal in juices and provide good color to the meat. Grease should be removed from the pan and the food is then covered and cooked gently in liquid until tender. For those who are anxious to eliminate as much grease as possible from their cooking, food can be browned in the oven instead of in fat or oil and then cooked in liquid.

Flambé

To pour warm liquor or liqueur, such as brandy, over cooked food and ignite it. Food must be free of any other liquid and be in a pan or flameproof dish. This is an impressive and elegant way to serve crepe or a special cut of meat. The alcohol will burn off, but the flavor will remain. Be sure to use a long match and extreme caution. Drafts or unusually long hair can create very serious problems.

Smoke

A technique used to cure certain kinds of meat, fish or poultry. Most smoking is done commercially. However, smokers are sold for home use and are used with special kinds of wood to provide unusual flavor to the smoked food. If you are interested in smoking food at home, you will need to purchase a smoker and follow the manufacturer's instructions carefully. You may also have to contend with friends and neighbors who will probably be standing in line waiting for a chance to sample your smoked food.

Frizzle

To fry food until crisp and curled.

Render

To cook solid fat, such as chicken fat, until fat has turned to liquid. Fat thus rendered can be used for cooking and will add special flavor to cooked food.

Sear

To brown the surface of meat quickly by intense heat.

Stir-fry

To cook small pieces of food in a small amount of hot fat or oil over very intense heat, usually in a wok. Food is cooked very quickly and must be stirred constantly during cooking.

Cooking in the Oven

There was a time when the only kind of oven found in the home was a standard gas or electric oven with a broiling unit that cooked food by radiant heat. Times have changed dramatically and many homes also now have a microwave oven, a convection oven or an oven that can do more than one kind of cooking, such as a combination micro-convection oven, micro-radiant oven or radiant-convection oven. Microwave ovens and convection ovens are not substitutes for radiant ovens, but rather additional aids to new kinds of cooking.

Broil

Food is placed in a broiler pan and cooked by direct heat to desired doneness. When cooked by this method, the food is placed below the source of heat. Food can also be placed on a grill and cooked in the same way with the source of heat below the food. In both cases, food is usually turned halfway through cooking in order to cook it on both sides. This is a dry-heat method of cooking. When meat is cooked this way, it should not be salted before cooking because salt will draw juice to the surface of the meat and dry it out. When very lean food is cooked in a broiler or on a grill, it is advisable to grease the cooking surface before food is added to keep it from sticking. Alternatively, food can be brushed lightly with fat or oil.

Roast

Meat or poultry are placed on a rack in a shallow roasting pan and cooked, uncovered, in a preheated oven to desired doneness. This is a dry heat method of cooking that will not tenderize meat and is usually reserved for food that does not require slow, moist cooking to tenderize it. Food often requires basting with pan juices or additional fat or liquid during cooking to keep the food from drying out. When poultry is cooked by this method, a coloring agent, such as paprika, is often sprinkled over the poultry for color and flavor enhancement. Occasionally a foil tent is placed over poultry for part of the cooking time to keep the skin from browning too much. Food cooked by this method will continue to cook after it has been removed from the oven and therefore should be cooked to about 10 degrees below desired doneness. Both meat and poultry should be allowed to stand out of the oven after roasting to allow the meat to "set" before carving.

Casserole Cooking

A combination of cooked or uncooked foods are combined in a heatproof dish, often with a sauce, and baked in a preheated oven. Casserole cooking can provide the cook with an opportunity to be imaginative in the development of new food combinations. Casseroles can be made ahead of time, frozen and reheated in the oven when needed. Occasionally cooked casseroles are placed under the broiler briefly to brown the top of the food. Casseroles can be cooked covered or uncovered, depending on whether or not it is necessary to retain moisture inside the dish.

Convection Oven

A convection oven differs from a radiant oven because there is a fan in the back of the oven that circulates the hot air. Professional bakers use convection ovens for baking. Food is cooked at a slightly lower temperature and in a somewhat shorter time than in a radiant oven. Convection heat is not a satisfactory method for heating food placed in a large deep casserole because the circulating hot air does not reach the center of the food.

Bake

Baking is the term used primarily for cooking such food as cakes, pies, cookies, breads, muffins, biscuits, vegetables or puddings. Food is placed in the center of a preheated oven and cooked at a specified temperature. It is important to place the pan in the center, away from the sides of the oven, to allow hot air to circulate freely around the food. When food such as cake or bread is baked, it must be cooked in the size pan given in a recipe. Since baking often involves a chemical formula, an arbitrary change in pan size can dramatically alter the cooking time and the result can be total disaster. The temperature at which food is cooked is also important and poor results may be due to inaccurate oven temperature. Ovens must be calibrated periodically in order to be accurate. Use an oven thermometer to be sure you are baking at the correct temperature. If your oven temperature is off, adjust the temperature following the reading on your oven thermometer.

Water Jacket

A small pan filled with food is placed in a larger pan. Enough boiling water is poured into the larger pan to come halfway up the sides of the smaller pan. Both pans are usually placed in the oven to cook. The water surrounding the small pan keeps the food moist during cooking.

Combination Ovens

Micro-convection ovens, micro-radiant ovens and convection-radiant ovens each cook in three ways. Micro-convection ovens, for example, can be used as a microwave oven, a convection oven or as an oven that cooks by both methods when programmed properly. These ovens offer cooks many advantages. A roast cooked in a microwave oven will not be as brown and juicy as a roast cooked in a radiant or convection oven, but it will cook very quickly. A roast cooked by the combination of microwaves and radiant or convection heat can be cooked quickly and will also be moist and beautifully browned.

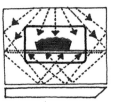

Microwave

Food and utensils respond to microwaves differently than they respond to radiant heat. Microwave cooking is a moist heat cooking method, and the time necessary to cook food depends on three things: the temperature, volume and density of food. For example, it takes the same amount of time to bake one potato or ten in a radiant oven, but in a microwave oven, each time you add a potato, you must increase the cooking time. Since the wattage of microwave ovens vary, cooking times will vary from oven to oven. Therefore it is important to follow manufacturer's instructions and to adjust all microwave recipes to the wattage of your particular oven. Microwaves cook from the outer edge of the food in toward the center. This means food should be arranged with the thickest part at the outer edge of the dish or stirred occasionally. Since food cooks very quickly in a microwave oven, it is important to undercook food and check frequently in order to avoid overcooking. Most food cooked in a microwave oven is covered in order to retain moisture in the dish and speed cooking as well as to prevent food from splattering inside the oven.

Combination Cooking

The more you use a microwave oven, the more you discover a microwave oven is not a substitute for a traditional radiant oven, rather an addition to it. As you understand what a microwave oven does well and what it does not do at all, or do satisfactorily, the more you can learn to use it in combination with traditional cooking methods. For example, you cannot broil chicken in a microwave oven. But you can still reduce the time necessary to broil or barbecue chicken by placing a split or cut-up chicken in the microwave oven; cover it with waxed paper and cook it at full power about 12 minutes. Then transfer the chicken to the broiler or grill and finish cooking it in very little time. This will reduce the amount of time necessary to broil chicken and produce chicken with moist tender meat and crisp skin. You can also bake a potato in a microwave oven in about 4 minutes and transfer it to a radiant oven for a few minutes to crisp the skin. There are many ways in which food can be partially cooked in a microwave oven to save time and then finished on top of the range or in a radiant oven. Use combination cooking to take full advantage of your microwave oven.

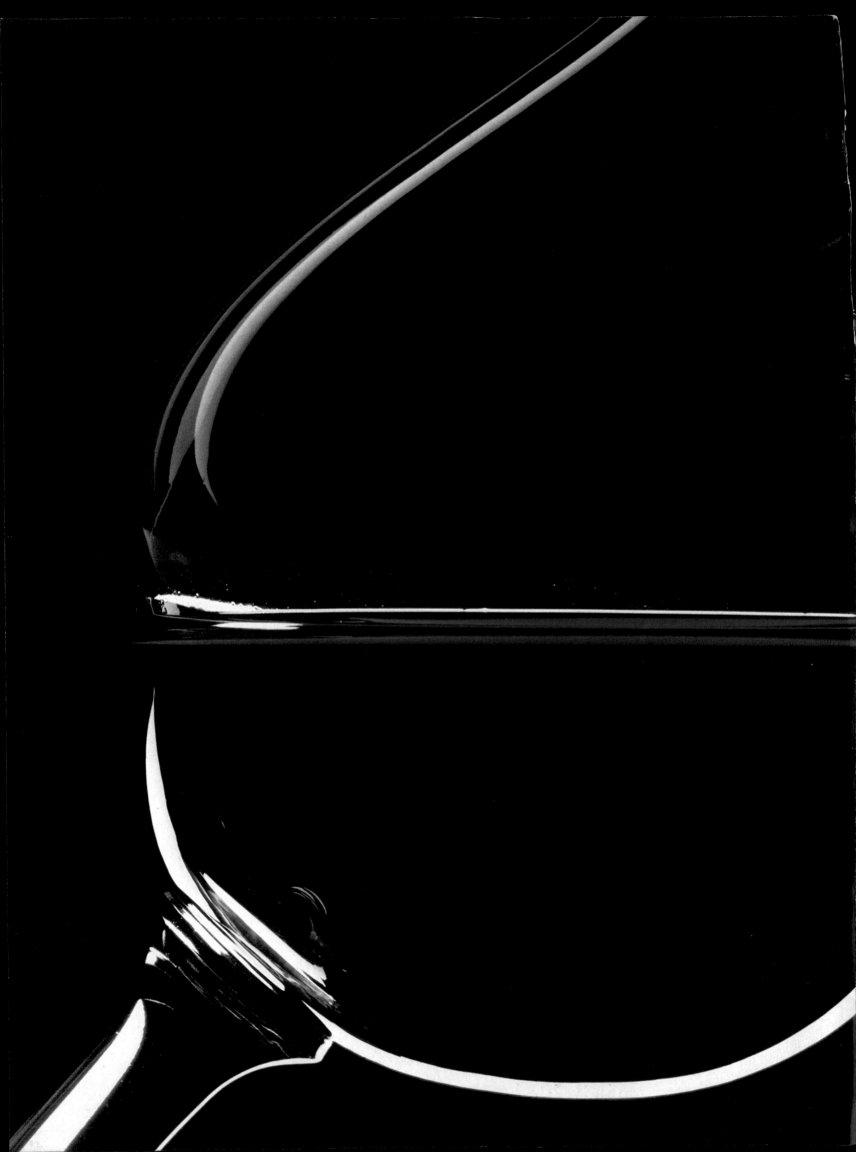

At the Table

What could be more enjoyable or more sociable than sharing a meal with friends? In ancient cultures, eating was something of a ritual. The Chinese court had banquets of 120 courses that lasted three days and three nights. Romans had mad orgies of eating. And at the court of the French Sun King, the pleasures of the table were constrained by strict ceremony, with more stress placed on etiquette than on the food. Nowadays, most of us are more relaxed about eating, but we still have rules and customs that have proven both practical and sensible over the centuries. Many of these customs have been updated or changed. Some have become obsolete, but the pleasures of the table remain the same. Eating and drinking with family and friends are still enjoyable experiences. And if a meal is shared with someone you love, so much the better.

Coffee: A Special Drink

To talk about coffee is to talk about Vienna. This old city on the Danube is as full of legends about coffee as it is filled with the wonderful strong aroma of freshly brewed coffee. Vienna's love affair with coffee began over 300 years ago when fleeing Turks left a wagonload of coffee beans behind. It progressed to the point where the Viennese coffeehouse became a beloved tradition, copied in most places around the world. James Joyce, Sigmond Freud and Trotsky could all be found at the Cafe Odeon, a coffeehouse in Zurich, discussing ideas that were destined to change the course of the world.

There were times when people in power looked upon the coffee bean with some suspicion. There were even occasions when coffee was prohibited. Frederick the Great sent "coffee spies" among his subjects and the church considered coffee to be a "hellish brew."

Initially, coffee was a drink "for men only" in Austria and Germany. It was not until the 18th century that it became acceptable for women to drink it too. This was the period when Bach was writing his famous Coffee Cantata and the advent of a coffeehouse open to people of all classes was just around the corner. At first, women were barely tolerated in coffeehouses. In this century, they have all but taken them over.

What was once a special pleasure, reserved for the small number of people in the upper classes, has become a drink enjoyed by almost everyone. There are few things more universally enjoyed than the very American custom known as *coffee break*. When coffee is prepared properly, and a bit of imagination added, there can still be an air of luxury and a touch of the exotic about it. The basic old recipe is still valid for well-made coffee today—"hot as hell, black as the devil, pure as an angel and sweet as love."

1. Cappuccino
Equal parts of coffee and hot milk, topped with lightly sweetened whipped cream and sprinkled with cinnamon.

2. Cafe Noisette
Coffee flavored with a dash of cherry brandy and sugar.

3. Espresso
Dark roasted coffee made in an espresso machine that forces hot steam through ground coffee; usually served with lemon peel.

4. Mocha Coffee
Equal amounts of hot unsweetened cocoa and coffee; usually served in a small cup.

5. Cafe au Lait
Equal amounts of strong coffee and hot milk; usually served in a large cup for breakfast.

6. Coffee Soda
Ice cream placed in a tall glass with cold, sweetened coffee and sparkling water poured over; topped with whipped cream and decorated with a maraschino cherry and grated chocolate.

7. Laced Coffee
Hot coffee flavored with rum, cognac, armagnac or whiskey.

8. Irish Coffee
Hot strong coffee flavored with 2 to 3 tablespoons Irish whiskey; topped with whipped cream and served in an Irish coffee glass.

9. Turkish Coffee
Made with dark, pungent Turkish coffee boiled with water and sugar in a special metal Turkish coffee pot.

10. Emperor's Coffee
Hot coffee to which egg yolk beaten with 2 teaspoons cream, sugar and brandy are added.

How to Brew Coffee

Select the correct grind of coffee for your coffeepot. Be sure the coffeepot has been thoroughly cleaned. Traces of coffee oil will spoil the flavor of freshly made coffee. Use fresh, cold tap water. Measure coffee and water accurately. Measures packed with coffee, and most cup measurements marked on coffeepots, are based on a 6-ounce cup. You will lose 1/2 ounce in brewing. It is important to take this into account if you want to serve 8-ounce cups of coffee. Never reuse coffee grounds. If you must use a filter with your coffeepot, be sure to use the correct size and type. When using a percolator, distribute ground coffee evenly in the basket; then perk coffee 6 to 8 minutes. Rinse a drip coffeepot in hot water before making coffee. Never allow coffee to boil.

Buying Coffee

Supermarket shelves are filled with a dazzling array of different coffee blends and grinds. The various grinds are marked on each package. You can buy regular coffee both caffeinated and decaffeinated in all grinds. You can also buy instant coffee, either powdered or freeze-dried, with or without caffeine. The newest method of packaging coffee is vacuum-sealed foil containers. If you don't need the coffee can to store coffee, you can usually save money by buying coffee this way.

Specialty food stores often carry fresh coffee beans that can be bought by the pound, then ground in the store or in small quantities at home. This is a wonderful, although expensive, way to buy coffee. You will probably want to experiment with different kinds of coffee to develop your own blend. If you decide to experiment with different blends, choose a store where they are willing to explain the characteristics of the coffee beans and offer advice and guidance on how to blend them. Some stores carry their own special blends, and if you find one you like, it will save you lots of trouble. Store coffee in a tightly closed container in a cool place up to 2 weeks. If you plan to store open ground coffee longer than 2 weeks, store it in the refrigerator up to 8 weeks. Beyond 8 weeks, it should be stored in the freezer.

Wine & Other Drinks

More and more people are adopting the custom of serving wine with dinner or having a glass of wine in place of any other alcoholic beverage. Those who are seriously interested in wine spend time to learn the characteristics of wines from different vineyards and make a study of which years the best wines were produced. For the novice, a helpful and informed wine merchant can be of invaluable assistance. The most important thing to remember is that a wine does not have to be expensive to be delicious. When you find a wine you like, save the label or make a note of the name and year so you can buy it again.

General Guidelines

Rules about serving wine should be viewed as guidelines, not as restrictions. You can drink any kind of wine you choose and in fact there are many people who, no matter what the menu, drink only red or only white wine. When you expect guests, it is a good idea to have both kinds of wine on hand.

Dry wine is served before dinner and with all courses except dessert, when a sweet wine is appropriate. On special occasions, champagne is appropriate as a cocktail or with dessert. And there are some hearty menus when beer is the ideal drink to serve. Keep the new non-alcoholic "wines," fruit juice or soda on hand for anyone who does not drink alcohol. Don't press someone to have "just one drink to be sociable" if they refuse an alcoholic drink.

Aperitif

An aperitif is an alcoholic drink taken before a meal to stimulate the appetite. Although sherry has been popular as an aperitif for a long time, other drinks are equally appropriate. The choice of drinks varies as tastes change and new trends become fashionable. At the present time Kir is very popular.

Basic Kir Recipe (above)

1 jigger crème de cassis
3/4 cup chilled dry white wine

Variation

Kir Royale:
1/2 jigger crème de cassis
1/2 jigger cherry brandy
3/4 cup chilled champagne or dry sparkling wine

White Wine

White wine should be served chilled. Place it in the refrigerator at least 2 hours prior to serving to chill it properly. Serve white wine in an all-purpose wine glass or in a glass that is smaller than the balloon glass generally used for red wine. Wine should be dry rather than sweet, unless it is to be served with dessert. Serve white wine with lightly flavored food, food with mild white sauces, light colored food such as poultry, fish or veal and with light meals.

Red Burgundy

The name Burgundy indicates the area in France where the grapes were grown that were used to make the wine. The Burgundy shown above is red, but there are also white wines that come from Burgundy. Open red wine 1 hour before you plan to serve it to allow it to "breathe." The serving temperature of the wine should be 65F to 70F (18C to 20C). Red wine can be served in an all-purpose wine glass or in the traditional balloon glass shown above. As with white wine, dry red wine should be served with the main part of the meal. Serve it with red meats, highly seasoned food, tomato-based sauces, brown-based sauces, game, stews and hearty foods.

Beer

Although it is not really inappropriate to drink beer directly from the can at a ball game or perhaps even at an informal picnic, chilled beer glasses or tankards are more appropriate at the dinner table. The fact that beer is always served thoroughly chilled in the United States is a cultural difference between America and most of the rest of the world. Warm or slightly chilled beer is served throughout much of Europe. Beer is growing in popularity with many people because imported beer is increasingly easy to buy and many companies are selling new light beers with reduced calories.

Red Bordeaux

As with Burgundy, the name indicates the area in France where the grapes were grown that were used to make the wine. Both red and white wines come from this area. Bordeaux wines are lighter and softer than Burgundy. Red Bordeaux is served in exactly the same way as Red Burgundy and White Bordeaux is served as all white wines are served. Wine glasses should never be filled to the brim. When serving white wine, fill the glass no more than two-thirds full. Glasses should only be half-full when serving red wine.

Brandy

Brandy is a distilled spirit made from grapes. Brandy glasses come in many sizes. The medium and moderately large glasses are preferable to the very small or enormously over-sized glasses. The wide bowl of a brandy glass allows you to swirl the brandy in the glass and enjoy the aroma as much as the flavor. Serve brandy at room temperature; then warm it further by holding the glass in both hands as you swirl it. Brandy improves with age before bottling. The older the brandy, the more expensive it is likely to be. The best way to serve brandy is in very small quantities as an after-dinner drink. It can also be combined with other ingredients to make a wide variety of cocktails or used in cooking for special dishes or to flambé food.

Champagne

Champagne is a sparkling wine, elegant and expensive. For wine to become champagne, a second fermentation is necessary. The process of handling the bottles while the champagne ages is both time-consuming and expensive. The real trick to serving champagne is to learn how to ease the cork out of the bottle with a sigh rather than allowing a shattering explosion. To accomplish this, hold the cork firmly in one hand and gently twist the bottle in the other hand. Serve champagne chilled in a narrow, tapered glass, shown above, with or without a stem, or serve in a flat, wide champagne glass. Champagne can be served before dinner, with dinner, after dinner or combined with other ingredients to make a cocktail.

Other Drinks

When you plan to serve highballs of scotch, rye or bourbon with sparkling water, or serve gin or vodka with quinine water, tomato juice or orange juice, you will need tall glasses and lots of ice. This is also true when you serve soft drinks. You should have a large punch bowl, small cups and a large block of ice in order to serve punch, which can be made with or without the addition of an alcoholic beverage.

Beautiful Table Settings

Table settings can be formal or informal and should reflect the kind of meal that will be served. Fine china, sterling silver and crystal are not appropriate for a children's birthday party or a meal of frankfurters and baked beans. On the other hand, an expensive fillet of beef, accompanied by fresh asparagus and Hollandaise Sauce should not be served on pottery or paper plates. Plan your table setting to fit the occasion and the food to be served.

Every table setting benefits from some kind of arrangement in the center of the table. Wild flowers can be lovely at an informal meal. Cultivated flowers and candles are ideal for a formal dinner. However, flowers are not the only thing you can use, and a traditional flower holder is not necessarily your only choice. Use your imagination to provide new ways to decorate your table. However, be sure your centerpiece is low enough for guests to see over it. Here are some centerpiece ideas.

● Place a bowl of flowers inside a hollowed-out pumpkin for a Thanksgiving table setting.
● Fill a glass bowl with Christmas tree ornaments and surround the bowl with evergreen branches. Use red or green candles.
● Place small potted plants or potted green herbs in a large basket for a spring or summer table setting.
● Arrange decorated dyed Easter eggs and Easter candies on shredded green cellophane.
● Use gourds, small dried corn husks and dried flowers to make fall centerpieces.
● Float a few single blossoms in a shallow bowl of water.
● Create a zoo of small stuffed animals for a children's party.
● Use fresh fruit or even colorful fresh vegetables for an edible centerpiece.

Formal Table Settings

- Use an elegant white tablecloth rather than place mats or a patterned or colored cloth.
- Use large cloth napkins to match or compliment the tablecloth.
- Use fine china in a simple pattern.
- Add silver or china place plates, if available.
- Use silver cutlery and stemmed crystal glasses.
- Add candles and a more elegant centerpiece.

Placement

Cutlery should be arranged with forks on the left and knives and spoons on the right. The butter knife can be placed on the butter plate or at the top of the place setting. Forks and spoons for dessert and coffee can also be placed at the top of the place setting, if desired, but only if the butter knife is placed elsewhere. Cutlery for the first course should always be placed on the outside. If salad is served before the main dish, the salad fork should be placed on the outside. If the main dish is served first, the salad fork should be placed on the inside. Proper placement will help guests know which piece of cutlery to use for each course.

Butter plates should be placed to the left of the place setting. Glasses should be placed to the right of the place setting. Napkins can be placed in the center on the place setting or on the left with the forks.

A Gala Menu

Many centuries ago, those who attended a feast found everything placed on the table at the same time. The guests worked their way through the food at their own pace. It was the French who improved this system and developed the classic menu, with one course succeeding another. Their aim was to serve a balanced meal and create an almost musical crescendo of taste sensations with the first courses serving as the overture to the high point of the meal—the main course. When properly planned, flavor and seasoning should increase as the menu progresses toward the main course and decrease as the meal ends. The taste possibilities of an eight or ten course nouvelle cuisine menu can be exciting. Since nouvelle cusine emphasizes small portions and light dishes, many courses can be served provided you are eating in a restaurant or have lots of help in the kitchen.

Nouvelle Cuisine Menu

Cold appetizer
Hot appetizer
Soup
Fish
Sorbet
Poultry
Meat
Cheese
Dessert
Fruit
Coffee/Pastry

Planning Menus

A simple menu can consist of three courses. The first course might be an hors d'oeuvre served in the living room with drinks, or a hot or cold appetizer, soup or salad served at the table. This is followed by a main course of meat, poultry or fish accompanied by a vegetable and starch. Dessert and coffee or tea provide a balanced meal.

A somewhat more elegant menu might have four or five courses consisting of an appetizer, soup, salad, main course and dessert. This basic outline can be varied. Some people prefer to serve salad before the main course, while others serve it after. The French often serve cheese with French bread and fruit as a separate course before dessert, while the Italians serve a pasta course before the main course. The European custom of serving a tart fruit sorbet between courses is designed to clear the palette. Coffee or tea may be served with dessert or after dessert, at the table or in the living room with after-dinner liqueurs.

There are no hard and fast rules for planning a menu. Common sense dictates that you take into consideration the amount of time you can devote to the preparation of the meal; budget; cooking equipment; space available for comfortable seating; whether or not you will have any help in the kitchen; and any medical dietary requirements of your guests.

Family Menu

P. 154-155	Pea Puree Soup
P. 188-189	Garnished Chicken Breast
P. 124-125	Braised Carrots
P. 102	Risotto
P. 271	Raspberry Bavarian

Hearty Menu

P. 146	Beef Consommé
P. 150	with Egg Flan
P. 138	Mixed Green Salad
P. 139	with Vinaigrette Dressing
P. 196-197	Tournedos with Herb Butter
P.110-113	Baked Potato with Cheese & Ham Topping
P. 274	Berry Compote

Italian Menu

Festive Menu

Planning a Dinner Party

A generation ago it was not unusual to assume there would be help in the kitchen if company was coming to dinner. More recently, even when help was not available, chances were reasonably good the hostess would have lots of time to prepare dinner. But today, with very little affordable help to be found and most people working outside the home, the question of how to give a successful dinner party can be difficult to answer. The key to the solution is good organization.

Dinner Party Pointers

- Plan your menu carefully. Resist the temptation to try a new recipe for the first time when you are cooking for company.
- Select dishes you can cook easily with the equipment you have. Remember, if you have only one oven, you can't heat an appetizer in the same oven in which you are cooking a soufflé.
- Plan to serve some dishes that can be cooked ahead of time and, if possible, frozen.
- Make a work schedule so you don't discover you forgot to make a salad dressing as you get ready to toss the salad.
- Get out dishes for every course before company arrives. Don't forget details like filling the cream pitcher and sugar bowl.
- Write yourself notes and post them around the kitchen as reminders of when certain things must be done.
- Make a list for yourself of everything you plan to serve. It can be very disheartening to discover a dish that took hours to prepare sitting in the refrigerator the morning after the party.
- Most important of all, relax. A party is supposed to be fun—even for the host and hostess.

Other Points to Consider

- If you are planning to use any silver, be sure to clean it ahead of time.
- Set the table the night before the party.
- A centerpiece for the table will add a festive touch. Plan for it ahead of time and, if you are going to use flowers, arrange them when you set the table.
- Be sure to put white wine in the refrigerator in time to chill properly. Remember to open red wine ahead of time to allow it to "breathe."
- Prepare salad greens before your guests arrive and wrap them in a damp dish towel. The only thing you will have to do the last minute is toss the salad with the dressing.
- If you have a warming drawer or free oven, heat the dinner plates. You can also heat dinner plates on the warm cycle of your dishwasher.
- Place cards are a nice touch, even at an informal dinner. Mix up your guests so husbands and wives don't sit together.

Creating New Menus

On the next ten pages, you will find ideas for combining recipes from various parts of this book to create new and exciting meals. There are ideas for dieters, economical meals, family meals, special-occasion meals and elegant entertaining. Try our ideas or create your own menus from the techniques and recipes in the chapters that follow. Take advantage of seasonal food and supermarket specials when planning meals.

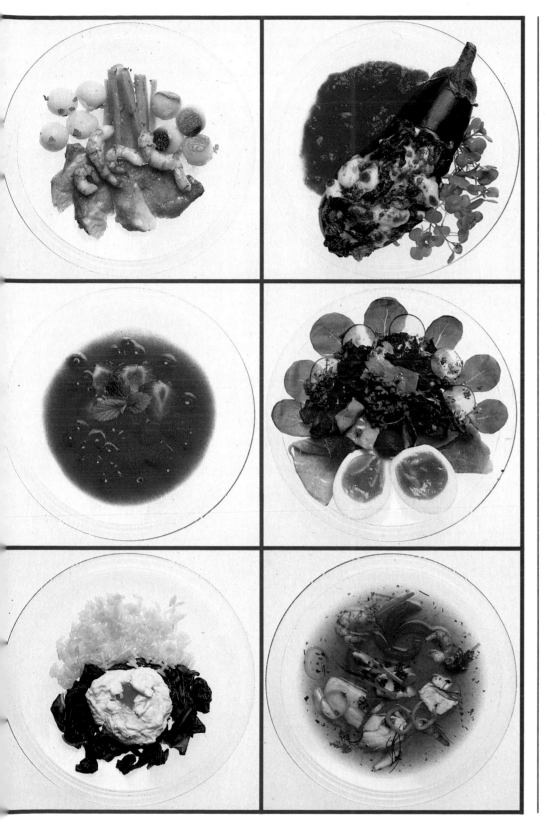

Ideas for Dieters

There are all kinds of diets that can be followed, but the best kind is one that includes interesting and nutritious food. Try some of the dishes suggested below and remember to serve small portions and eat slowly. A healthy diet will not produce dramatic weight loss overnight, but rather a gradual loss of weight based on intelligent eating habits that reduce both calorie and fat intake.

1. Marinated Eye Round Steak, page 202, with blanched pea pods, page 128, and carrot balls, page 130.

2. Poached turbot fillet, pages 164-165, with blanched celery, page 130, and Peeled Boiled Potatoes, pages 110-111.

3. Carrot & Potato Puree, page 115, with blanched garden peas, page 128.

4. Sautéed chicken breast, page 189, with shrimp, blanched carrot sticks, page 130, kohlrabi, page 126, and zucchini balls, page 136.

5. Strawberry Puree, pages 262-263, with red currants, raspberries and sliced strawberries.

6. Poached Egg, pages 62-63, on spinach, page 126, with rice, page 96.

7. Eggplant, pages 136 and 225, with Spinach & Ricotta Filling, page 89, and Fresh Tomato Sauce, page 82.

8. Mixed salad of radicchio, lamb's tongue, lettuce, iceberg lettuce, radishes and watercress with Vinaigrette Dressing, pages 138-139, boiled ham and hard-cooked eggs, pages 62-63.

9. Light Seafood Soup, page 180, with tomatoes, cod, shrimp, leek, carrot strips, dill and chervil.

Economical Meals

When you don't have to consider cost, meal planning is very easy. But when money is tight, planning interesting and delicious meals can be a challenge. With careful planning, you can find many ways to stretch your food dollars and still serve wonderful meals. Be flexible when you market and don't hesitate to change a menu when you find prices too high.

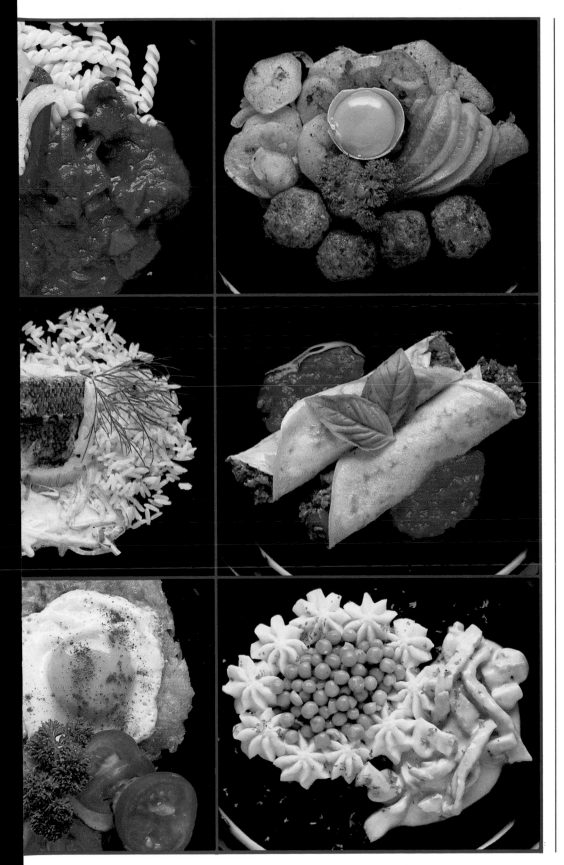

1. Hamburgers, page 214, with sautéed eggplant and zucchini, page 136, and French-Fried Potatoes, pages 110-111.

2. Stuffed Cabbage, page 226, with diced cooked bacon and onion and noodles, pages 80-81.

3. Crumb-coated chicken leg, page 191, with Pilaf, page 103.

4. Hungarian Goulash, page 238, with pasta twists, page 92, and sweet peppers.

5. Poached fish fillet, pages 164-165, with rice, page 96.

6. Potato Pancakes, page 116, with fried eggs, cherry tomato and cucumber slices.

7. Fried Potatoes & Onions, pages 110-111, with Meatballs, page 215, sliced pickle, egg yolk and parsley. The egg yolk is stirred into the fried potatoes at the table.

8. Crepes, pages 62-63, with meat filling, pages 72-73, and Fresh Tomato Sauce, page 82.

9. Piped Mashed Potatoes, page 114, with blanched garden peas, page 128, and Swiss Veal Strips, page 207.

Family Meals

It is not very likely there are many people who genuinely enjoy cooking seven days a week. But when there is a hungry family waiting to be fed, it can be very difficult to avoid the inevitable. Try at least one new dish every week to add interest and a challenge to the task of family cooking. Before long, you will have a whole new repertoire of family dishes, and a reputation as an exciting and innovative cook.

1. Beef Roulades, page 210, with Potatoes Anna, page 120, and blanched kohlrabi with cream and chives, page 126.

2. Lentil-Vegetable Soup, page 158.

3. Poached cod steak, pages 164-165, with tomato rice, page 100, cucumber in Herb & Wine Butter, page 250.

4. Stuffed Pepper, page 225, with Fresh Tomato Sauce, page 82, and Cream-Style Potatoes, page 118.

5. Fresh Herb Pasta, pages 80 and 87, with grated cheese.

6. Tomato Soup, page 153, with rice, page 96.

7. Chicken Curry, page 193, with apricots, coconut, bananas and cherries, pages 188-189.

8. Meatball kabob, page 220, and Fresh Tomato Sauce, page 82, over rice, page 96.

9. Pork Loin in Beer, page 233, with Mashed Potatoes, page 114, and Sauerkraut, page 140.

Special-Occasion Meals

Food, the gift of love, is always appropriate as a way to celebrate a special occasion. Whether the celebration is at breakfast, lunch or dinner; whether it is a family affair or a meal for guests; special food is in order. Serve a typical American meal, or plan a meal with an ethnic theme. Take advantage of the wide variety of ethnic foods available in most supermarkets to plan a special menu.

1. Tortellini, page 88, with Mornay Sauce, page 254, grated Parmesan cheese and steamed broccoli, pages 124-125.

2. Boiled shrimp, page 171, over Risi e Bisi, page 106.

3. Veal Marsala, page 208, with noodles, pages 80-81, and celery, page 130.

4. Beef Loin Porterhouse Steak, page 204, with Baked Potato, pages 110-111, broiled tomato and herb-butter garnish, page 33.

5. Breaded Veal Cutlet, page 207, with Potato Croquettes, page 116, and sautéed mushrooms, page 137.

6. Beef Roulade, page 210, with Brussel sprouts, page 127, and Peeled Boiled Potatoes, pages 110-111.

7. Won-Ton, page 90, with rice, page 96, and sautéed bean sprouts, page 136, and Sweet & Sour Sauce, page 192.

8. Sauerbraten, pages 236-237, with Red Cabbage, page 133, and Peeled Boiled Potatoes, pages 110-111, and Bread-Crumb Butter, page 250.

9. Pork Chop, page 206, and bacon with kale, page 133, and Caramelized Potatoes, page 118.

10. Scrambled Eggs, pages 62-63, and buttered shrimp, pages 171, over pumpernickel bread.

Elegant Entertaining

Planning food for a formal dinner can be intimidating. But, with careful planning, it can also be lots of fun. Choose dishes that don't require much last-minute preparation, and don't try a new recipe for the first time when you are cooking for company. Work out your menu well in advance and make a careful marketing list. Prepare as much food as possible the day before the party and leave yourself enough time to dress and relax before your guests arrive.

1. Pork Loin in Beer, page 233, with steamed broccoli, pages 124-125, and noodles with Herb Cream Sauce, pages 80-82.

2. Pot Roasted Beef Brisket, page 233, with Peeled Boiled Potatoes, pages 110-111.

3. Duck with Cherry Sauce, page 185, Potatoes au Gratin, page 120, and braised savoy cabbage, page 132.

4. Beef tenderloin with Béarnaise Sauce, pages 197 and 253, with blanched pea pods, page 128, braised carrots, pages 124-125, and sautéed chanterelles, page 137.

5. Chocolate Mousse, page 262-263, Strawberry Sorbet, page 269, Cranberry Ice Cream, page 275, Kiwi Puree, page 266, with sliced strawberries, nectarines and raspberries.

6. Rabbit with Prunes, page 236, Spatzle, page 81, and sautéed mushrooms, page 137.

7. Boneless Chicken Breast with julienned carrots and leeks, page 189, Rice Parcels, page 99, and Cream Sauce, pages 244-245.

8. Trout Amandine, page 177, with Peeled Boiled Potatoes, pages 110-111, sliced cucumbers with Vinaigrette Dressing, page 139.

9. Sliced Venison Steak with Cranberries and Grapes, page 206, Duchess Potatoes, page 117, and Cream Sauce, pages 244-245.

Eggs: A Miracle of White & Gold

Eggs are one of our most versatile foods—perfectly formed, universally useful and miraculously prepackaged. Ever since man first foraged for food, eggs have been part of our diet. They have long been regarded as the beginning of life, provided you get beyond the old dilemma of which came first—the chicken or the egg. In almost every culture the egg is the symbol of spring and fertility. Most cooks consider the egg almost indispensable, and regard it so highly that many of the great chefs of the world have created their own special egg dishes.

Cooking Eggs

Whether you are cooking eggs for an egg dish or using eggs as a binding agent, rising agent or thickening agent, they must be handled with care. Generally eggs should be cooked over medium or low heat. They should be broken and separated carefully. The only time an egg can be treated roughly is when you beat egg whites.

Buying Eggs

When buying eggs, look for two things—the grade and the size. One has nothing to do with the other. Government grades are U.S. Grade AA or fresh fancy, U.S. Grade A and U.S. Grade B. Top-grade eggs have the largest proportion of thick white surrounding a high, firm yolk. They give superior appearance for poaching and frying. Grade B eggs are excellent for combining with other ingredients in cooked dishes. Grade or shell color does not affect food value. Egg sizes are Jumbo, Extra Large, Large, Medium and Small. Size is based on an ounce weight per dozen. Extra Large, 27 ounces per dozen; Large, 24 ounces per dozen; and Medium, 21 ounces per dozen. Most recipes tested for cookbooks are based on the use of Large Eggs.

Storing Eggs

Store eggs in the refrigerator, large-end up. Whenever possible, use eggs within 1 week. Place leftover yolks in a container; then cover with cold water. Cover the container and refrigerate up to 2 days. Drain before using. Store leftover egg whites in a tightly covered container in the refrigerator 1 to 2 days. For longer storage, place in freezer. Use promptly when thawed.

Beating Egg Whites

Separate eggs carefully. Even a tiny drop of egg yolk in the egg whites will inhibit foaming. For greatest volume, bring egg whites to room temperature before beating. Beat egg whites in an unlined copper bowl or add 1 teaspoon cream of tartar for each 1 cup of egg whites to increase stability. Do not add sugar until egg whites have been beaten to a soft peak stage. The addition of sugar decreases volume but increases stability. Add in small amounts. Beat egg whites until stiff, but not dry. They will still be moist and glossy. Beaten egg whites lose volume when allowed to stand; use promptly. Fold beaten egg whites into other ingredients.

Hard-Cooked Eggs

1. Prick egg carefully at large end with an egg piercer or needle, if desired.

2. Place egg on a spoon; lower slowly into simmering water.

Poached Eggs

1. Bring lightly salted water to a boil. Add 1 tablespoon white vinegar.

2. Reduce heat to simmering. Break egg into cup.

Scrambled Eggs

1. Break eggs into bowl.

2. Beat well; season to taste with salt and pepper.

3-Egg Omelet

3 eggs
Salt to taste
2 drops hot-pepper sauce
2 tablespoons water
1 tablespoon butter
(also pages 74-75)

1. Lightly beat eggs in a small bowl. Beat in salt, pepper sauce and water.

2. Melt butter in a skillet over medium-high heat. Pour in egg mixture.

Crepes

3 eggs
1-1/2 cups milk
1/4 teaspoon salt
3/4 cup all-purpose flour
2 tablespoons sugar, if desired
Butter for cooking
(also pages 76-79)

1. Beat eggs, milk and salt in a bowl until well blended.

2. Beat in flour and sugar, if desired, 1 tablespoon at a time.

3. When cooked, plunge egg into cold water to stop cooking.

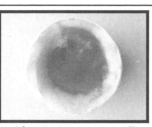

4. After 4 minutes, egg yolk will be soft and waxy; white will not be firm.

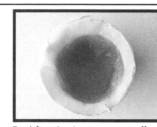

5. After 6 minutes, egg yolk will be soft; white will be firm.

6. After 12 to 14 minutes, both yolk and white will be firm.

3. Slide egg carefully into simmering water.

4. Use spoon to push egg white toward center of egg and shape neatly.

5. Cook gently 4 minutes. Remove egg from water with slotted spoon.

3. Melt butter in a skillet over medium heat.

4. Pour beaten eggs into skillet.

5. As eggs begin to set, stir or scramble with a spoon or fork.

6. Cook to desired doneness; serve immediately.

3. Stir mixture briefly. Finish cooking without stirring.

4. When eggs are almost set, lift and fold over. Tilt pan; slide omelet to edge.

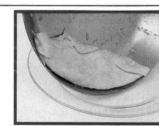

5. Slide finished omelet onto plate. Garnish as desired.

3. Melt 1 teaspoon butter in a crepe pan or skillet over medium heat.

4. Add just enough batter to cover bottom of pan when pan is tilted.

5. Turn crepe over when lightly browned on bottom.

6. Cook until lightly browned on second side. Repeat with remaining batter and butter.
Makes 12 to 14 crepes

Eggs Transformed

There are very few ingredients that can be used in as many different ways as eggs. Anyone on a low-cholesterol diet will tell you that if you are not permitted to eat eggs, the list of foods you cannot eat is almost mind boggling. Among other things, egg yolks are used to add color to pale sauces, thicken thin sauces, transform melted butter into hollandaise sauce and turn olive oil into mayonnaise. Beaten egg whites lighten cake mixtures, cause soufflés to rise, clarify consommé and stock, can be turned into meringues and are used in endless other ways. Both egg yolks and egg whites can be used as a glaze.

Eggs in a Glass

(top left)
Place warm, peeled, soft- or hard-cooked eggs in a pretty glass instead of an egg cup. Add a small amount of butter; sprinkle with finely chopped herbs, salt and pepper.

Sliced Eggs

(bottom left)
Hard-cooked eggs can be sliced or cut in wedges. Use as garnish or in a recipe.

Colored Eggs

(top center)
Hard-cooked eggs can be dyed or painted. Generally used at Easter. If not allowed to sit around too long, they can still be peeled and eaten.

Raw Egg Yolk

(center)
Serve individual portions of Steak Tartare with an egg yolk in the center.

Deviled Eggs

(center)
Cut hard-cooked eggs in half lengthwise. Carefully scoop out yolks; place in a bowl. Blend with a small amount of mayonnaise, dairy sour cream or whipping cream. Season as desired with salt, pepper, mustard, ketchup, Worcestershire sauce, hot-pepper sauce or herbs. Pipe yolk mixture into egg whites; garnish as desired.

Sieved Egg Yolk

(in small spoon)
Press hard-cooked egg yolk through a fine sieve. Sprinkle over spinach, asparagus, smoked fish, black-bean soup, salads or white sauce.

Chopped Egg White

(in large spoon)
Finely chop hard-cooked egg white; use to garnish salads, soups and vegetables.

Pickled Eggs

(top right)
Bring salted water to a boil. Add bay leaf, peppercorns, rosemary, caraway seed, whole cloves and a few tablespoons dry red wine. Let stand until cool. Pour into a jar. Crack shells of hard-cooked eggs; do not peel. Add eggs to jar; cover and let stand 1 to 2 days before eating. When ready to eat, peel eggs; cut in half lengthwise. Remove yolks; fill whites with a mixture of oil, vinegar, mustard and spices. Replace yolks and serve.

Sunshine Toast

(bottom right)
Butter a piece of toast; place on a heat-proof dish. Place raw egg yolk in center of toast. Beat egg whites; pipe around yolk. Bake in preheated 425F (220C) oven 4 to 5 minutes or until whites are lightly browned.

Meringue

(not shown)
Beat egg whites with cream of tartar and sugar to stiff peak stage. Use to make a wide variety of baked desserts.

Egg Snow

(not shown)
Drop meringue by spoonfuls into hot milk; poach gently. Serve on top of fruit purees or custard.

65

Scrambled Eggs

There are very few cooking procedures easier than making scrambled eggs. It is also possible to make them in a microwave oven. Although scrambled eggs are delicious unadorned, they lend themselves to all kinds of interesting combinations, which is probably why so many chefs felt challenged to look for new ways to prepare them. Even the famous Chef Escoffier felt the challenge. When he prepared scrambled eggs for his good friend, the famous actress Sarah Bernhardt, he stuck a peeled garlic clove on the end of a knife and used the knife to stir the eggs. This can be a wonderful way to cook eggs for someone who loves garlic, but probably is better served at mid-day or late in the evening rather than for breakfast. If you scramble eggs in the morning before your eyes are quite open, you may not feel inspired to experiment. But scrambled eggs are a wonderful dish to serve for Sunday brunch, a weekend lunch or a late-night snack. You may find some of the following ways to serve them worth the minimal extra effort. Try our ideas or create some of your own.

24 Ways to Serve Scrambled Eggs

1. Garnish eggs with sliced pimento-stuffed olive and parsley.
2. Garnish eggs with strips of smoked salmon.
3. Serve eggs with tiny cooked shrimp; garnish with dill.
4. Add sliced mushrooms, cooked or raw, to eggs.
5. Cook diced bacon until crisp; drain, then cook eggs in same skillet.
6. Serve eggs with cooked peas.
7. Garnish eggs with sliced truffles.
8. Cook eggs with strips of sweet red pepper; garnish with parsley.
9. Mix sliced artichoke bottom with eggs; garnish with chervil.
10. Garnish eggs with dairy sour cream.
11. Stir anchovy fillet into eggs; garnish with radish sprouts.
12. Stir cooked julienned carrot and leek into eggs; garnish with parsley.
13. Mix eggs with chopped cress or radish sprouts.
14. Serve eggs with strips of bologna or cooked ham.
15. Garnish eggs with gherkins.
16. Stir snipped chives into eggs before cooking. Use chives as a garnish.
17. Stir grated cheese into eggs.
18. Cook eggs with green peppercorns.
19. Garnish eggs with caviar.
20. Crumble blue cheese into eggs before cooking.
21. Mix eggs with finely chopped, cooked spinach.
22. Stir smoked white fish into eggs; garnish with dill.
23. Mix eggs with chopped tomato; garnish with fresh oregano.
24. Mix eggs with corn; garnish with parsley.

French Omelets

Although there is more than one way to make an omelet, the French method is very special. When done properly, it can be the basis for a wonderful light meal. Making a French omelet properly is not difficult, but it does take practice. Once you have mastered the art, you will look for excuses to serve omelets as often as possible. Serve them plain, with a filling, as a light dish, a main dish or even for dessert.

Making a Perfect Omelet

If you are going to take omelet making seriously, invest in a heavy omelet pan with rounded sides that make it easy to slide the finished omelet out of the pan. Season the pan by heating a small amount of butter or oil in the pan. Sprinkle with salt and rub all over with a paper towel. Don't use the pan for anything but omelets. Never wash the pan. When you are finished cooking, sprinkle the pan with coarse salt; then wipe with a paper towel.

Beat eggs lightly; add salt, hot-pepper sauce and water, page 62. Melt butter in omelet pan over medium-high heat. Spread butter over bottom and side of pan. Pour eggs into pan; stir with flat side of a fork in a circular motion to create layers of lightly cooked egg. Shake pan as you stir. Spread cooked eggs evenly over bottom of pan; cook until remainder of eggs are nearly set. If you want to roll a filling inside the omelet, add it at this point. Roll omelet and slide out of pan onto a warm plate. Serve immediately.

Omelet Fillings

Although omelets are delicious plain, they can be even more delicious when filled. The filling can be spread over the omelet before rolling or a slit can be made down the center of the omelet and the filling arranged in the slit.

Herb Omelet

Stir 2 tablespoons chopped mixed herbs, such as basil, sage, chervil, marjoram, oregano, tarragon or parsley, into egg mixture. Cook as directed; garnish with additional herbs.

Asparagus Omelet

Cut 1/4 pound white or green asparagus into small pieces; sauté in 1 to 2 tablespoons butter; season with salt and pepper to taste. Arrange warm asparagus in an omelet; garnish with chopped chervil or parsley.

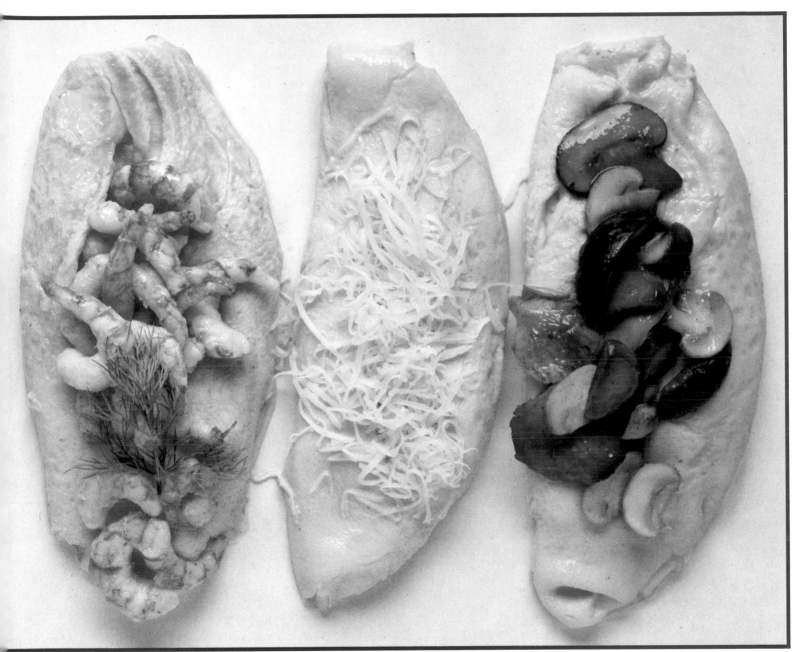

Shrimp Omelet

Cook 1/4 pound peeled small shrimp. Season as desired; arrange warm shrimp in omelet. Garnish with dill.

Cheese Omelet

Sprinkle 2 tablespoons grated Swiss or Cheddar cheese over omelet in pan before eggs finish cooking. Roll omelet, then sprinkle with additional cheese.

Mushroom Omelet

Sauté 1/4 pound sliced mushrooms in 1 tablespoon butter; season with salt and pepper to taste. Arrange warm mushrooms in omelet.

Tips:
● To make a sweet dessert omelet, spread omelet with jam or jelly or use some of the sweet crepe fillings suggested on the following pages.
● Heat diced leftovers in a small amount of butter. Use to fill omelets.

Crepes: An International Favorite

Crepes have become almost as much a part of the fast-food scene as pizza and hamburgers. Almost every country has their own version. Whether they are called *palatschinken, blini, blintz, pfannkuchen, enchilada, egg roll, crespelle* or just *thin pancakes*, they are delicious and easy to make.

Pointers for Making Crepes

● Crepe batter can be made with a wooden spoon, whisk, mixer, blender or food processor. You can use any method you like.

● Once crepe batter has been made, it should be allowed to stand at room temperature at least 1 hour. This allows the flour to expand. If batter thickens during standing time, thin it out with a little milk. Batter must be thin to make thin crepes.

● Crepe batter can be made ahead of time; then kept covered in the refrigerator up to 24 hours.

● Sugar should only be added to batter if crepes are going to be used for dessert.

● Add 1 tablespoon melted butter to crepe batter for added flavor.

● If you have a special crepe pan, season and care for it in the same manner as an omelet pan, page 68.

5 Ways to Shape a Crepe

1. Twist into cone shapes and fill as shown.
2. Fold into triangles to flambé.
3. Roll and serve plain or filled.
4. Build into a tower, then serve plain with sauce poured over or spread filling between layers. If a tower is made of many crepes, cut like cake and serve wedges.
5. Spoon filling in center; then fold opposite sides of crepe in toward center. Fold in remaining sides to make parcels.

12 Ways to Garnish Dessert Crepes

1. Powdered sugar
2. Granulated sugar
3. Brown sugar
4. Shredded or flaked coconut
5. Chopped, slivered or sliced nuts
6. Sweetened whipped cream
7. Grated chocolate
8. Chocolate sprinkles
9. Warm maple syrup
10. Honey
11. Jam or jelly
12. Liqueur

Sweet & Savory Crepe Fillings

It can be lots of fun to experiment with fillings for crepes because you can use anything from leftover turkey to an elegant crème patisserie. Try some of the suggestions on the next page or make your own fillings. Add a sauce if you like, or simply garnish or decorate the crepes with an ingredient that compliments the filling.

It is a good idea to make a batch of crepes whenever you have free time. Store them in the freezer. Slide a piece of waxed paper between each cooled crepe; wrap tightly in freezer bags and store up to 4 months. Bring crepes to room temperature before using; then heat in a conventional oven or microwave. You can use the crepes whenever you have unexpected company or just fill them with leftovers for a quick, inexpensive, but delicious light meal.

Savory Crepes

(left)

1. Fill with Chicken Fricassee, page 193; garnish with a lemon wedge and chervil.

2. Fill with sautéed chicken livers and chopped herbs; garnish with basil.

3. Fill with strips of cooked ham and onion rings; garnish with parsley.

4. Fill with flaked tuna; garnish with onion rings and dill.

5. Fill with mixed vegetables; garnish with watercress.

6. Fill with cooked ground meat, sweet peppers and onion; garnish with red-pepper strips and parsley.

Sweet Crepes

(right)

1. Fill with sautéed apple slices and raisins; sprinkle with Calvados and sliced almonds.

2. Spread with orange marmalade; sprinkle with orange liqueur, strips of blanched orange peel and powdered sugar.

3. Spread with melted chocolate; sprinkle with grated chocolate.

4. Spread with Raspberry Puree, page 266, and vanilla ice cream; sprinkle with nut topping.

5. Fill with sautéed banana slices; sprinkle with flaked coconut.

6. Sprinkle with lemon juice and chopped pistachios; garnish with a lemon slice and additional nuts.

Pancakes: Close Kin to Crepes

There are few foods more delicious than fresh hot pancakes, spread with sweet butter and smothered in real maple syrup that has been warmed. But whatever you do, don't spoil the treat by counting calories.

Pancake batter is thicker than crepe batter and pancakes are thicker and usually larger than crepes. As a result, they are a heartier dish. As with crepes, the batter can be mixed by hand, in a mixer, blender or food processor and should be allowed to rest after it has been made. Small lumps in pancake batter are not a serious problem and can be ignored. Although additional ingredients are usually added to crepes as a separate filling, ingredients such as berries can be added directly to pancake batter because the batter is thicker. Either milk or buttermilk can be used in pancake batter. When buttermilk is added, 1/2 teaspoon baking soda must be added for each cup of buttermilk.

Make pancakes on a lightly greased griddle or skillet. The griddle will be the correct temperature when a few drops of cold water dance and sputter when dropped on the hot surface. If the water does not dance, the griddle is not hot enough. If the water evaporates immediately, the griddle is too hot. Place the batter in a pitcher, then pour it onto the hot griddle, making pancakes the desired size. Cook 2 to 3 minutes or until bubbles appear on the surface. Turn with a spatula; cook 1-1/2 minutes or until bottoms are lightly browned. Keep warm until ready to serve.

Basic Pancakes

1-1/2 cups sifted
  all-purpose flour
3 tablespoons sugar
1-1/4 teaspoons baking
  powder
1 teaspoon salt
2 eggs, beaten
1 to 1-1/4 cups milk
3 tablespoons melted
  butter

1. Sift flour, sugar, baking powder and salt into a medium bowl.
2. Beat eggs and milk until blended. Gradually add melted butter, beating well.
3. Pour milk mixture into dry ingredients, stirring constantly until almost smooth.
4. If time permits, let batter stand 30 minutes to 1 hour.
5. Heat a large skillet or griddle; grease lightly. If making 9- or 10-inch pancakes, use a skillet with a heatproof handle.
6. Pour batter onto hot surface; cook until bubbles appear on pancake surface. Turn pancakes to finish cooking. For a large pancake, place skillet under a preheated broiler, 6 inches from heat source, to cook the top surface.
7. Slide pancake onto a warm plate; keep warm until ready to serve.
8. Repeat with remaining batter.
Makes 4 (9- to 10-inch) or 14 (4-inch) pancakes.

Cherry Pancakes

Cut 1 pound sweet cherries in halves, removing pits. Simmer in a small amount of water 2 to 3 minutes. Drain and spoon over pancakes.

Blueberry Pancakes

Rinse 1 to 2 cups fresh or frozen blueberries; pat dry with paper towels. Fold gently into batter.

Bacon & Onion Pancakes

Omit sugar from batter. Cook 1/2 pound bacon; drain on paper towels. Break into small pieces. Slice 1 onion; sauté in a small amount of bacon drippings or butter. Drain on paper towels; combine with bacon. Spoon over pancakes.

Plum Pancakes

Cut 1-1/2 pounds red plums in quarters, removing pits. Simmer in a small amount of water 2 to 3 minutes. Drain and spoon over pancakes.

Apple Pancakes

Peel, core and slice 2 or 3 large apples. Sauté in a small amount of butter. Spoon over pancakes; sprinkle with sugar and cinnamon, if desired.

Crespelle

12 cooked crepes, pages 62-63

Filling:
3 tablespoons butter
1 onion, diced
1 garlic clove, crushed
1/4 lb. mushrooms, sliced
3 tablespoons all-purpose flour
1 cup chicken broth
1/4 cup dry white wine
1/4 cup whipping cream
3 cups diced cooked chicken, veal or tongue, or 1 cup each
Salt and pepper to taste

Cheese Sauce:
3 tablespoons butter
3 tablespoons all-purpose flour
1-1/2 cups milk
2 egg yolks
1/2 cup grated Parmesan cheese

1. Prepare crepes.
2. To make filling, melt butter in a large saucepan over medium heat. Add onion and garlic; sauté until onion is transparent. Add mushrooms; sauté 3 minutes. Sprinkle flour over mushrooms; stir and let cook 1 minute.
3. Gradually add broth; cook, stirring constantly, until mixture thickens. Add wine and cream; cook, stirring constantly, until sauce thickens and comes to a boil. Remove from heat. Stir in meat. Season with salt and pepper.
4. Spoon filling down center of crepes; roll and place seam-side down in a single layer in a large greased baking dish.
5. Prepare Cheese Sauce according to directions for Béchamel Sauce, pages 244-245 through step 6.
6. Beat egg yolks in a small bowl. Stir 1/2 cup hot sauce into beaten egg yolks until blended. Return mixture to remaining sauce, stirring gently. Cook over low heat, stirring constantly, until sauce is thickened. Add 1/4 cup Parmesan cheese; stir until cheese is melted.
7. Preheat oven to 400F (200C). Pour sauce over crepes. Sprinkle with remaining 1/4 cup cheese. Bake 10 to 15 minutes or until sauce is bubbly and golden brown on top.
Makes 6 servings.

Palatschinken

12 cooked crepes, pages 62-63

Filling:
1-1/2 cups prepared prune or plum puree or jam
2 to 3 tablespoons plum brandy or cognac
1/4 cup melted butter
Powdered sugar

1. Prepare crepes.
2. Preheat oven to 425F (220C).
3. Place prune puree in a small bowl; break up with a fork. Add brandy; stir until blended.
4. Spread 2 tablespoons puree over each crepe; roll crepe. Place seam-side down in a single layer in a greased baking dish.
5. Brush liberally with melted butter.
6. Bake 8 to 10 minutes.
7. Dust with powdered sugar. Serve immediately.
Makes 6 servings.

Nockerin

4 egg yolks
1/4 cup all-purpose flour
1/2 teaspoon vanilla extract
6 to 8 egg whites
3/4 cup sugar
3 tablespoons butter
Powdered sugar

1. Beat egg yolks until thick and pale yellow in color. Beat in flour until smooth. Stir in vanilla.
2. Beat egg whites in a large bowl until soft peaks form. Gradually add sugar, beating until stiff and glossy.
3. Stir 2 tablespoons beaten egg whites into egg-yolk mixture to lighten. Fold in remaining egg whites.
4. Melt butter in a 10-inch skillet with a heatproof handle; tilt pan to coat bottom and side.
5. Preheat oven to 275F (135C).
6. Spoon mixture into hot skillet by heaping tablespoonfuls. Cook over low heat 4 to 5 minutes or until lightly browned on bottom.
7. Place skillet in preheated oven. Bake 10 minutes or until lightly browned on top.
8. Dust with powdered sugar. Serve immediately.
Makes 6 to 8 servings.

Kaiserschmarrn

2/3 cup all-purpose
flour
3 tablespoons
granulated sugar
2 eggs, separated
1 cup milk
3 tablespoons golden
raisins
3 tablespoons butter
Powdered sugar

1. Stir flour and
granulated sugar in a
medium bowl.
2. Beat egg yolks and
milk until blended. Add
egg-yolk mixture to
flour; beat with a wire
whisk until smooth.
3. Stir in raisins.
4. Beat egg whites until
stiff peaks form. Stir 2
tablespoons beaten egg
whites into batter to
lighten. Fold in
remaining egg whites.
5. Melt 2 tablespoons
butter in a large skillet
over medium heat. Pour
in batter.
6. Cook, turning once,
until golden brown on
both sides.
7. Remove from skillet;
break into bite-sized
pieces with 2 forks.
8. Melt remaining 1
tablespoon butter in
skillet. Add pancake
pieces; sauté 3 minutes.
9. Spoon onto a serving
plate; dust with
powdered sugar.
Makes 2 servings.

Blinis

1-1/2 teaspoons active
dry yeast
1 teaspoon sugar
1 cup half and half,
warmed to 105F to
115F (40C to 45C)
1 cup buckwheat flour
1/2 cup all-purpose
flour
1/2 teaspoon salt
4 eggs, separated
1/4 cup melted butter
Caviar
Dairy sour cream

1. Sprinkle yeast and
sugar over warm half
and half; stir to
dissolve. Let stand 5 to
10 minutes or until
foamy.
2. Stir flours and salt
together in a medium
bowl.
3. Beat egg yolks until
blended. Add beaten
egg yolks, yeast mixture
and butter to flour. Stir
with a wooden spoon
until blended.
4. Cover bowl with a
clean towel; let rise in a
warm place, free from
drafts, until doubled in
bulk.
5. Beat egg whites until
stiff peaks form. Fold
into batter.
6. Drop batter by
tablespoonfuls onto a
greased griddle or
skillet. Cook until lightly
browned on both sides.
7. Remove to a serving
plate; keep warm.
Repeat with remaining
batter. Serve with caviar
and dairy sour cream.
Makes about 36 Blinis.

Orange Soufflé

Butter for greasing
1 to 2 tablespoons sugar
3 tablespoons butter
3 tablespoons
all-purpose flour
3/4 cup milk
4 egg yolks
1/2 cup granulated sugar
1/3 cup Grand Marnier
Grated peel of 1 large
orange
Grated peel of 1 lemon
6 egg whites
Powdered sugar

1. Butter a 1-1/2 quart
soufflé dish. Sprinkle 1
to 2 tablespoons sugar
in dish; tilt from side to
side to coat bottom and
side of dish. Invert dish
and tap out excess
sugar.
2. Melt 3 tablespoons
butter in a medium
saucepan. Add flour;
cook stirring constantly,
1 minute.
3. Add milk slowly;
cook over medium heat,
stirring constantly, until
mixture thickens and
comes to a boil. Remove
from heat.
4. Beat in egg yolks, 1
at a time. Add 1/2 cup
granulated sugar; beat
into mixture. Stir in
Grand Marnier and
orange and lemon peel
until blended.
5. Beat egg whites until
stiff peaks form. Stir 2
tablespoons beaten egg
whites into orange
mixture to lighten. Fold
in remaining egg
whites.
6. Preheat oven to 350F
(180C). Spoon mixture
into prepared dish. Bake
30 to 35 minutes or until
puffed and golden
brown.
7. Dust with powdered
sugar; serve
immediately.
Makes 4 to 6 servings.

Pasta: A Gift from Italy

According to history books, it was Thomas Jefferson who introduced pasta to the United States. He brought a spaghetti die when he returned to the United States from a tour of duty as a diplomat in Europe. As President, he is reported to have served pasta in the White House. Although pasta may have been considered a special luxury food in Jefferson's time, it is enjoyed by everyone today as a delicious and unbelievably versatile food that is also inexpensive. When you think about it, it really is quite amazing how many different kinds of pasta and pasta dishes begin with the simple combination of flour, eggs, salt and oil. The basic recipe for pasta has not changed over the centuries, but the method for making it certainly has been simplified.

Fresh & Dry Pasta

When you plan to serve pasta, you have several choices. You can buy dry pasta in the supermarket, either domestic or imported. Or, if you have already discovered how much more delicious fresh pasta is than dry, but you don't want to make it yourself, you can buy fresh pasta in many supermarkets and in Italian-food stores. But if you want to eat the very best pasta of all, you will make it yourself. It is easier to make than you may think, and you don't have to buy a pasta machine to get started, although it certainly saves time if you have one.

Many Ways to Serve Pasta

Pasta can be added to soup, served as a first course, a main dish, a side dish, a salad or as a light meal. When pasta is cooked prior to being used in a casserole, it should be slightly undercooked because it will continue to cook when the casserole is finished in the oven. Allow 2 to 4 ounces uncooked pasta per person for a main dish. Reduce the amount by about half when making an appetizer or side dish. Although you will not really save time by cooking pasta in a microwave oven, a microwave is ideal for reheating leftover pasta or heating a pasta dish that was made in advance.

Basic Pasta

4 cups unbleached
   all-purpose flour
4 eggs
4 teaspoons vegetable
   oil
1 teaspoon salt

1. Take out ingredients and equipment before you start to work.

2. Sift flour onto a clean work surface, making a well in center with a fork.

3. Break eggs into well.

4. Add oil to well.

5. Add salt to well.

6. Using a fork, beat eggs lightly.

7. Gradually incorporate flour, pushing it under dough to keep it from sticking to board.

8. Begin kneading dough when half the flour has been incorporated.

9. Continue kneading until dough is smooth and elastic.

10. Cover dough with a clean towel; let rest 30 minutes.

11. Divide dough into 4 pieces; flatten each. Set rollers to wide setting. Roll 1 piece of dough at a time.

12. Lower setting and feed dough through rollers again.

13. Repeat passing of pasta through rollers down to lowest setting.

14. Pass dough through cutting blades to make wide or thin noodles.

How to Cook Pasta

Fill a large pot with 6 quarts of water for each pound of pasta to be cooked. Add 1 tablespoon salt and 1 tablespoon vegetable oil. The addition of oil will help prevent pasta from sticking together. Bring water to a rolling boil; add pasta. Reduce heat enough to keep water from boiling over, but high enough to keep water boiling. Cook, uncovered, to desired doneness. Depending on size of pasta, dry pasta will take about 10 minutes to cook; fresh pasta will cook in about 4 minutes. Remove a piece of pasta and taste it near the end of cooking time to determine if it is fully cooked. Pasta should be cooked *al dente* or tender but firm to the bite. Pasta should not be overcooked because it will get soft and mushy. However, it must be cooked long enough to eliminate the taste of raw flour. Stir during cooking only if necessary to prevent pasta from sticking. If stirring is necessary, stir very gently. Drain cooked pasta immediately to stop cooking. Do not rinse unless you want to cool pasta quickly for salad. Toss hot pasta with seasoned butter and grated Parmesan or Romano cheese, or cover with sauce and sprinkle with grated cheese.

If pasta is to be combined with other ingredients for a casserole, undercook it slightly and add it to other ingredients while still warm.

1. Heat 6 quarts water in a large saucepan. Add 1 tablespoon salt.

2. Add 1 tablespoon oil; bring water to a rolling boil over high heat.

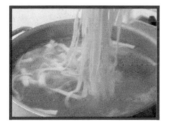

3. Add pasta to rapidly boiling water; reduce heat slightly.

4. Stir gently only if necessary to prevent pasta from sticking.

5. Pour pasta into strainer or colander; drain thoroughly.

6. Rinse pasta only if necessary to cool quickly for salad.

7. Melt butter in thoroughly dried pan; season to taste.

8. Add drained pasta; cook 1 to 2 minutes or until pasta is reheated. Serve immediately.

Making Pasta Without a Pasta Machine

Make pasta as shown in photos through step 10. Divide dough into 4 pieces. Place dough on a lightly floured work surface; roll out thinly and evenly with a lightly floured rolling pin. Sprinkle dough lightly with additional flour, if necessary. Spread sheets of dough on clean dish towels to dry. When dough is dry, cut into strips of desired width with a sharp knife or make other shapes as shown on pages 92-93.

Spatzle

2-1/3 cups all-purpose flour
1/2 teaspoon salt
2 eggs
2/3 cup water or stock
1/3 cup butter
Salt and pepper to taste
Grated nutmeg

1. Stir together flour and salt in a medium bowl.
2. Beat eggs and water or stock until blended. Add to flour; beat vigorously. Knead in bowl to make a smooth, soft dough.
3. Bring 4 quarts lightly salted water to a boil.
4. Cut off thin slivers of dough and drop into boiling water. Or press dough through a large-hole colander or spatzle maker.
5. Cook 3 to 5 minutes. Spatzle will rise to surface when cooked.
6. Drain well; place in a warm serving bowl.
7. Melt butter; pour over spatzle. Season with salt and pepper; toss lightly to coat. Sprinkle with nutmeg. Serve immediately. Makes 4 servings.

Traditional Pasta Sauces

Although pasta is delicious served with nothing more than melted butter, salt, pepper and freshly grated Italian cheese, it usually is served with a sauce. Most sauces are variations on three basic recipes—tomato sauce, cream sauce or green sauce. Once you have learned how to make the pasta and the sauces, you are ready to make almost any kind of pasta dish you wish.

Carbonara
(top right)

2 tablespoons olive oil
1 tablespoon butter
3 garlic cloves, crushed
1/3 lb. pancetta or boiled ham, diced
4 egg yolks
1/4 cup whipping cream, warmed
1/2 cup grated Parmesan or Romano cheese
Black pepper to taste
1 lb. fresh ribbon noodles

1. Heat oil and butter in a skillet. Add garlic; sauté until golden brown. Remove and discard garlic.
2. Add pancetta; cook over low heat until lightly browned. Set aside in skillet.
3. Place egg yolks, cream, cheese and pepper in a deep serving bowl; beat with a fork until thoroughly blended. Set aside.
4. Cook noodles in lightly salted boiling water; drain well. Add to egg-yolk mixture; toss to coat.
5. Reheat pancetta until very hot. Add to pasta; toss lightly. Sprinkle with additional pepper. Serve immediately.
Makes 4 to 6 servings.

Basic Cream Sauce

1/4 cup unsalted butter
2 tablespoons olive oil
1 small onion, finely chopped
1 to 2 garlic cloves, crushed
2 cups whipping cream
1/2 cup grated Parmesan or Romano cheese
White pepper to taste
Grated nutmeg

1. Heat butter and oil in a medium saucepan. Add onion and garlic; sauté until onion is transparent.
2. Add cream; bring to a boil. Cook over medium heat until sauce is reduced by half.
3. Remove pan from heat; add cheese. Stir until melted. Season with white pepper and nutmeg.
Makes about 1-1/4 cups.

Mushroom & Cream Sauce
(bottom center)

Prepare Basic Cream Sauce as directed above. Add 1/4 pound sautéed sliced mushrooms.

Herb Cream Sauce
(top center)

Prepare Basic Cream Sauce as directed above. Add 2 tablespoons freshly chopped herbs, such as basil, thyme, parsley, oregano or tarragon.

Pesto Sauce
(bottom left)

Recipe on page 147.

Fresh Tomato Sauce

2 lbs. ripe plum tomatoes
2 tablespoons olive oil
1 onion, finely chopped
2 garlic cloves, crushed
2 tablespoons freshly chopped basil
Salt and pepper to taste

1. Plunge tomatoes into boiling water 30 seconds. Peel and discard seeds; coarsely chop flesh.
2. Heat oil in a medium saucepan. Add onion and garlic; sauté until onion is transparent.
3. Add chopped tomatoes; cook over medium heat 15 to 20 minutes or until sauce thickens.
4. Add basil, salt and pepper; simmer 5 minutes.
Makes about 2-1/2 cups.

Hot Tomato Sauce
(bottom right)

8 bacon slices, diced
2 to 3 red chili peppers, seeded, diced
Fresh Tomato Sauce, above
1/2 cup grated Parmesan cheese

1. Cook bacon in a skillet until crisp. Remove bacon with a slotted spoon; drain on paper towels.
2. Drain off all but 2 tablespoons drippings. Add diced chilies; cook 2 minutes or sauté in butter.
3. Add bacon and chili to Fresh Tomato Sauce; simmer 5 minutes.
4. Stir in cheese before serving.
Makes about 2-1/2 cups.

Bolognese Sauce
(top left)

Recipe on page 226.

30 Ingredients to Combine with Pasta

Many ingredients blend well with pasta dishes. Mix and match the 30 suggestions on these pages and create your own new, innovative dishes. Use any shape pasta you wish. If you add sauce, be sure additional ingredients go well with the ingredients in the sauce. When you create a new dish, make a note of the ingredients and amounts you use so you can make the dish again in the same way, or make an adjustment you think will improve the dish.

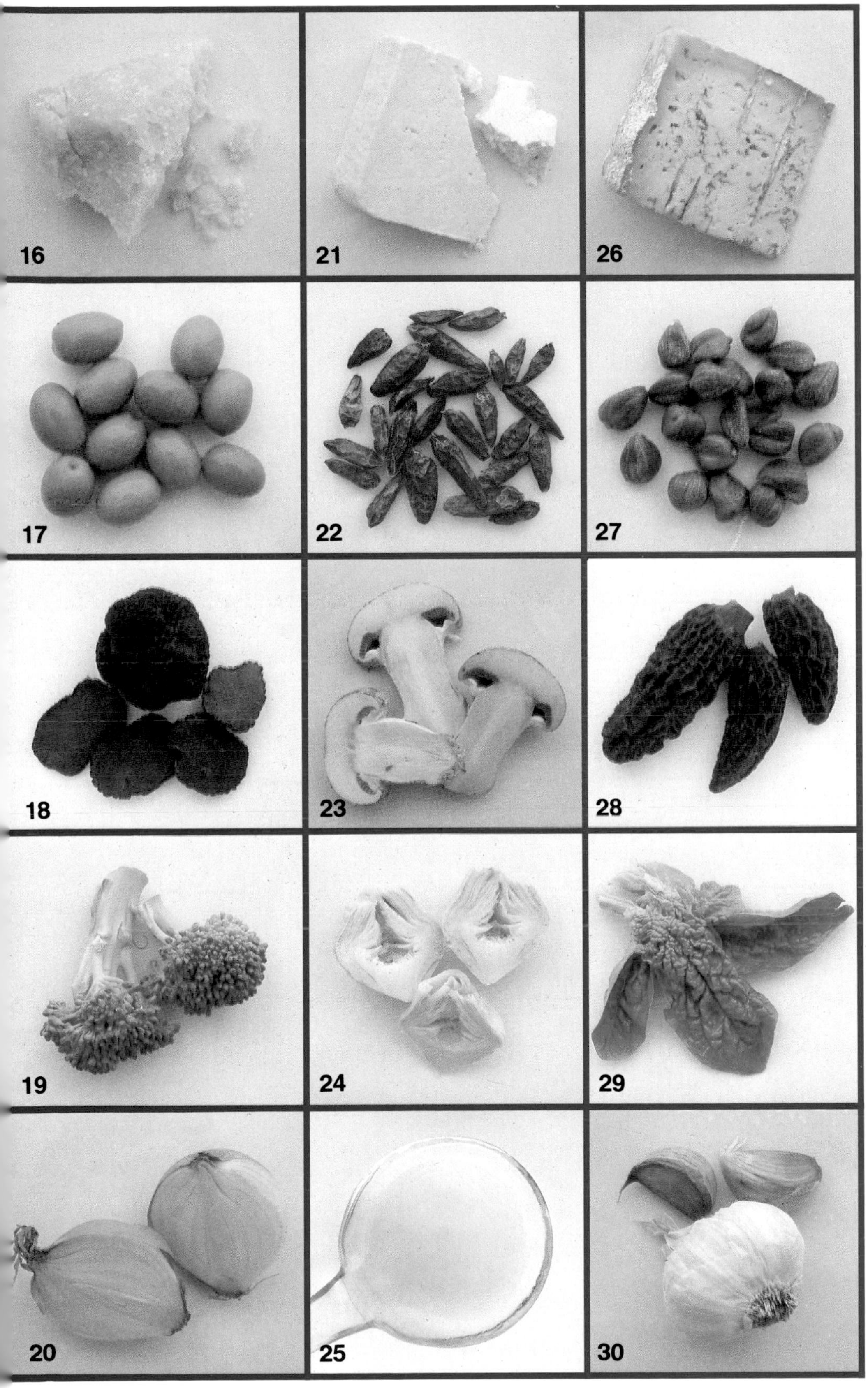

16

21

26

17

22

27

18

23

28

19

24

29

20

25

30

1. Mussels, cooked in white wine until opened.

2. Salami, cut into strips.

3. Egg yolk, stirred into pasta.

4. Tomato Paste, combined with wine and other ingredients to make sauce.

5. Basil, finely chopped.

6. Fresh cooked shrimp.

7. Prosciutto, diced or sliced.

8. Butter, melted and tossed with pasta.

9. Fresh chili peppers, seeded and chopped.

10. Rosemary, finely chopped.

11. Squid, cooked 8 to 10 minutes in white wine.

12. Bacon, cooked and crumbled.

13. Crème Fraîche or whipping cream, stirred into pasta.

14. Tomatoes, quartered for pasta salad or cooked for sauce.

15. Oregano, finely chopped.

16. Parmesan cheese, grated and sprinkled over pasta.

17. Olives, finely chopped.

18. Truffles, sliced and used as a garnish.

19. Cooked broccoli, added to pasta with melted butter and seasoning.

20. Onion, finely chopped and sautéed.

21. Ricotta cheese, finely crumbled and stirred into pasta.

22. Dried chili peppers, crushed and used sparingly.

23. Mushrooms, sliced, sautéed and added to hot pasta, or sliced and added raw to pasta salad.

24. Artichoke hearts, quartered and tossed with pasta.

25. Olive oil, heated and tossed with pasta.

26. Gorgonzola cheese, finely crumbled and mixed with pasta.

27. Capers, whole or finely chopped.

28. Morels tossed with pasta.

29. Blanched spinach, chopped and tossed with pasta.

30. Garlic, crushed, sautéed in olive oil and stirred into pasta.

The Art of Coloring Pasta

It is typical of the artistic nature of many Italians that, in addition to developing pasta and all kinds of wonderful shapes for it, they also discovered ways in which pasta could be colored naturally. By using colored pasta, you can change the look of a simple dish into something quite special, particularly if you blend pastas of different colors. Use your own sense of color to create beautiful dishes. Serve red pasta with fresh green broccoli, but not with tomato sauce. Serve green pasta with a lovely white cream sauce and garnish it with a touch of paprika.

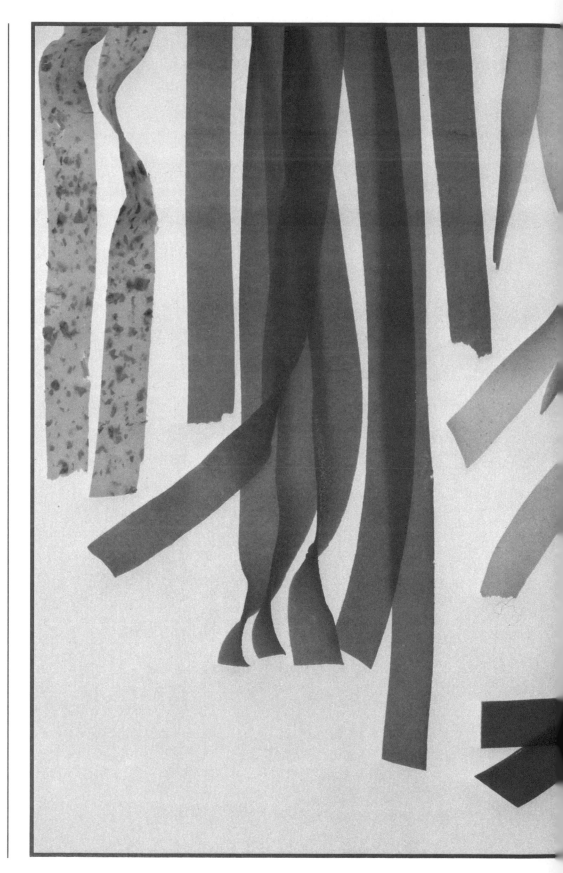

Prepare pasta using Basic Pasta, page 80.

Herb Pasta

Add 2 to 3 tablespoons finely chopped herbs to eggs; work into flour to make a smooth dough.

Tomato Pasta

Beat 2 to 3 tablespoons tomato paste into eggs; work into flour to make a smooth dough.

Saffron Pasta

Dissolve 1 teaspoon ground saffron in 1 tablespoon hot water; add along with eggs. Work into flour to make a smooth dough.

Beet Pasta

Add 1 to 2 tablespoons cooked pureed beets to eggs; work into flour to make a smooth dough.

Variations

● There are many other ways in which color can be added to pasta. Try adding 1 or 2 tablespoons cooked pureed carrots or spinach, or add some paprika to the dough.

Making Pasta Shapes

Once you have learned how to make and color pasta, you can go on to make pasta in a variety of different shapes. Be as creative as you like, but remember one essential rule. Once you have made the pasta dough, don't allow it to dry out. If the dough is dry, it will be crumbly and impossible to work with. Cover the dough with a damp cloth to keep it moist until you are ready to shape it. Several classic shapes are shown here.

Prepare Basic Pasta, page 80. Roll pasta by hand or in a pasta machine.

Lasagna (bottom left)

Prepare 2-1/2 cups Bolognese Sauce, page 226, and 1-1/2 cups Béchamel Sauce, pages 244-245. Cut pasta dough into strips, about 2 inches wide and 10 inches long. Cook about 4 minutes in lightly salted boiling water. Drain and arrange in layers in a greased baking dish. Spread Bolognese sauce between layers of noodles. Top with Béchamel Sauce. Sprinkle with Parmesan cheese. Bake in 450F (230C) oven about 15 minutes.

Variation
● Substitute Meat Sauce for Bolognese Sauce.
● Add a layer of mozzarella cheese.

Cannelloni (above left)

Cut thin sheets of pasta dough into 4- or 5-inch squares. Cook pasta squares quickly in lightly salted boiling water. Drain, fill and roll. See recipe, page 90.

Tortellini
(top left)

Cut thin sheets of pasta dough into 2-inch squares. Spoon a little filling, recipes opposite, onto each square. Fold squares over to make triangles; press edges together. Turn 2 outer points in toward center; press together.

Ravioli
(above center)

Cut thin sheets of pasta dough into 2-inch circles with a plain or fluted cutter. Spoon a little filling, recipes opposite, onto each circle. Fold circles over filling; press edges together.

Ricotta-Spinach Filling for Tortellini & Ravioli
(above center)

1 lb. fresh spinach
2 eggs, lightly beaten
1 cup ricotta cheese
1 cup grated Parmesan cheese
Salt and pepper to taste

1. Wash spinach several times under cold running water; discard coarse stems. Cook spinach in 1/4 cup lightly salted boiling water 3 minutes or until wilted. Drain well, squeezing out excess moisture; finely chop.
2. Place spinach and remaining ingredients in a bowl; blend well.
3. Use to fill any kind of pasta.
Additional fillings can be found on following pages.

Meat Filling for Ravioli & Tortellini
(above top)

1 tablespoon butter
1/4 lb. turkey or chicken breast, minced
1/4 lb. boneless veal, minced
1/2 lb. bulk sweet Italian sausage
2 eggs, lightly beaten
3/4 cup grated Parmesan cheese
Salt and pepper to taste
1/4 teaspoon grated nutmeg

1. Melt butter in a medium skillet. Add turkey or chicken, veal and sausage; cook over medium heat, stirring until sausage is no longer pink.
2. Drain off excess fat; place meat in a bowl. Add remaining ingredients; blend well. Refrigerate until ready to fill pasta.

Noodles
(far right)

Noodles can be cut in a pasta machine or by hand. To cut by hand, sprinkle rolled dough lightly with flour; fold over several times to make a flat roll. Cut roll into slices of desired width with a sharp knife, then unroll. To make wavy-edged noodles, cut strips from a flat sheet of dough with a decorator's knife or fluted pastry wheel.

Special Pasta Dishes

Occasionally questions are raised about whether Marco Polo brought pasta to Italy from China in the 13th century, or whether it was already there. No matter what the origin, it is the Italians who perfected pasta making and they, along with other countries, have created an array of pasta dishes.

Ravioli

1 recipe Basic Pasta, page 80
1/2 lb. lean ground pork
1/4 lb. lean ground beef
1 small onion, minced
1 lb. fresh spinach, blanched, coarsely chopped
1 teaspoon freshly chopped thyme or 1/2 teaspoon dried leaf thyme
1 tablespoon dry bread crumbs
Salt and pepper to taste
1 qt. stock or water
3 tablespoons butter
Grated Parmesan or Romano cheese, if desired

1. Prepare pasta through step 9, page 80. Cover with a damp cloth; set aside.
2. Place ground pork and beef in a medium skillet; cook until no longer pink.
3. Add onion; cook until transparent. Remove from heat; drain off fat.
4. Add spinach, thyme, bread crumbs, salt and pepper; blend well. Let cool.
5. Roll out each piece of pasta to a thin sheet; cut into 5" x 4" rectangles.
6. Place 1 tablespoon cooled filling in center of each rectangle. Brush edges of pasta with water; fold pasta over filling. Press edges firmly together to seal.
7. Bring stock or lightly salted water to a boil over medium heat. Add filled ravioli. Reduce heat and simmer 12 to 15 minutes or until pasta is cooked. Drain well.
8. Melt butter; drizzle over ravioli. Toss lightly. Serve with grated cheese, if desired.
Makes 4 to 6 servings.

Cannelloni

1 recipe Basic Pasta, page 80
3/4 lb. lean ground beef
2 oz. lean prosciutto, chopped
1 large onion, chopped
1 garlic clove, crushed
1 tablespoon all-purpose flour
1/4 cup tomato paste
1/2 cup dry red wine
1 teaspoon freshly chopped thyme or 1/2 teaspoon dried leaf thyme
Salt and pepper to taste
1-1/2 cups Béchamel Sauce, pages 244-245
Grated Parmesan or Gruyère cheese
Butter

1. Prepare pasta through step 9, page 80. Cover with a damp cloth; set aside.
2. Place ground beef and prosciutto in a medium skillet; cook until no longer pink.
3. Add onion and garlic; cook until transparent. Drain off fat.
4. Sprinkle flour over meat mixture; cook, stirring, 1 minute.
5. Blend tomato paste and wine; stir into mixture. Add thyme, salt and pepper. Simmer, stirring occasionally, until liquid has evaporated. Remove from heat; set aside.
6. Roll out each piece of pasta to a thin sheet; cut into 6" x 4" rectangles.
7. Bring 2 to 3 quarts lightly salted water to a boil. Drop 2 to 3 pasta rectangles into boiling water; cook 5 minutes. Remove with a slotted spoon; place on a damp towel. Repeat with remaining pasta.
8. Preheat oven to 375F (190C). Grease a large baking dish.
9. Place 2 tablespoons meat filling on each pasta rectangle; roll up. Arrange filled pasta, seam-side down, in a single layer in greased dish.
10. Spoon Béchamel Sauce over pasta. Sprinkle with grated cheese; dot with butter.
11. Bake in preheated oven 15 to 20 minutes or until cheese is melted and top is golden brown.
Makes 4 to 6 servings.

Won-Ton

1 recipe Basic Pasta, page 80
3/4 lb. lean ground pork
1/4 lb. mushrooms, minced
2 teaspoons dry sherry
1 teaspoon sesame oil
1 egg, lightly beaten
Salt and pepper to taste

1. Prepare pasta through step 9, page 80. Cover with a damp cloth; set aside.
2. Combine remaining ingredients, blending well.
3. Roll out each piece of pasta to a thin sheet; cut into 2-inch squares.
4. Place 1/2 teaspoon pork mixture in center of each square. Brush edges of pasta squares with water; bring edges up to meet in center, as shown.
5. Place about 1-inch water in a large saucepan. Arrange Won-Tons in steamer basket; cover and steam 30 minutes or cook in a Chinese wooden steamer following manufacturer's instructions.
Makes 4 to 6 servings.

A Variety of Pasta Shapes

Although you probably are familiar with pasta shapes such as macaroni, noodles, vermicelli and shells, you may not have encountered some of the unusual shapes available. Most Italians can reel off at least two dozen types of pasta without pausing to take a breath, many of which are not familiar to the average cook outside Italy. Some of the shapes, usual and unusual, are shown on the right. Many of them are available in the supermarket.

Pasta Shapes

(top left to right)
1. Maruzze, also known as conchiglie or shells. Available in several sizes.
2. Anellini rigati, used in soup.
3. Mezzani, also known as tubetti lunghi or macaroni.
4. Mostaccioli rigati
(center left to right)
5. Ditali, 1/2-inch tubes
6. Fusilli, spirals
7. Acini di Pepe, used in soup.
8. Gemelli, twin twists
9. Spaghetti
(bottom left to right)
10. Farfalle or bows
11. Cellophane noodles, made from mung beans, used in Oriental cooking.
12. Lumache or snails

Rice: Delicious, Nutritious & Easy to Cook

According to legend, rice arrived in America as a gift from grateful sea captain. His ship, in need of repair, was carrying rice to England from Madagascar in the late 17th century when it went off course and found its way to South Carolina. The only thing the captain had to give the colonists in appreciation for their help was rice. What he gave them was just one small bag! Rice grew so well in South Carolina that it became a source of great wealth for rice farmers. Although Arkansas, Louisiana and Texas are the main rice-growing states today, the origin of rice in this country is still evident in what is known as the Carolina rice industry. In the western world, rice is just one of many versatile foods, high in nutrients and good to eat. In many parts of the world, rice is the main source of food for millions of people. In spite of the many varieties of rice, and the many ways in which it can be cooked, it remains a food that can be prepared quickly and more easily than many think. Best of all, it goes well with a great many other foods.

How to Store & Cook Rice

The way in which rice is cooked depends on the type of rice as well as the recipe. Once plain rice has been cooked, it can be stored in the refrigerator or freezer, ready to use in soups, casseroles, desserts, fried or seasoned, heated and served as a base on which other food can be arranged. Rice is a major ingredient in many ethnic dishes, and each country has its own favorite method for preparation and seasoning.

The Myth That Will Not Die

Just about every package of rice sold carries the admonition "do not wash rice before cooking." But nonetheless, for some mysterious reason, people continue to wash rice, and sometimes even rinse it again after it has been cooked. Probably one reason some people wash rice is because they saw their mothers do it and have never given it a second thought. It probably is also true that there are those who think of rice incorrectly as they think of vegetables—a food that has been grown and handled before it reaches the kitchen, and therefore must be washed in the same way fresh fruit and vegetables are washed. There was a time when rice was coated with talc and glucose, and washing was necessary. But little, if any, coated rice is still sold and, in any case, according to law, it must be labeled "coated." In the unlikely event you come across a package of coated rice, don't buy it. Then you will never again have to wonder if it is necessary to wash rice. The rice you buy will have been washed, cleaned and milled before packaging. When you wash it at home, you accomplish only one thing—washing away nutrients.

Storing Rice

Store uncooked rice in a covered container in a cool, dry place. It will keep almost indefinitely. Store cooked rice in a covered container in the refrigerator up to 1 week. It can also be stored in the freezer about 8 months.

Cooking Rice

The first rule in cooking rice is to read the instructions on the package. Different kinds of rice require different amounts of water and different cooking times. With most white rice, the basic cooking method is to add rice and salt to boiling water, then cover and cook over low heat until most of the water has been absorbed. Do not stir. Allow cooked rice to stand, covered, about 5 minutes until all the water has been absorbed. Fluff with a fork, season and serve immediately.
If cooked rice is not going to be served immediately, place in a colander, cover and keep warm over simmering water. Rice can also be reheated in a covered dish in a microwave oven.

How Much Rice to Cook

● Estimate about 1/2 cup cooked rice per serving.
● 1 cup uncooked white rice will make about 3 cups cooked rice.
● 1 cup uncooked converted, parboiled or brown rice will make about 4 cups cooked rice.
● 1 cup instant precooked rice will make about 2 cups cooked rice.

1. Measure 1 cup long-grain rice and 2-1/2 cups water.

2. Pour water into a large saucepan; bring to a boil over high heat. Add rice.

3. Add 1/2 teaspoon salt and 1 tablespoon butter, if desired.

4. Stir once with a wooden spoon. Reduce heat, cover and simmer 20 minutes or until most liquid has been absorbed.

5. Let stand 5 minutes. Fluff rice with a fork; stir in additional butter and seasoning, if desired.

Variation
For added flavor, dissolve 1 bouillon cube in boiling water before adding rice. Omit salt. Garnish cooked rice with freshly chopped parsley.

Types of Rice

Rice grows in three lengths—long, medium and short, although medium-grain rice is very difficult to find. Depending on what part of the country you live in, you many find it all but impossible to buy both short and long-grain rice. Curiously, some parts of the country sell almost nothing but long-grain rice, while other parts of the country sell mostly short-grain rice. When cooked, medium and short-grain rice is soft and the grains tend to stick together. Properly cooked long-grain rice will hold its shape and the grains of rice will remain separate.

The difference between brown and white rice is not in what is grown, but in how the rice is milled after it has been harvested. When the outer hulls of the rice have been removed, the rice that remains has a light brown nutritious covering called *bran*. This is called *brown rice*. It has a delicious, nutty flavor, takes longer to cook than white rice and cannot be stored as long as white rice. When the bran layer is removed, the rice that remains is white rice. Although it is the bran layer that contains the largest amount of nutrients, most modern processing methods use a procedure that returns many of the nutrients to the white rice. This makes it a very nutritious food—providing the nutrients are not washed off before cooking!

As shown on the right, both short-grain and long-grain rice are available in many forms:

Brown Rice

Natural rice with bran layer. Cook in same manner as white rice, but cook about 45 minutes.

Enriched White Rice

Usually sold as Carolina rice. Polished rice with nutrients added.

Converted Rice

Treated during milling to force nutrients from bran layer into grains. Some of bran layer left on grains giving uncooked rice a yellow tint, rice is white when cooked. Parboiled, steamed and dried before packaging.

Precooked Rice

Cooked and dried before packaging. Requires minimal amount of cooking.

Wild Rice

Although wild rice is not an annual cereal grass as other rice is, it is almost always linked with rice. Wild rice is the seed of a different grass that grows wild in the northern part of the United States. Since it must be picked by hand, it is costly to harvest and very expensive to buy. Unlike regular rice, it is not milled and must be carefully and thoroughly washed and picked over to remove foreign particles. Wild rice is often combined with regular rice. When cooked alone it is cooked in more water than regular rice and must be cooked about 40 minutes.

Short-Grain Rice

Brown Rice

Enriched White Rice

Italian Rice

Precooked Rice

Long-Grain Rice

Brown Rice

Enriched White Rice

Converted Rice

Precooked Rice

Wild Rice

Serving Rice

The easiest way to serve rice is to cook it, season it and spoon it into a serving dish. But it can be served in many other ways. A molded ring of rice can be served hot or cold with a filling for a special company dish. Rice can also be packed into almost any shape well-greased container and unmolded onto a serving plate. The variations are almost endless and molded rice will add a festive touch to any meal.

Rice Molds

Prepare rice according to directions on page 96 or follow package directions. Season rice or mix with other ingredients. Pack into a well-greased mold, cover and place in refrigerator several hours to chill if rice is to be served cold. If rice is to be served hot, place filled mold in pan of hot water; bake in a preheated 350F (175C) oven 20 minutes. Invert onto a serving dish; remove mold.

Rice Ring

(top left)
Use a well-greased, 2-quart ring mold for 1 cup cooked rice. Fill center of hot rice ring with creamed chicken, fish, mushrooms or cooked fresh vegetables, such as peas. Fill center of cold ring with chicken, shellfish or vegetable salad.

Rice Parcels

(bottom left)
Separate sheets of rice paper and place on a damp cloth 15 minutes or until pliable. Spoon seasoned cooked rice, combined with cooked, diced vegetables or meat, if desired, onto center of rice paper. Dot with butter; then wrap. Arrange in a single layer in a steamer; cover and steam about 5 minutes. Rice paper can be bought in Oriental food stores. It tears easily and must be handled very carefully.

Rice Bowls

(top center)
Serve rice in the Oriental manner. Spoon rice into small bowls; top with well-seasoned cooked meat, poultry or fish. Eat with chopsticks.

Rice Timbals

(bottom center and top right)
Pack cooked rice into well-greased small soufflé dishes or nicely shaped small bowls. Bake or chill as directed above; unmold onto a serving dish.

Base of Rice

(bottom right)
Spoon rice onto a serving dish; top with kabobs, chili, cooked vegetables or cooked creamed poultry or fish.

24 Ingredients to Serve with Rice

Plain, unseasoned rice can be dull eating. Because rice combines so well with many ingredients, it is very easy to find ways to dress it up. Try some of the seasoning or ingredients shown here to create a wide range of interesting rice dishes. Use them alone or in combination with other foods for family or company meals.

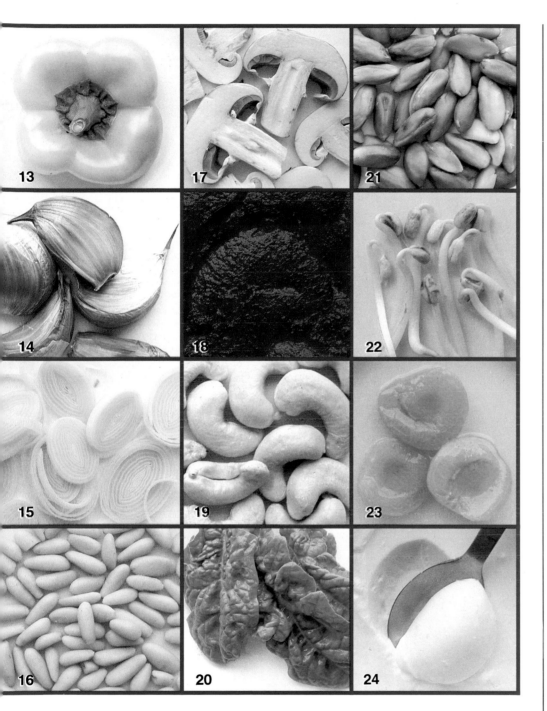

1. Herbs, freshly chopped and cooked with rice; added to cooked rice or used as garnish.
2. Tomatoes, peeled, seeded and chopped; cooked with rice or added, uncooked, to rice salad.
3. Saffron threads cooked with rice or saffron powder stirred into cooked rice.
4. Curry powder, cooked with rice or stirred into cooked rice.
5. Bacon, cooked, crumbled and stirred into cooked rice.
6. Sliced almonds, plain or sautéed and stirred into cooked rice.
7. Raisins, soaked in liquid and stirred into sweetened or unsweetened cooked rice.
8. Gingerroot, peeled, finely chopped and cooked with rice.
9. Cheese, grated and stirred into cooked rice.
10. Shrimp, cooked and served over rice with sauce.
11. Asparagus, cooked and served over cooked rice.
12. Peas, cooked and stirred into cooked rice.
13. Peppers, chopped, sautéed and stirred into cooked rice.
14. Garlic, minced, sautéed lightly and stirred into cooked rice.
15. Leeks, sliced, cooked and stirred into cooked rice.
16. Pine nuts stirred into cooked rice.
17. Mushrooms, sliced, sautéed and stirred into cooked rice.
18. Tomato sauce stirred into cooked rice, then heated.
19. Cashews, chopped and stirred into cooked rice.
20. Spinach, coarsely chopped, cooked and stirred into cooked rice.
21. Pistachios, finely chopped and stirred into cooked rice.
22. Bean sprouts stirred into rice salad.
23. Apricots, pitted, peeled, chopped and stirred into cooked, sweetened or unsweetened rice.
24. Dairy sour cream stirred into cooked, sweetened rice.

2 Classic Rice Dishes

Risotto from Italy and Pilaf from the Near and Middle East are two of the most famous and popular ethnic rice dishes. Although rice is the basic ingredient in both dishes, each dish has many versions. The variations are created by the addition of a wide variety of other ingredients.

Risotto

Risotto is made with short-grain rice. Meat, fish, poultry or vegetables can be added. The finished dish is served as a main course.

Basic Risotto

1 onion, finely chopped
1 garlic clove, crushed
1/2 cup butter
2-1/2 cups Italian Arborio or short-grain rice
1 cup dry white wine
5 to 6 cups hot chicken broth
1 cup grated Parmesan cheese
1 lb. cooked sliced mushrooms, if desired
1 lb. cooked small shrimp, if desired
1 lb. cooked spinach, if desired

This version comes from the Swiss Canton of Tessin rather than from Italy. It is usually made with *cepes,* a type of mushroom readily available throughout Europe. If you cannot find cepes, substitute button mushrooms, as shown.
Makes 8 to 10 servings.

1. Sauté onion and garlic in 6 tablespoons butter.

2. Add rice; sauté 2 minutes over medium heat.

3. Add wine; stir and bring to a boil.

4. Cook until liquid is reduced by half; add 1 cup hot broth.

5. Cook, stirring, until liquid is absorbed. Add remaining broth, 1 cup at a time.

6. Cook 20 to 25 minutes or until all liquid is absorbed, stirring frequently.

7. Stir in remaining 2 tablespoons butter and cheese.

8. Add mushrooms, shrimp or spinach, if desired.

1. Sauté onion in butter until transparent.

4. Cover tightly and reduce heat. Cook 20 to 25 minutes.

2. Add rice; sauté 2 minutes.

5. Stir in additional butter, if desired.

3. Add salt and broth; bring to a boil.

6. Add curry powder, raisins and apricots.

Pilaf

Pilaf is made with long-grain rice. It is popular in the Near East, Middle East and Eastern Mediterranean regions. Each country has a slightly different name for the dish, such as *Pilaff, Pilau, Pilaw, Pulau* or *Polo.*

Basic Pilaf

1 onion, finely chopped
1/4 cup butter
2 cups long-grain rice
1 teaspoon salt
4 cups hot chicken broth or beef broth
1 teaspoon curry powder
1 cup raisins
1 cup chopped apricots

In Middle Eastern countries, popular additions to rice pilaf include lamb, mutton, vegetables, nuts, aniseed or fennel seed. In Central Europe, chicken or turkey are usually added with paprika or pepperoni as additional choices. Makes 6 servings.

Paella

1 lb. mussels
1/2 cup olive oil
1/2 lb. boneless pork,
  diced
Salt and pepper to taste
2-1/2 lbs. chicken pieces
1 lb. chorizo or Spanish
  sausage, thickly
  sliced
2 onions, chopped
3 garlic cloves, minced
3 tomatoes, seeded,
  chopped
1 red-bell pepper,
  seeded, chopped
3 to 4 cups chicken
  broth
1/2 teaspoon dried leaf
  thyme
1 teaspoon saffron
  threads or 1/2
  teaspoon ground
  saffron
1/2 cup dry white wine
2 cups long-grain rice
1/2 lb. shrimp, peeled,
  deveined
1 (9-oz.) pkg. frozen
  artichoke hearts,
  thawed
1/2 cup frozen green
  peas
Lemon slices to garnish

A Spanish Specialty

Paella is a classic Spanish rice dish that usually includes shellfish, poultry, sausage and spices. As with many classic dishes, variations on the basic recipe can be found throughout the country. Paella is a major Spanish contribution to international cuisine that tastes of the sun and the sea. It is as beautiful to look at as it is delicious to eat.

1. Scrub mussels under cold running water. Remove beards. Discard any open mussels.

2. Heat 1/4 cup oil in a large skillet. Add diced pork; sauté until browned on all sides. Remove with a slotted spoon; set aside.

3. Season chicken pieces with salt and pepper; add to skillet. Cook until browned on all sides. Remove from skillet; set aside.

4. Add chorizo to skillet; cook until browned on all sides. Remove from skillet; set aside.

5. Add onions and garlic to skillet; sauté until onions are transparent.

6. Add tomatoes and red pepper; stir well. Cook 6 minutes.

7. Heat remaining 1/4 cup oil in a large paella pan. Add 1 teaspoon salt, 3 cups broth, thyme, saffron, wine and rice; stir well.

8. Add reserved pork, chicken, chorizo and tomato mixture. Bring to a boil; cover and simmer 10 minutes.

9. Preheat oven to 350F (175C). Add mussels, shrimp, artichoke hearts, peas and more broth, if necessary. Cover and bake 5 to 10 minutes.

10. Uncover and discard any mussels that are not open. Bake 5 to 10 minutes longer or until all liquid has been absorbed.

11. Season to taste; garnish with lemon slices.
Makes 6 to 8 servings.

Risi e Bisi

6 tablespoons butter
1 onion, chopped
1-1/2 cups Italian
    Arborio or short-grain
    rice
1/2 cup dry white wine
4 cups hot chicken
    broth or beef broth
1/4 teaspoon salt
2 cups fresh green peas
    or 1 (10-oz.) pkg.
    frozen green peas
1/3 lb. boiled ham, cut
    into strips
1/2 to 3/4 cup grated
    Parmesan cheese

1. Melt 1/4 cup butter
in a large saucepan.
Add onion; sauté until
transparent.
2. Add rice; sauté 2
minutes. Add wine;
cook until reduced by
half.
3. Add 2 cups hot
broth; cook, stirring
occasionally, until liquid
is absorbed.
4. Add salt, peas, ham
and remaining 2 cups
broth. Cook until rice
and peas are tender,
about 12 to 15 minutes,
stirring occasionally.
5. Stir in remaining 2
tablespoons butter and
cheese. Serve
immediately.
Makes 6 servings.

Serbian Meat & Rice

1/4 cup vegetable oil
1 lb. boneless pork,
    diced
3 onions, finely
    chopped
1 garlic clove, crushed
1 (16-oz.) can whole
    peeled tomatoes,
    chopped
3 tablespoons tomato
    paste
2-3/4 cups beef broth or
    water
1 teaspoon dried leaf
    thyme
1 tablespoon paprika
Salt and pepper to taste
1-1/4 cups long-grain
    rice
2 red-bell peppers,
    seeded, chopped
1 chili pepper, seeded,
    chopped
Freshly chopped parsley

1. Heat oil in a large
saucepan. Add pork;
cook until browned on
all sides.
2. Add onions and
garlic; sauté until onions
are transparent.
3. Add tomatoes with
juice, tomato paste and
broth or water; mix
well. Stir in thyme,
paprika, salt and
pepper. Bring to a boil;
reduce heat. Cover and
simmer 30 minutes.
4. Add rice, red
peppers and chili
pepper; stir well. Cover
and cook over low heat
20 to 25 minutes or until
all liquid has been
absorbed. Season to
taste; garnish with
parsley.
Makes 4 to 6 servings.

Fried Rice

2 garlic cloves, minced
1/4 cup soy sauce
5 tablespoons vegetable
    oil
1 lb. boneless beef or
    pork, cut into thin
    strips
4 slices boiled ham, cut
    into strips
4 cups cooked rice
1 bunch green onions,
    chopped, tops
    included
1/2 lb. shrimp, peeled,
    deveined
2 eggs, lightly beaten
Pepper to taste
Shredded Egg Flan,
    page 150

1. Combine garlic, soy
sauce and 2 tablespoons
oil in a glass bowl. Add
beef or pork; stir to
coat. Marinate 1 hour at
room temperature.
2. Heat remaining 3
tablespoons oil in a
large skillet or wok.
Add ham; stir-fry 1
minute.
3. Drain meat, reserving
marinade; add meat to
skillet. Stir-fry until
meat is cooked through.
4. Add rice; stir-fry
about 3 minutes.
5. Reserve 2
tablespoons onions.
Add remaining onions,
shrimp, and 2 to 3
tablespoons reserved
marinade. Stir well and
cook 5 minutes.
6. Add beaten eggs;
cook 2 to 3 minutes,
stirring constantly, until
eggs are set.
7. Season with pepper;
garnish with shredded
Egg Flan and reserved
green onions.
Makes 6 to 8 servings.

Nasi Goreng

1/4 cup vegetable oil
1 bunch green onions, chopped, tops included
2 garlic cloves, minced
1 onion, chopped
1/2 lb. beef top round, cut into thin strips
2 tablespoons curry powder
Salt and pepper to taste
3 cups cooked long-grain rice
1/2 lb. shrimp, peeled, deveined

1. Heat 2 tablespoons oil in a large skillet or wok. Reserve 2 tablespoons green onions. Add remaining green onions, garlic and onion; sauté until onion is transparent.
2. Add beef; stir-fry until meat is no longer pink. Add curry powder, salt and pepper; mix well. Cook 2 minutes.
3. Add remaining 2 tablespoons oil and rice; stir-fry until rice is coated and heated through.
4. Add shrimp; cook 5 minutes, stirring occasionally.
5. Spoon into a serving dish; garnish with reserved green onions. Makes 4 to 6 servings.

Rice Pudding with Stewed Fruit

1 (8-oz.) pkg. dried mixed fruit
1 cup short-grain rice
6 cups milk
3/4 cup sugar
1/4 teaspoon salt
1/2 (3-inch) cinnamon stick
2 teaspoons vanilla extract
2 cups dry white wine
1 cup whipping cream

1. Place dried fruit in a bowl. Add enough warm water to cover; let stand 1 hour.
2. Place rice, milk, 1/2 cup sugar, salt and cinnamon stick in a saucepan; stir well.
3. Bring to a boil over medium heat. Reduce heat; cover and simmer 1 hour or until rice is very soft, stirring occasionally.
4. Remove from heat; discard cinnamon stick.
5. Stir in vanilla. Cover and refrigerate until chilled.
6. Drain fruit and place in a saucepan. Add remaining 1/4 cup sugar and wine. Bring to a boil over medium heat. Boil rapidly 5 minutes.
7. Beat cream in a medium bowl until firm. Fold whipped cream into chilled rice pudding.
8. Spoon pudding into serving dishes; serve with drained stewed fruit.
Makes 6 to 8 servings.

Shireen Polo

1-1/2 cups long-grain rice
8 cups water
Salt to taste
Grated peel of 2 oranges
2 tablespoons butter
3 carrots, very thinly sliced
1/4 cup sugar
1/2 cup chopped pistachios
1/2 cup chopped blanched almonds
1/2 teaspoon ground saffron
1/4 cup vegetable oil
2-1/2 lbs. chicken pieces
1 onion, chopped

1. Place rice, 6 cups water and salt in a medium saucepan; bring to a boil. Cook 7 minutes.
2. Drain rice well; set aside.
3. Blanch orange peel in boiling water 1 minute. Drain and set aside.
4. Melt butter in saucepan. Add carrots; sauté 5 minutes. Add sugar, reserved orange peel, pistachios, almonds and saffron; cook over low heat, stirring until sugar is dissolved. Remove from heat; set aside.
5. Heat oil in a large skillet. Season chicken with salt; add to skillet. Brown on all sides. Add onion and remaining 2 cups water to skillet. Bring to a boil. Reduce heat and simmer 5 minutes.
6. Arrange reserved rice and reserved carrot-nut mixture over chicken. Cover and simmer 25 to 30 minutes or until chicken is tender and rice is cooked.
Makes 4 to 6 servings.

Potatoes: Delicious in So Many Ways

Potatoes made their way to North America in a very 'round about way. Native to South America, it is believed that Sir Francis Drake brought potatoes to England in the 16th century and from there they were introduced in Ireland. It was not until the 18th century that potatoes were imported from Ireland to North America for cultivation. Since that time, they have become increasingly popular and many well-known chefs have devoted much of their time and talent to the development of interesting and unusual ways to cook potatoes. Highly nutritious, the lowly potato has been much maligned as a fattening food. The fact is that unadorned potatoes are very low in calories, but when combined with such things as butter, dairy sour cream or gravy, they can indeed become fattening.

For best results when cooking potatoes, choose the right kind of potato for the recipe you are preparing. Although the all-purpose potato can be used for many recipes, Idaho and Russet potatoes are best for baking. Small, new potatoes are best for boiling and roasting.

Potatoes

Foil-Baked Potatoes

Use Idaho or Russet potatoes for baking. Wrap in foil or rub skins with butter or margarine; then bake. Serve with butter or a favorite topping.

1. Prick potatoes several times with a fork or wooden skewer.

2. Wrap potatoes tightly in foil. Bake in preheated 375F (190C) oven about 1 hour.

3. Unwrap and cut across on top.

Unpeeled Boiled Potatoes

Potatoes cooked in their skins retain most of their nutrients. This cooking method is ideal for small new potatoes, particularly those with thin skins.

1. Sort potatoes, choosing potatoes similar in size.

2. Scrub potatoes thoroughly; rinse under cold running water.

3. Place in a large saucepan; cover with water. Add salt and herbs, if desired. Bring to a boil; reduce heat.

Fried Potatoes & Onions

Boiled potatoes can be peeled and sliced, or diced and fried with onions. Add minced garlic for a superb flavor treat. Garnish with paprika and freshly chopped parsley.

1. Peel and slice boiled potatoes. Slice onions; separate into rings.

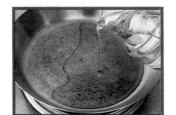

2. Heat vegetable oil in skillet.

3. Add potatoes; cook over medium heat 8 to 10 minutes, turning occasionally.

Peeled Boiled Potatoes

Potatoes can also be peeled before boiling. This method is recommended for large potatoes that should be cut before boiling.

1. Peel potatoes with a vegetable peeler or sharp paring knife.

2. Rinse under cold water; cut into even-sized pieces.

3. Place in a large saucepan; cover with water. Add salt; cover and bring to a boil.

French-Fried Potatoes

Prepare potatoes for frying ahead of time; then place in iced water until ready to fry. Dry thoroughly before cooking.

1. Peel potatoes; cut into 1/2-inch-thick strips.

2. Rinse under cold water; pat dry with a clean towel.

3. Heat oil in a deep-fryer to 400F (200C). Cook 1 cup potatoes in hot oil about 3 minutes.

4. Squeeze potato on bottom to open.

5. Dot with butter; season with salt and pepper or spoon topping over.

Recipes and photographs of delicious toppings for baked potatoes can be found on pages 112-113.

4. Cover and simmer 20 to 25 minutes. Drain well; peel, if desired.

Serve potatoes in skins with butter, or peel and mash, pages 114-115, or make Potato Croquettes, page 116.

4. Add onion; cook until potatoes are golden brown.

5. Season with salt and pepper.

Potatoes can be fried in vegetable oil, a combination of oil and butter or in clarified butter. Don't fry potatoes in unclarified butter because the butter will burn.

4. Reduce heat and cook 20 to 25 minutes or until fork tender.

5. Drain well.

Slightly undercook potatoes that are going to be cooked further, such as home-fried potatoes. Potatoes that are going to be mashed should be very tender, but not overcooked.

4. Remove and drain well; set aside.

5. Just before serving, deep-fry again 2 to 3 minutes or until golden brown.

Drain potatoes after second frying; sprinkle with salt. Serve hot. See variations for fried potatoes, page 117.

Toppings for Baked Potatoes

Baked potatoes can be served with a plain pat of butter, seasoned butter or a special topping. Try some of the combinations suggested here or create your own. Special butters or toppings can turn a simple baked potato into delicious company fare.

Onion & Bacon Butter

Cook 4 bacon slices until crisp; drain on paper towel. Crumble bacon; set aside. Sauté chopped onion in 1 tablespoon butter or bacon drippings until transparent. Remove with a slotted spoon. Add crumbled bacon and sautéed onion to 1/3 cup softened butter; blend well. Season with pepper and snipped chives, if desired.

Herb Butter

Add 3 tablespoons freshly chopped herbs, such as parsley, basil, tarragon or chives; 1 to 2 teaspoons lemon juice; 1 crushed garlic clove; and a dash of red (cayenne) pepper to 1/3 cup softened butter; blend well. Season to taste.

Dill Butter

Add 1-1/2 tablespoons freshly chopped dill and 1 to 2 teaspoons lemon juice to 1/3 cup softened butter; blend well. Season to taste.

Anchovy Butter

Add 2 teaspoons anchovy paste and 1 teaspoon lemon juice to 1/3 cup softened butter; blend well.

Curried Cream Cheese

Add 1 mashed small banana, 1 teaspoon curry powder and 1 to 2 tablespoons whipping cream to 3 ounces softened cream cheese; blend well. Season to taste.

Salmon Topping

Dice 2 slices smoked salmon. Add salmon and 1 to 2 teaspoons lemon juice to 1/3 cup dairy sour cream; blend well. Season to taste.

Cheese & Ham Topping

(top left)
Combine 3 ounces cream cheese; 2 tablespoons freshly chopped herbs, such as parsley, dill, chives, basil or thyme; and 2 tablespoons whipping cream. Season to taste. Cut 1 slice boiled ham into julienne strips. Spoon cheese topping onto 4 to 6 potatoes; top with strips of ham. Garnish with herbs.

Shrimp Topping

(center left)
Arrange small cooked shrimp on potato. Top shrimp with 1 tablespoon dairy sour cream. Garnish with sprig of basil.

Remoulade Topping

(bottom left)
Dice 4 sweet gherkins, 1 teaspoon drained capers, 2 anchovy fillets, 1 small onion and the white of 1 hard-cooked egg. Combine with 1/4 cup mayonnaise; season to taste. Spoon remoulade onto 4 potatoes. Garnish with sieved egg yolk, capers, parsley sprig and tiny gherkins cut into fan shapes.

Green-Peppercorn Topping

(top right)
Spread 1 to 2 tablespoons softened butter on top of each potato. Garnish with drained green peppercorns.

Blue-Cheese Topping

(center right)
Mash 2 to 3 ounces Gorgonzola or blue cheese with 1/4 cup dairy sour cream. Add 1 teaspoon lemon juice; season with freshly ground pepper. Spoon onto 4 to 6 potatoes; garnish with sprigs of fresh herbs.

Tomato & Cognac Topping

(lower right)
Combine 1 tablespoon ketchup with 1/4 cup mayonnaise. Add 1 to 2 teaspoons cognac and salt and pepper to taste. Spoon onto 4 to 6 potatoes; garnish with strips of peeled tomato and sprigs of chervil.

A New Look for Mashed Potatoes

Once potatoes have been boiled, it doesn't take long to turn them into light, fluffy mashed potatoes. But it takes a bit of practice to keep them from getting lumpy or gluey. It is very important to drain boiled potatoes thoroughly. To be sure your mashed potatoes will not be watery, return the cooked potatoes to the empty pan and shake them over low heat until all the excess moisture has been absorbed. Press potatoes through a potato ricer, mash well with a potato masher or puree in a food processor. Don't try to mash potatoes with a small fork because you will not be able to prevent lumps. When you add milk, add it slowly, beating constantly. The amount of milk necessary will depend on the size and type of potatoes used. If you add milk too quickly, or add too much, the potatoes will turn to glue. Be sure to season potatoes well before serving. Unseasoned mashed potatoes can taste very dull.

Mashed Potatoes Plus

It is not uncommon for better restaurants to serve pureed vegetables with the main course these days. Although this may seem to be a new fashion in food, it is in fact nothing more than an extension of an old familiar theme. Mashed white or sweet potatoes and mashed turnips are familiar to everyone. And when mashed properly, they are in effect pureed. But somehow many cooks have ignored the possibilities of serving other vegetables in puree form, unless they are preparing food for an infant. Almost any vegetable can be cooked, pureed and imaginatively seasoned. They add an elegant touch to a meal. And well-seasoned pureed vegetables can be combined with simple, old-fashioned mashed potatoes for a delicious new taste treat.

Mashed Potatoes

2 to 2-1/2 lbs. potatoes, peeled (about 6 medium)
1/4 to 1/2 cup butter
About 1 cup milk or half and half, warmed
Salt and pepper to taste
Paprika
Freshly chopped parsley

1. Boil potatoes in lightly salted water until fork tender.
2. Drain well and mash in potato masher, press through potato ricer or puree in food processor.
3. Add butter; stir until melted and well combined. Add milk gradually, beating constantly.
4. Season with salt and pepper.
5. Return potatoes to low heat; cook, stirring, until heated through.
6. Spoon into a warm serving dish. Garnish with paprika and parsley.
Makes 4 to 6 servings.

Pea & Potato Puree

1-1/2 lbs. potatoes, peeled, cooked (about 4 medium)
1/4 cup butter
2/3 cup milk
2 cups fresh green peas or 1 (10-oz.) pkg. frozen green peas
Chicken broth
Salt and pepper to taste
Mint sprig

1. Prepare mashed potatoes as above using 1/4 cup butter and 2/3 cup milk; set aside.
2. If using fresh peas, place peas and 1-1/4 cups chicken broth in saucepan; bring to boil. Reduce heat and simmer 5 to 7 minutes or until tender. If using frozen peas, prepare according to package directions, substituting chicken broth for water.
3. Drain well. Reserve 1 tablespoon peas; puree remaining peas in a blender or food processor fitted with a metal blade.
4. Combine pureed peas with mashed potatoes in saucepan; stir until well blended. Season with salt and pepper; cook over low heat until thoroughly warmed.
5. Spoon into a warm serving dish; garnish with warmed reserved peas and a sprig of mint.
Makes 4 to 6 servings.

Herbed Potato Puree

1 recipe Mashed Potatoes, above
1 tablespoon freshly snipped chives
1 tablespoon freshly chopped parsley
1 tablespoon freshly chopped thyme
Salt and pepper to taste
Herb sprigs

1. Prepare mashed potatoes.
2. Add chopped herbs; stir well. Season with salt and pepper.
3. Reheat, if necessary. Spoon into a warm serving dish. Garnish with sprigs of fresh herbs.
Makes 4 to 6 servings.

Additional Ideas for Serving Mashed Potatoes

1. Stir in grated Parmesan, Cheddar or other grated cheese.
2. Combine with applesauce, mashed turnips or other pureed vegetables.
3. Top with fried onion rings.
4. Sprinkle with cooked, crumbled bacon or crumbled blue cheese.
5. Spoon tomato sauce or gravy over.
6. Use as a casserole topping.
7. Make Potato Croquettes, page 116.

Carrot & Potato Puree

1-1/2 lbs. potatoes, peeled, cooked (about 4 medium)
1/4 cup butter
2/3 cup milk
2 cups peeled, sliced carrots
1-1/4 cups chicken broth
Salt and pepper to taste
Chervil

1. Prepare mashed potatoes as opposite using 1/4 cup butter and 2/3 cup milk; set aside.
2. Place carrots and broth in a saucepan; bring to a boil. Reduce heat; cook 10 to 12 minutes or until tender.
3. Drain well. Reserve 4 to 6 carrot slices; puree remaining carrots in a blender or food processor fitted with a metal blade.
4. Combine pureed carrots with mashed potatoes in saucepan. Stir until well blended. Season with salt and pepper. Cook over low heat until thoroughly warmed.
5. Spoon into a warm serving dish; garnish with warmed reserved carrots and chervil.
Makes 4 to 6 servings.

Tomato & Potato Puree

1-1/2 lbs. potatoes, peeled, cooked (about 4 medium)
1/4 cup butter
2/3 cup milk
2 to 3 ripe tomatoes
Salt and pepper to taste
Tomato wedges
Basil sprig

1. Prepare mashed potatoes as opposite using 1/4 cup butter and 2/3 cup milk; set aside.
2. Plunge tomatoes into boiling water 30 seconds; peel tomatoes.
3. Coarsely chop tomatoes, discarding seeds. Puree flesh in a blender or food processor fitted with a metal blade.
4. Combine tomato puree and mashed potatoes in saucepan. Stir until well blended. Season with salt and pepper. Cook over low heat until thoroughly warmed.
5. Spoon into a warm serving dish; garnish with tomato wedges and a sprig of basil.
Makes 4 to 6 servings.

Mashed Potatoes with Elegance

There are many elegant potato dishes that can be made using mashed potatoes as the base. Potato Croquettes are made by adding a few ingredients to mashed potatoes, shaping and coating the mixture, and then cooking the potatoes in a deep-fat fryer. Potato Pancakes, often made with grated raw potatoes, can also be made with mashed potatoes. And when elegance is really called for, mashed potatoes can be piped and heated in the oven to make Duchess Potatoes. All of these special potato dishes are illustrated on the right.

Potato Croquettes (top right)

4 to 5 cooked, peeled potatoes
4 egg yolks, beaten
1/8 teaspoon grated nutmeg
Salt and pepper to taste
3 tablespoons all-purpose flour
3 tablespoons fine dry bread crumbs
Vegetable oil for deep-frying

1. Mash potatoes while still warm.
2. Add 2 beaten egg yolks, nutmeg, salt and pepper; blend well.
3. Shape mixture into 1-inch-thick logs. Cut logs into 2-inch lengths.
4. Coat each piece in flour; then dip in remaining egg yolks and roll in bread crumbs. Place on waxed-paper-lined baking sheets.
5. Heat oil in a deep-fat fryer or skillet; fry croquettes, a few at a time, until golden brown. Remove with a slotted spoon; drain on paper towels.
Makes 4 to 6 servings.

Variations
● Potato Croquettes can be shaped into short or long logs, balls or cones.
● In addition to a classic coating of flour, egg and bread crumbs, the croquettes can be rolled in sliced almonds before they are rolled in bread crumbs. They can also be rolled in crushed cellophane noodles or vermicelli instead of bread crumbs.
● To make a light and delightfully puffy croquette, double-fry as in French-Fried Potatoes, pages 110-111.

Potato Pancakes (lower left)

1 recipe Potato Croquettes, coating omitted
6 bacon slices
1 tablespoon butter
2 onions, finely chopped
1/4 cup freshly chopped parsley
1 egg yolk
Vegetable oil for frying

1. Prepare Potato Croquettes through step 2; set aside.
2. Cook bacon in skillet until crisp; drain on paper towels. Heat butter in a small skillet; sauté onion until transparent. Remove with a slotted spoon; drain on paper towels.
3. Crumble bacon; stir into potato mixture. Add onion, parsley and egg yolk; stir until blended.
4. Shape mixture into small flat cakes. Pan fry in hot oil over medium heat until golden brown on both sides. Remove and drain on paper towels.
Makes 4 servings.

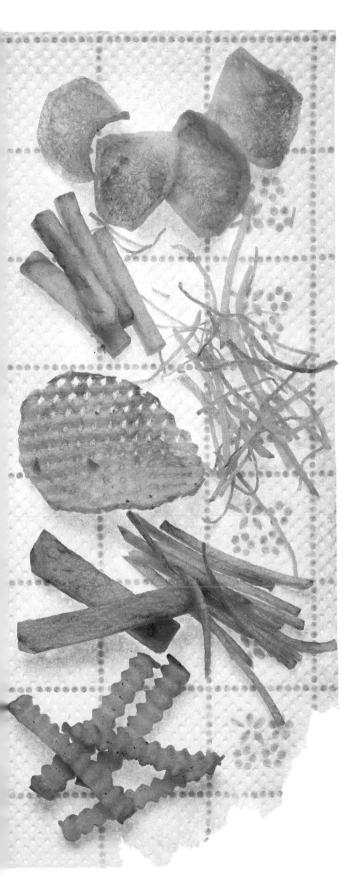

Duchess Potatoes
(bottom far left)

1 recipe Potato
   Croquettes, coating
   omitted
2 egg yolks
1 tablespoon butter,
   softened
2 tablespoons melted
   butter

1. Prepare Potato
Croquettes, through step
2; set aside.
2. Line baking sheets
with parchment paper;
grease paper. Preheat
oven to 400F (200C).
3. Add egg yolks and
softened butter to potato
mixture; blend well.
4. Spoon mixture into a
pastry bag fitted with a
large open star tip. Pipe
in small mounds onto
lined baking sheets.
Drizzle a little melted
butter over each potato
mound.
5. Bake in preheated
oven 5 to 10 minutes or
until golden brown on
top. Remove with a
spatula; arrange on a
platter around roast
meat.
Makes 4 servings.

Deep-Fried Potatoes

Deep-fried potatoes come in a wide
variety of shapes and sizes. They are a
welcome addition to any menu and
surely a favorite food of children and
adults alike. See pages 110-111 for cooking method.

(left, top to bottom)

Potato Chips

Thinly slice potatoes; deep-fry once.
Drain on paper towels and sprinkle
with salt.

Thin French-Fried Potatoes

Cut potatoes into sticks, 1/4 inch thick
and 2 inches long. Deep-fry once; drain
and salt.

Potato Straws

Cut potatoes into thin, narrow strips;
fry as above.

Potato Gaufrettes

Cut potatoes according to directions on
pages 26 and 31; fry as above.

Matchstick Potatoes

Cut French-Fried Potatoes in half
lengthwise; fry as above.

French-Fried Potatoes

Cut potatoes into strips 1/2 inch thick
and 2 inches long with a straight-edge
or decorator's knife; deep-fry once or
twice. Drain and salt.

Shallow-Fried Potatoes

Boiled potatoes can be turned into all kinds of unusual dishes by combining them with other ingredients and pan frying.

Cream-Style Potatoes

4 to 5 medium potatoes, boiled
3 tablespoons vegetable oil
2/3 cup milk
2/3 cup whipping cream
Salt and pepper to taste

1. Peel and dice cooled potatoes.
2. Heat oil in a medium skillet; add potatoes. Cook until golden brown, stirring occasionally.
3. Add milk and cream; bring to a gentle boil. Cook until sauce thickens, stirring frequently.
4. Season with salt and pepper; serve immediately.
Makes 4 servings.

Caramelized Potatoes

1-1/2 lbs. small new potatoes, boiled
2 tablespoons butter
3 tablespoons sugar

1. Peel potatoes, if necessary.
2. Melt butter in skillet; add sugar. Cook, stirring until sugar is completely dissolved and light caramel in color.
3. Add potatoes to syrup in pan; cook, stirring constantly, until potatoes are well coated. Serve immediately.
Makes 4 servings.

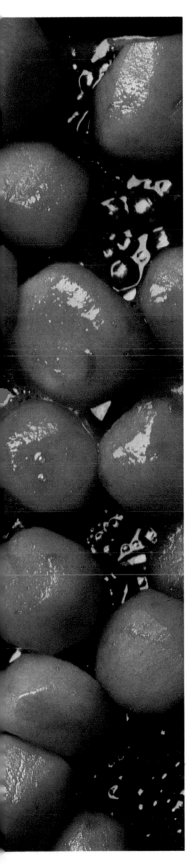

Country Breakfast

2 large potatoes, boiled
4 bacon slices, cut in
  half
3 tablespoons butter
2 small onions, thinly
  sliced
4 to 6 mushrooms,
  sliced
2 eggs, beaten
Salt and pepper to taste

1. Peel, if necessary, and dice cooled potatoes; set aside.
2. Cook bacon in skillet until crisp. Drain on paper towels; set aside.
3. Melt butter in a medium skillet; add onions. Sauté about 2 minutes. Add mushrooms; sauté 3 minutes.
4. Add potatoes; cook about 4 minutes, stirring, until potatoes are browned.
5. Return bacon to pan; stir. Stir in eggs; cook 2 to 3 minutes or until eggs are set.
6. Season with salt and pepper. Serve immediately.
Makes 2 servings.

Wonderful Ways to Bake Sliced Potatoes

These three classic recipes are all made with sliced raw potatoes. Prepare them ahead of time; then place in the oven 1 hour before you are ready to eat. Once they are in the oven, you can forget about them while you prepare the rest of the meal.

Scalloped Potatoes (opposite)

4 medium potatoes
2 tablespoons
  all-purpose flour
1/4 cup butter
1-1/4 cups half and half
  or milk
Pinch grated nutmeg or
  dry mustard
Salt and pepper to taste

1. Peel and thinly slice potatoes.
2. Grease a round 10-inch baking dish. Preheat oven to 350F (175C).
3. Arrange half the potato slices in bottom of prepared dish. Sprinkle with half the flour; dot with half the butter. Repeat with remaining potatoes, flour and butter.
4. Heat milk or half and half in a small saucepan until tiny bubbles begin to form around inside edge of pan. Season with nutmeg or dry mustard, salt and pepper. Pour evenly over potatoes.
5. Bake in preheated oven 1 hour or until potatoes are fork tender. Makes 4 servings.

Potatoes au Gratin (top left)

1 recipe Scalloped
  Potatoes, left
1/4 teaspoon paprika
3/4 cup shredded Swiss
  or Gruyère cheese
2 tablespoons fine dry
  bread crumbs

1. Prepare Scalloped Potatoes through step 3.
2. Add paprika and half the cheese to hot milk; stir until cheese is melted. Pour over potatoes.
3. Scatter remaining cheese on top of potatoes; sprinkle with bread crumbs.
4. Bake in preheated 350F (175C) oven about 1 hour or until potatoes are tender and top is golden brown. Makes 4 servings.

Potatoes Anna (center left)

4 medium potatoes,
  peeled
Salt
5 to 6 tablespoons
  butter, melted

1. Preheat oven to 400F (200C). Butter an 8 or 9-inch pie plate.
2. Thinly slice potatoes; place in iced water. Let stand 10 minutes. Drain well and pat dry with paper towels.
3. Sprinkle potatoes lightly with salt; toss gently.
4. Arrange potatoes, slightly overlapping, in prepared dish. Drizzle melted butter on top. Cover with foil; bake in preheated oven 20 minutes. Uncover and bake 45 minutes or until potatoes are tender and top is golden brown. Makes 4 servings.

Tip:
● Potatoes are not the only vegetable that can be cooked this way. You can substitute almost any root vegetable, although baking time may have to be adjusted. Check periodically after half the cooking time; bake until vegetables are fork-tender.

Vegetables: Healthy & Delicious

A slow walk down the aisle in the produce department of a modern supermarket, with mounds of fresh vegetables piled high on either side, is an exciting shopping experience that can engage most of our senses. The profusion of bright colors, the wonderful mixture of earthy smells, the varied textures and the anticipation of delicious, healthy eating, all can combine to make choosing fresh vegetables the high point of food shopping.

5 Ways to Prepare Vegetables

Of the five methods shown for preparing vegetables, only one method, sautéing, is a dry heat method. Generally vegetables are cooked by moist heat, and sometimes a combination of methods is used. For example, vegetables can be blanched and frozen, then cooked by another method after defrosting. Or they can be parboiled and then fried or baked. Almost all vegetables can be prepared by any of the methods shown. In addition, they can be baked, deep-fried, stir-fried and cooked in a microwave oven.

Vegetable Storage

There is no single rule for storage of fresh vegetables because different kinds of vegetables require different storage. Vegetables such as onions and white potatoes can be stored safely for several weeks or longer if they are kept in a cool, dry, dark place. Beets, cabbage and carrots can be kept in the refrigerator as long as 2 weeks. On the other hand, many fragile vegetables, such as asparagus and spinach, should be stored only 1 or 2 days, and used as soon as possible after purchase. When vegetables are stored in the refrigerator, they should be placed, unwashed, in a plastic bag and kept in the crisper drawer. Restrict your purchase of fresh vegetables to the amount you can use while still in prime condition.

Blanching

Brief cooking in boiling water prior to freezing, peeling or cooking by another method.

1. Trim ends off 1 pound of green beans; rinse under cold running water.

2. Place enough water to cover and salt in a large saucepan. Bring to a boil.

Steaming

Cooking in steamer basket over a small amount of boiling water in a tightly covered pan.

1. Trim and wash 1 pound of broccoli. Arrange in a steamer basket.

2. Pour 1-inch water into a large saucepan.

Braising

Cooking sliced or chopped vegetables in butter and a small amount of water or stock.

1. Melt 1 tablespoon butter in a saucepan or skillet.

2. Add 1 pound sliced carrots; stir to coat.

Boiling

Cooking whole or cut vegetables in lightly salted boiling water.

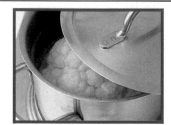

1. Rinse cauliflower in cold water.

2. Place in a large saucepan of lightly salted water; cover.

Sautéing

Cooking evenly cut vegetables quickly in butter and oil over high heat.

1. Trim ends from 1 pound zucchini; cut into matchstick pieces.

2. Heat 2 tablespoons butter and 1 tablespoon oil in skillet or wok over high heat.

3. Add beans to rapidly boiling water.

4. Cook 5 minutes. Beans should remain crisp and firm.

5. Remove with a slotted spoon; rinse under cold water to stop cooking.

3. Place filled steamer basket inside saucepan.

4. Cover tightly and bring to a boil over high heat.

5. Reduce heat and simmer 8 to 10 minutes or until broccoli is crisp-tender.

3. Add about 1/2 cup water or stock; bring to a boil.

4. Cover and reduce heat; simmer 10 to 12 minutes or until tender.

3. Bring to a boil over high heat; cook about 15 minutes.

4. Remove with a large skimmer or slotted spoon; drain thoroughly.

5. Season and serve with butter or sauce.

3. Add zucchini to skillet. Season with salt and pepper.

4. Cook over high heat, stirring constantly.

5. Check after 3 minutes. Zucchini should be crisp-tender. Cook longer, if necessary.

Finding Out About Vegetables

It might be fun to speculate why some vegetables are familiar to all of us and some rarely, if ever, appear on our dinner plates. Until recently vegetables were often considered a necessary evil, the food children had to finish eating before they could have dessert. Familiarity with one vegetable as opposed to another is probably related to limited availability in the past, or to the taste preferences of the cook who planned the meals of our childhood. If, as you were growing up, you were never served a specific vegetable, the chances are reasonably good you will hesitate before purchasing it. But, as healthy eating grows in popularity, and more and more vegetables are available year-round, interest in new ways to prepare familiar and unfamiliar vegetables has increased. The more we learn about the many kinds of vegetables available, the more we are able to vary menus and provide meals that are as nutritious as they are delicious.

Kohlrabi

The pale green, thickened stem of this member of the cabbage family can be eaten raw or cooked. Occasionally the leaves of very young tender plants are also eaten.

Availability—Peak season is June and July. Also available May to November.

Selection—Choose small or medium bulbs with fresh green leaves. Large bulbs may have a woody texture.

Preparation—Trim bulbs and peel before or after cooking. Cut into julienne strips to serve raw in salad or as crudite. Slice, cube or julienne; cook in lightly salted water 20 minutes or until just tender. Season with butter, nutmeg, salt and pepper. May also be steamed, braised, baked or fried, and can be served with a cream sauce and grated cheese.

Yield—1 pound kohlrabi will yield 2 to 3 servings.

Spinach

Fresh spinach is available loose by the pound, or packaged in plastic bags, usually about 10 ounces each. Serve raw in salad or cook and serve whole or chopped.

Availability—Peak season is early spring, but available all year.

Selection—Choose crisp green leaves, the younger the better. Avoid limp, yellowed, moist leaves that look bruised.

Preparation—Trim off roots and heavy stems. Wash several times under cold running water to remove sand and grit. After washing, soak 5 minutes in cold water to release any stubborn sand still clinging to leaves. Drain and place in a large non-aluminium pan with nothing but the water that clings to the leaves. Cover; cook gently 5 minutes. Drain well. Leave whole or chop and season with your choice of butter, lemon juice, vinegar, Worcestershire sauce, nutmeg, salt and pepper. Combine with cream sauce and cheese; use to make soufflé or quiche; wrap in phyllo dough; or use as a base under seafood, creamed chicken or eggs.

Yield—1 pound fresh spinach will yield about 1 cup cooked spinach, about 2 servings.

Broccoli

Like cauliflower, broccoli is related to cabbage. It is sold in bunches and can be eaten raw or cooked.

Availability—Peak season is October to May, but available all year.

Selection—Choose firm, tightly packed heads that are dark green or purple. Avoid bunches with any sign of wilt or tinge of yellow.

Preparation—Trim off leaves and bottoms of stems. Peel and trim stems or cut into flowerets. Steam about 12 minutes, cook in lightly salted boiling water about 8 minutes or until fork-tender, parboil and stir-fry, use in casseroles or serve with Hollandaise Sauce, pages 252-253, or bread-crumb topping.

Yield—1 bunch broccoli weighs about 2 pounds and yields 4 to 6 servings.

Sweet Bell Peppers

Bins filled with bright green-bell peppers are a familiar sight. At certain times of the year, you will find a supply of glorious red peppers next to them. They are in fact identical vegetables, the red pepper having been left on the vine long enough to change from green to red. Since red peppers require more care to produce, they are also more expensive and usually slightly sweeter. Yellow peppers are a different variety of pepper, expensive and often difficult to find. On rare occasions white or deep purple peppers can also be found, but they are even more expensive than yellow peppers. All sweet peppers can be served raw or cooked.

Availability—Green peppers are available all year, other peppers are available seasonally.
Selection—Choose very firm peppers that are not wrinkled or bruised.
Preparation—Remove stem end and seeds. Cut into strips and serve raw; dice or cut into strips and sauté to combine with other food; blanch or char to remove skin if desired; stuff and bake whole or halved.
Yield—1 large pepper will yield about 1 cup diced pepper.

Tomatoes

There are many varieties of tomatoes from big beefsteaks to small cherry tomatoes. The real difference in tomatoes is not in the variety as much as the season. Locally grown tomatoes, available during summer months, bear no resemblance in flavor, texture or smell to the chemically ripened tomatoes sold during the winter. Although some of the expensive imported tomatoes available in winter are of good quality, winter is the time to use canned tomatoes instead of fresh. Fresh tomatoes are eaten raw or cooked in every imaginable way.

Availability—Good fresh tomatoes are available from late June to early October. Canned tomatoes are available all year.
Selection—Choose firm plump tomatoes with a fresh distinctive odor. Avoid soft bruised tomatoes with cracked or pale skin.
Preparation—To peel tomatoes, blanch 30 to 45 seconds; peel off skin. To remove seeds, cut in half and squeeze gently through strainer. Discard seeds; use pulp and juice. Use fresh tomatoes in salads, sandwiches and as a garnish. Use cooked tomatoes as a baked or stewed vegetable, in sauces, casseroles, stews and soup.
Yield—1 pound fresh tomatoes will yield 1-1/2 cups cooked tomato.

Brussels Sprouts

This tiny member of the cabbage family grows in tight little buds in circles around a heavy stalk topped by a cabbage rose. This unusual wonder of nature makes a unique centerpiece. Although Brussels sprouts can be used cold in a salad, they are always cooked first.

Availability—Peak season is October to May because sprouts are thought to benefit from a touch of frost before harvesting.
Selection—Buy the smallest sprouts available with bright green color and firm to the touch.
Preparation—Wash carefully and check for insects between the leaves. Trim stem end and remove any damaged outer leaves. Cut an X in the bottom of each sprout for even cooking. Steam or cook in lightly salted water 8 to 10 minutes. Do not overcook. Season with butter, lemon juice, salt and pepper. Combine with nuts, particularly chestnuts, or with cream sauce.
Yield—1 pound Brussels sprouts will yield about 4 servings.

Additional Vegetable Know-How

The most important rule about cooking vegetables by any method is to avoid overcooking. Properly cooked vegetables should have a bit of crunch to them and should never be served limp or soggy. The longer a vegetable is cooked, the more nutrients it will lose and the less appealing it will be to eat.

Any vegetable that can be cooked in lightly salted boiling water can also be steamed. Steaming has the advantage of keeping the color of a vegetable bright and eliminating the need to pour off cooking liquids filled with nutrients. When a vegetable has been boiled, it must be drained as soon as it is cooked or it will continue to cook while it sits in hot water. The same principle is true for steamed vegetables. If they are allowed to remain in the steamer after they are cooked, they will go on cooking. If necessary, a quick reheating is preferable to keeping a vegetable hot in water or over steam.

Unfortunately there still are cooks who do not understand the need to drain vegetables thoroughly and properly. Vegetables served in a puddle of cooking liquid can spoil the appetite of even the most determined eater.

Not only do vegetables have to be drained in a colander or strainer, but before butter or a sauce are added, the vegetables should be returned to the empty pot and placed over low heat briefly to evaporate any remaining liquid, a process the English call *sweating*. Even the smallest amount of liquid remaining in the pot or on the vegetables will dilute a butter or cream sauce.

Few, if any, vegetables are appealing if they are served without some seasoning. The quickest and easiest seasoning is a little butter, salt and pepper. The flavor of many vegetables is further enhanced by a few drops of fresh lemon juice. Simple cream sauces, or more elegant sauces, such as Hollandaise Sauce, pages 252-253, go well with many vegetables, as do toppings that can include nuts, cheese, herbs or sautéed bread crumbs.

Special Legumes

Beans and peas are both legumes, vegetables with seeds that form inside a pod. Sometimes only the seeds are eaten, as with green peas and mature fava beans. When the pod is tender, as the pods of edible pea pods and string beans are, the whole vegetable is eaten. In addition to the peas and beans shown on the right, there are many others familiar to most cooks, menu favorites like wax beans, lima beans and a whole catalogue of dried beans, all filled with exceptional nutritional value. String beans grow in a rainbow of colors that include the familiar: green and yellow along with the less familiar red, pink, purple, black, brown, tan, white and even multi-colored beans. There are two types of peas: green peas and edible pea pods. Green peas vary considerably in size and, if you are a gardener, you can grow peas with wonderful names like "Mammoth Melting Sugars" or "Little Marvels." The natural sugar in peas turns to starch soon after they are picked, which means the flavor diminishes with each day fresh peas sit on a grocer's shelf. There are several varieties of edible pea pods including snow peas and sugar snap peas.

Edible Pea Pods

A staple of Chinese cooking, this variety of peas has gained great popularity in Western cooking. Both pod and seed are eaten.
Availability—All year.
Preparation—Trim ends and remove strings, if necessary. Cook in lightly salted boiling water about 3 minutes or stir-fry 2 minutes.
Yield—1 pound pea pods will yield 4 servings.

Garden Peas

A favorite, eaten raw or slightly cooked. Peas should be eaten as soon as possible after picking. When fresh peas are unavailable, substitute frozen peas.
Availability—Peak season is March through November.
Preparation—Shell peas; blanch 3 to 4 minutes. Longer cooking may be needed for older peas. Add to casseroles without cooking or puree cooked peas to serve as vegetable or in soup.
Yield—1 pound fresh peas will yield 2 servings.

Young Green Beans

Young tender string beans, when available, are much to be desired. Unfortunately they are usually mixed with older beans and there are only two ways to get them. Grow them and pick them while still young, or stand over a bin of loose beans and carefully pick out those that are young and tender.

Availability—May to October.

Preparation—Trim ends, then steam or cook in small amount of lightly salted water 5 minutes or less.

Yield—1 pound beans will yield 4 servings.

String Beans

Most beans today do not have strings. They grow on low bushy plants or climb poles.

Availability—Peak season is May to October, but available all year.

Preparation—Trim ends, then cook whole, julienne or cut into short lengths. Steam or cook in lightly salted boiling water 15 minutes or until crisp-tender.

Yield—1 pound beans will yield 4 servings.

Fava Beans

Fava Beans are similar to lima beans and can be interchanged. Pods of young fava beans can be eaten.

Availability—Spring and summer.

Preparation—Remove seeds from pods. Cook in lightly salted boiling water 25 to 30 minutes.

Yield—3/4 pound fava beans yields 1 serving.

A Potpourri of Stalks, Roots & Bulbs

Stalk vegetables are plant stems, such as fennel, asparagus and celery shown on the right, as are Swiss chard and bok choy. Root vegetables include salsify, carrots and celeriac shown, along with all kinds of potatoes, parsnips, turnips, beets and Jerusalem artichokes. Green onions and leeks are part of the bulbous onion family that includes a wide variety of onions, garlic and shallots. All these vegetables are welcome additions to family and company meals and can be served in a variety of ways.

Fennel

This dense fleshy stalk can be served as a cooked vegetable or used raw in salad.
Availability—August to April.
Preparation—Cut off leaves and any woody stalks. Wash, cut in half lengthwise and cut into quarters or strips. Braise about 25 minutes. Toss in butter, season to taste with salt and pepper and sprinkle with chopped fennel leaves or dill. Or blanch fennel halves and scoop out some flesh. Dice flesh and mix with seasoned cooked ground meat and dairy sour cream. Fill halves and sprinkle with grated cheese. Bake in preheated 375F (190C) oven about 20 minutes.
Yield—6 small heads or 3 large heads yield 4 servings.

Asparagus

Although both green and white asparagus are sold, white asparagus is scarce and usually expensive.
Availability—March to June.
Preparation—Soak in cold water to remove sand. Rinse in cold water several times; snap off woody ends at point where stalk breaks naturally. Trim ends to make stalks even lengths. Peel stems, if desired. Steam or cook in lightly salted boiling water 8 minutes or until crisp-tender. Serve with lemon butter or Hollandaise Sauce, pages 252-253. Or place in a baking dish; season with salt and pepper. Dot with butter. Cover with foil; bake in 350F (175C) oven 20 minutes.
Yield—1 pound asparagus will yield 16 to 20 spears or about 3 servings.

Celery

This popular crunchy stalk is used raw and cooked. It is also used as seasoning in stocks and as part of a bouquet garni, page 145.
Availability—Peak season is October to April but available all year.
Preparation—Trim ends and remove leaves. Use leaves to flavor stock. Wash thoroughly in cold water; remove strings from outer stalks, if necessary. Use whole, cut into short lengths, sliced or chopped. Braise 10 to 15 minutes and season with butter, salt and pepper. Or cut celery into 2-inch lengths. Braise as above until crisp-tender. Mix with 1 cup cream sauce and garnish with paprika, or mix with 1 cup tomato sauce.
Yield—1 bunch will yield 4 to 6 servings.

Black Salsify

Salsify has limited appeal, possibly because it is not always easy to find. Black salsify is a black radish. White salsify is often called *oyster plant*.
Availability—October and November.
Preparation—Wash and peel roots; place in acidulated water to keep from discoloring. Slice or julienne; keep in acidulated water until ready to cook. Cook 10 minutes in a large amount of lightly salted boiling water to which a little lemon juice or vinegar has been added. Drain well; season with lemon butter, salt and pepper. Or thinly slice salsify; cook as above. Combine with cream sauce; sprinkle with bread crumbs. Bake in 350F (175C) oven until heated through.
Yield—1 pound salsify will yield 3 servings.

Carrots

Carrots grow long, short, fat and thin. They are one of our most nutritious vegetables. Sweet, tender, fresh baby carrots have the best flavor, but large carrots are also delicious when properly cooked and seasoned.
Availability—All year.
Preparation—Scrape young carrots, do not peel. Peel older carrots when necessary. Slice, julienne, grate, puree or serve whole, either raw or cooked. Cook carrots in 1- to 2-inches lightly salted boiling water. Cooking time will vary according to age and size of carrot pieces. Undercook carrots to be added to stews or casseroles, cook until soft to puree. To serve as a side dish, cook until fork-tender, then season with butter, lemon juice, dill, salt and pepper. Or melt butter and sugar or honey in skillet. Add thinly sliced carrots; toss to coat. Cook until just tender; season with freshly snipped dill, salt and pepper. Try cooking carrots in lightly salted water until just tender. Drain and chill. Toss with vinaigrette dressing; serve cold. Also puree and combine with mashed potatoes, page 115.
Yield—1 pound, about 1 bunch, yields 3 to 4 servings.

Celeriac

This root is related to celery and similar in flavor. It is also called *celery root* or *knob celery*. Occasionally it is available canned.
Availability—September through April, but often difficult to find.
Preparation—Peel and slice, julienne or leave whole. Place in acidulated water until ready to cook or serve raw in salad. Cook in lightly salted water 25 minutes or longer if knobs are cooked whole, about 10 minutes if sliced or julienne. Drain and season with butter, nutmeg, salt, pepper, parsley or chives. Puree cooked celeriac and combine with mashed potatoes, pages 114-115. Or grate raw celeriac and combine with mayonnaise-type dressing. Serve on lettuce.
Yield—1 pound celeriac yields 3 servings.

Green Onions

A young onion is also known as a *scallion, green onion* or *spring onion*. Most green onions sold are very young onions, picked in the spring before the onion bulb has formed.

Unlike mature onions, green onions must be stored in the refrigerator and used within a few days.

Availability—All year.

Preparation—Rinse, trim off roots, trim green end if desired and peel if necessary. Serve whole or sliced. Slice, sauté and combine with other foods or use in stir-fry recipe. Use as a garnish. Use raw in salad or as crudite.

Yield—1 bunch will yield about 2 cups chopped.

Leeks

Leeks are mild-flavored, sweet members of the onion family. Leeks are not served raw.

Availability—Peek season is winter, but available all year.

Preparation—Leeks require thorough washing to remove sand embedded between leaves. Rinse under cold running water, pulling leaves gently apart. Trim off root, trim leaf end; cook whole or sliced. Cook sliced leeks in salted boiling water 8 minutes or until fork-tender. Drain well; season with butter, nutmeg, salt, pepper and parsley. Puree cooked leeks and combine with pureed potatoes. Add stock and cream; season to make leek and potato soup. Serve hot or cold, as Vichyssoise, page 160. Or puree cooked leeks; stir in small amount of cream. Season with butter, salt and pepper. Braise whole leeks 10 minutes; place in a baking dish. Add braising liquid; cover and bake in 350F (175C) oven 30 minutes or until fork-tender. Drain and serve with buttered bread crumbs and crumbled cooked bacon.

Yield—about 2 whole leeks per serving.

White or Green Cabbage

A firm, round compact head with smooth, light-green leaves. Choose heads that feel heavy for their size and have fresh-looking green outer leaves.
Availability—Peak season is from end of summer to early spring, but available all year.
Preparation—Remove and discard thick outer leaves. Cut cabbage in half and cut again into quarters. Remove core. Shred, thinly slice, cut into small wedges or pull leaves apart. Cook, covered, in lightly salted water until crisp-tender, about 5 minutes for shredded cabbage and 10 minutes for wedges. Drain well; season with butter, caraway seeds, salt and pepper.

Variations
● Shred cabbage and use raw to make coleslaw or sauerkraut.
● Braise in butter or bacon fat.
● Combine cooked cabbage with cream sauce or dairy sour cream.
● Braise whole leaves and use leaves to make Stuffed Cabbage, page 226.
● Add to soup, stews or casseroles.

Savoy Cabbage

Savoy cabbage is similar to white or green cabbage but the leaves are darker green and curly, and the head is less compact.
Availability—Easy availability is limited to September through March.
Preparation—Use in the same way as white or green cabbage.

Cabbages & Kings

To reword Lewis Carroll's famous poem somewhat, "the time has come to talk of cabbages, (if not) of kings." Although surely there must have been kings down through the centuries who found a dish of well-cooked cabbage to their liking. Five kinds of cabbage are shown here, and all of them can be eaten raw or cooked. Cabbage is very popular in Germany, and is a staple of the Russian diet. As coleslaw, cabbage is surely an American favorite. Corned Beef and Cabbage, Irish in origin, is so closely associated with New England that many think of it as an American dish. In one form or another, cabbage dishes can be found in almost every country. Cooked, it is something of a down-to-earth vegetable, not likely to appear on an elegant company menu, but nonetheless nutritious and good to eat.

Red Cabbage

Red cabbage is also similar to white or green cabbage except for its wonderful reddish-purple color. It can be used very effectively with white or green cabbage to make a bright and attractive coleslaw.

Availability—Easy availability is limited to September through March.

Preparation—Vinegar or lemon juice must be added to red cabbage when it is cooked in order to keep the bright red from turning an odd blue. Prepared with a sweet and sour sauce, red cabbage goes particularly well with pot roast of beef, page 230, or breaded veal cutlets, page 207.

Sweet & Sour Red Cabbage

2 tablespoons butter
1 onion, chopped
1/4 cup firmly packed
 brown sugar
5 to 6 cups shredded
 red cabbage, about
 1-1/2 lbs.
1 tart apple, peeled,
 cored, diced
1/2 cup dry red wine
1/4 cup cider vinegar
1/4 teaspoon ground
 cloves
1/4 teaspoon allspice
Salt and pepper to taste

1. Melt butter in a large saucepan. Add onion; cook until transparent.
2. Stir in brown sugar until melted. Add cabbage, apple, wine, vinegar, cloves, allspice, salt and pepper; stir well.
3. Cover and cook over medium heat 45 minutes, stirring occasionally. Adjust seasoning before serving.
Makes 4 to 6 servings.

Chinese Cabbage

Choy, or cabbage in Chinese, is available in many varieties. Chinese cabbage, Napa cabbage, bok choy and celery cabbage are all names used somewhat interchangeably, and not always accurately, for cabbages that are both identical and those that are merely similar. The leaves tend to be longer than white, green, Savoy or red cabbage and the heads are less compact. The flavor is closer to celery or chard than cabbage.

Availability—Available all year.

Preparation—Chinese cabbage can be used the same way other cabbage is used and is also often used in stir-fry dishes. It can be used successfully in a salad in place of shredded lettuce.

Kale

Although kale is actually a member of the cabbage family, it is more often associated with collard greens.

Availability—All year, peak season is winter through early spring.

Preparation—Kale can be served raw or cooked like collard greens. Very young tender kale can be cooked like spinach.

Southern-Style Kale

3 lbs. fresh kale
1 smoked ham hock
Grated nutmeg
Salt and pepper to taste

1. Wash kale. Discard tough or wilted leaves; trim stems. Break leaves into large pieces.
2. Place in a large saucepan with ham hock. Add water to cover; bring to a boil. Reduce heat, cover and simmer 1-1/2 to 2 hours.
3. Remove hock. Cut meat from bone; dice meat. Drain kale; combine with ham. Season to taste with nutmeg, salt and pepper.
Makes 4 servings.

Vegetables for Mealtime Pleasure

These six vegetables include the familiar and popular cauliflower, corn, beets and turnips, along with artichokes, familiar to most, and okra, almost a staple in many southern homes. Each vegetable has its own unique flavor and texture, and all are worthwhile additions to family and company meals.

Cauliflower

Choose compact heavy heads, creamy white and free of blemishes.
Availability—Peak season is September through November, but available all year.
Preparation—Remove green outer leaves and trim core. Rinse in cold water. To boil, see pages 124-125. Also can be served raw, steamed, stir-fried or baked. Serve cooked cauliflower with Hollandaise Sauce, pages 252-253; or Mornay Sauce, page 254.

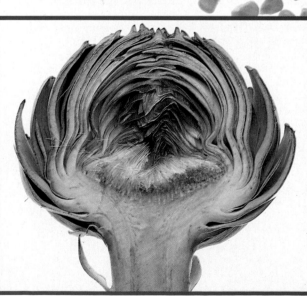

Corn-on-the-Cob

There is a significant flavor difference between freshly picked corn and corn that is several days old. As soon as corn is picked, the sugar begins to turn to starch. When it is picked, cooked and eaten the same day, it is very sweet. Even one day old, there is a major loss of flavor.
Availability—Summer for fresh picked.
Preparation—Remove husks and silk; trim stem. Bring a deep kettle of unsalted water to a boil. If desired, add sugar and milk. Cover and cook 5 minutes, no longer! Drain and serve with melted butter, salt and pepper. Corn can also be steamed or cooked over grill. Remove kernels from leftover ears, then use for fritters or in casseroles.

Artichokes

Choose tightly closed artichokes with flat, relatively unblemished leaves.
Availability—Peak season is March through May, but available all year.
Preparation—Rinse under cold running water, pulling leaves slightly apart to rinse between leaves. Cut stem flat with bottom; rub with lemon juice to prevent discoloration. Trim off sharp tips of leaves, if desired. Do not use an aluminum pan. Cook in lightly salted, acidulated, boiling water 30 to 45 minutes, depending on size. Serve with a dipping sauce, such as melted butter.

Okra

First brought to the "New World" from Africa, okra is used in many traditional southern dishes. Choose firm, young tender pods.
Availability—Peak season is July through October, but available all year.
Preparation—Wash and trim stem ends. Cook whole unless very large. Cook in lightly salted boiling water about 5 minutes. Drain; season with butter and lemon juice. Can also be breaded and deep-fried or pickled. Used in stews and casseroles, such as gumbo which is the African name for okra, often as a thickening agent. Combine with other vegetables, such as corn and tomatoes.

Beets

Choose small or medium firm, deep-colored beets.
Availability—Peak season is June through October, but available all year.
Preparation—Trim stems leaving a 1-inch stem. Trim root, but do not cut off. Wash gently. Cook in lightly salted boiling water 30 to 45 minutes depending on size. Drain; cool and slip off skins. Serve whole, sliced, julienned or diced; hot or cold; seasoned with butter, lemon juice, salt and pepper or in a sauce.

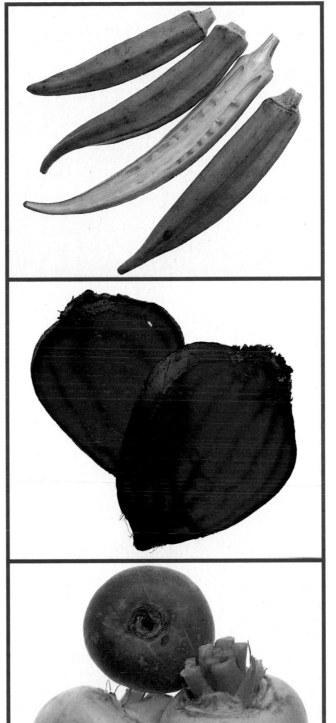

Turnips

Two kinds of turnips are available: small white turnips or large yellow turnips, not shown. Choose small or medium white turnips. Both kinds should be firm and unblemished.
Availability—All year.
Preparation—Peel and dice, slice or cut into julienne strips. Serve raw or cook in lightly salted boiling water 20 minutes or until tender. Drain and season; or mash, season and combine with mashed potatoes.

135

Vegetables to Sauté

Many vegetables lend themselves beautifully to sautéing in butter or oil. A single vegetable can be sautéed or a combination of vegetables can be cooked this way, with or without the addition of meat. Use a heavy skillet that will distribute the heat evenly, or stir-fry in a wok, Chinese-style. Cook in oil or a combination of butter and oil. Butter alone will burn over high heat unless it has been clarified, page 250.

Eggplant

To sauté eggplant, peel, if desired; cut into 1/2-inch-thick slices. Sprinkle slices with salt; place in a colander to drain 30 minutes. Pat dry with paper towels. Heat olive oil in a large heavy skillet. Press 2 garlic cloves through a garlic press; add to oil. Place eggplant slices in skillet in a single layer; sauté until lightly browned. Turn slices over; sauté. Remove with a spatula; drain on paper towels. Cook remaining slices, adding additional oil, if necessary.

Variations
• Sauté with other vegetables to make Ratatouille, page 140.
• Eggplant can also be baked, steamed, stuffed or served cold.

Zucchini

To sauté zucchini, peel if desired; slice, dice or cut into julienne strips. Heat olive oil in a large heavy skillet. Press 2 garlic cloves through a garlic press; add to oil. Add zucchini to skillet; sauté until tender. Remove with a slotted spoon; drain on paper towels. Salt to taste.

Variations
• Sauté with other vegetables to make Ratatouille, page 140.
• Coat sliced zucchini lightly with flour before cooking; sauté with sliced onions.
• Shred, soak in iced water, drain, pat dry, coat with flour and deep-fry. Salt to taste.
• Zucchini can also be served raw in salad, baked, stuffed, and used in quick breads, cakes or muffins.

Bean Sprouts

For many years bean sprouts were available only in canned form. Because of the great interest in Oriental cooking, it is now possible to buy bean sprouts fresh, and it is unbelievably easy to grow them yourself in 4 to 5 days. They can be sautéed quickly in oil and seasoned with soy sauce and pepper. More often, they are added to a stir-fry dish and cooked quickly with other foods in a skillet or wok. They can also be added to salads without cooking or added to eggs as they cook.

Button Mushrooms

Choose firm, plump, unblemished mushrooms with tightly closed caps. As the mushrooms begin to age, the caps open and the mushrooms get soft and dark. Size does not effect quality. Large mushrooms are ideal for stuffing. Some packaged mushrooms have a preservative added; this information is printed on the package. Mushrooms that are snowy white because a preservative has been added, turn dark very quickly when the package is opened. Whenever possible, buy button mushrooms that do not have any preservatives added. If mushrooms are to be served raw or used as a garnish without cooking, sprinkle with lemon juice to keep them from discoloring.

Cepes

Cepes are a boletus mushroom often used in French cooking. They are not always easy to find and may be expensive. Cepes have good flavor and are dark brown in color. The family of boletus mushrooms includes shiitakes from Japan and porcini from Italy.

Oyster Mushrooms

Oyster mushrooms are large whitish-gray mushrooms, elegant in appearance. They go particularly well with meat, fish, poultry and game, and are increasingly available due to recent cultivation.

Chanterelles

Chanterelles are funnel-shaped, orange mushrooms, usually fairly large. They have good flavor, but require longer cooking than other mushrooms.

Enoki

Enoki are small, attractive Japanese mushrooms, easy to find because of increased cultivation. They do not have a strong flavor, but are a good addition to Oriental stir-fried dishes and salads because of their crisp texture.

Morels

Morels cannot be cultivated and therefore are hard to find and very expensive. They have a wonderful smoky flavor.

Mushrooms

Until recently, almost the only mushrooms available were cultivated mushrooms known as *button mushrooms*, no matter how big they were. Most markets now sell a wide variety of mushrooms, many of them popular in Europe and the Far East for many years. Button mushrooms are available all year. Other varieties may be more difficult to find at any time, but are most likely to be available from September through January.

All mushrooms should be wiped clean with a damp cloth, but none of them should be washed unless absolutely necessary. They should not be peeled because much of the flavor is in the skin. Mushrooms can be cooked whole, sliced or chopped, and sautéed in butter until they have released their liquid and the liquid has evaporated. Minced garlic and chopped green onion provide added flavor. Mushrooms can also be eaten raw or can be pickled and add flavor, cooked or raw, to salad, soup, stews, casseroles, vegetables, meat, fish, poultry and egg dishes. Refrigerate mushrooms loosely wrapped. They will keep fresh 1 to 2 days only.

The A to Z of Salad

A beautiful crisp, green salad, tossed with a simple homemade dressing, is a delicious and nutritious addition to any meal. Take advantage of whatever greens are available in the market, then combine different greens to make an interesting flavor combination. Greens can be washed and torn ahead of time, then wrapped loosely in a damp cloth, ready to toss with dressing just before serving. A salad can be made with greens and nothing else, or it can include radishes, cucumbers, celery, nuts, onions, tomatoes, croutons, cold vegetables, diced cheese or just about anything that can be eaten cold.

There seems to be no universal agreement about the proper time to serve salad. Some people prefer to serve salad as a first course, some serve it with the main dish and some serve it between the main course and dessert. Any time you choose is appropriate, as long as the salad is freshly made.

Pointers for Making Salad

- Choose greens with an eye for color contrast and flavor combinations.
- Wash greens in cold water; shake or spin dry.
- Keep greens wrapped in a damp cloth until ready to serve.
- Add salad dressing just before serving. If dressing is added too soon, the greens will get limp.
- Don't add too much dressing; use just enough to coat leaves.
- Make more than one kind of dressing; then serve salad without dressing and pass dressings at the table.

Salad Greens

The variety of salad greens available is almost endless. Greens pictured on the right are included here.

Iceberg lettuce
Large, firm, tightly packed heads; darkish green outer leaves, pale green inner leaves; pale green to yellow center called "heart"; crisp and easy to shred.

Radicchio
Also called *Italian red chicory*; red leaves with slightly bitter flavor.

Chicory
Also called *curly endive*; yellow at base of stem, dark green spike-shaped leaves; slightly bitter flavor.

Butterhead lettuce
Includes Boston, bibb, and buttercrunch lettuce; small heads, loosely formed; darkish green outer leaves, very light green to yellow inner leaves; fragile and perishable.

Cress
Also called *radish sprouts* and *Tsu-mamina*; small bright green shoots, Japanese in origin, sold in cartons; fairly new to U.S. market; somewhat spicy or peppery flavor.

Lamb's tongue
Also called *lamb's lettuce*, *corn salad* or *mache*; smooth green leaves that grow wild in the United States and are cultivated extensively in Europe.

Belgian endive
Greenish, white, tightly packed long leaves with slightly bitter flavor. It is a variety of chicory.

Watercress
Small dark green leaves that grow out from stem; tender and spicy and often used as garnish.

Other salad ingredients shown on the right:

Summer radishes
Small round bright red radishes; sold in bunches; flavor can vary from mild to very sharp; large radishes tend to be tough and woody and should be avoided; usually sliced or chopped for salad, but can be served whole or cut into "roses" for garnish.

Winter radishes
White or black, round or elongated; have strong flavor and should be used sparingly.

Cucumbers
Available in many sizes and varieties; long dark green cucumbers found most often in the market are often waxed to prolong shelf life and must be peeled before using; unwaxed cucumbers can be used without peeling unless the particular variety has a very tough skin; welcome addition, sliced or chopped, to any salad.

Red onions
Ideal for salads because they usually have a sweet flavor and add color to salad as well.

Bean sprouts
Also called *soybean sprouts*; pale ivory color; should be used when very crisp and can be refreshed in ice water.

Creamy Blue-Cheese Dressing

1 cup mayonnaise or
  dairy sour cream
1 to 2 teaspoons sugar
1 tablespoon grated
  onion
Dash Worcestershire
  sauce
1/4 lb. blue cheese,
  crumbled
1 to 2 tablespoons cider
  vinegar

1. Blend mayonnaise, sugar, onion and Worcestershire in a small bowl. Fold in crumbled cheese.
2. Add vinegar, 1 tablespoon at a time, depending on desired thickness; stir well.
3. Refrigerate at least 1 hour before serving. Makes about 1-1/2 cups.

Vinaigrette Dressing

3/4 cup olive oil
1/4 cup red-wine
vinegar, tarragon
vinegar or cider
vinegar
2 to 3 tablespoons
freshly chopped
herbs, such as
parsley, chives,
tarragon, thyme or
chervil
1/2 teaspoon dry
mustard
Salt and pepper to taste

1. Place oil, vinegar, herbs, mustard, salt and pepper in a screw-top jar. Shake vigorously until well blended. Makes about 1 cup.

Thousand Island Dressing

1 cup mayonnaise
1/4 cup prepared chili
sauce
1 tablespoon minced
green onion
2 tablespoons minced
green- or red-bell
pepper
1 hard-cooked egg,
finely chopped
1 tablespoon freshly
minced parsley

1. Stir together mayonnaise and chili sauce in a medium bowl; add onion, green pepper, chopped egg and parsley. Stir until blended.
2. Cover and refrigerate 2 to 3 hours. Spoon dressing over crisp salad greens or lettuce wedges.
Makes about 1-1/3 cups.

Ratatouille

1/4 cup olive oil
3 medium onions,
  sliced
2 garlic cloves, minced
1 eggplant, about 1 lb.,
  peeled, cut in chunks
1 large red-bell pepper,
  seeded, cut in thin
  strips
1 large green-bell
  pepper, seeded, cut in
  thin strips
1-1/2 lbs. fresh
  tomatoes, peeled,
  seeded, coarsely
  chopped or 1 (28-oz.)
  can whole peeled
  tomatoes, chopped
3/4 lb. zucchini, sliced
2 tablespoons freshly
  chopped mixed herbs,
  such as parsley, basil
  and thyme
Salt and pepper to taste

1. Heat oil in a dutch
oven or large saucepan
over medium heat.
2. Add onions and
garlic; sauté until onion
is transparent.
3. Add eggplant; sauté
5 minutes.
4. Add red- and
green-pepper strips; stir
well and cook 5
minutes.
5. Add tomatoes,
zucchini, chopped
herbs, salt and pepper;
blend well.
6. Bring to a boil.
Reduce heat, cover and
simmer 30 to 35 minutes
or until vegetables are
tender.
Makes 6 servings.

Sauerkraut

2 tablespoons bacon
  drippings or butter
2 onions, chopped
1-1/2 lbs. fresh
  sauerkraut or 1
  (28-oz.) can
  sauerkraut, drained
1 potato, peeled, grated
1-1/4 cups dry white
  wine
6 to 8 dried juniper
  berries or 2 to 4
  whole cloves
1 bay leaf
Pinch sugar
Salt and pepper to taste

1. Heat bacon drippings
in a dutch oven or large
deep skillet.
2. Add onions; sauté
until transparent.
3. Add sauerkraut and
potato; mix well.
4. Add wine, juniper
berries and bay leaf; stir
well.
5. Bring to a boil;
reduce heat. Cover and
simmer 30 minutes.
6. Remove bay leaf and
discard. Season with
sugar, salt and pepper.
Makes 4 to 6 servings.

Bean Casserole

1/2 lb. (about 1-1/4 cups)
  dried Great Northern
  or navy pea beans
4 cups hot water
1/4 lb. salt pork, diced
2 large onions, chopped
1 large garlic clove,
  crushed
4 to 6 cups stock or
  water
1 (6-oz.) can tomato
  paste
3 tablespoons red-wine
  vinegar
2 tablespoons prepared
  mustard
Salt and pepper to taste
3 medium, tart apples,
  peeled, diced
2 carrots, thinly sliced

1. Sort beans; rinse
under cold running
water. Place in a large
bowl; add hot water.
Soak overnight.
2. Cook salt pork in a
2-quart heatproof
casserole until crisp.
Add onion and garlic;
cook until onion is
transparent.
3. Preheat oven 250F
(120C).
4. Drain beans. Add to
casserole. Add 4 cups
stock, tomato paste,
vinegar and mustard;
stir well. Season with
salt and pepper.
5. Cover and bake in
preheated oven 5 hours,
adding more stock, if
necessary, to keep beans
moist. Uncover; add
apples and carrots.
Blend well.
6. Cover and bake 2 to
3 hours or until beans
are tender.
Makes 6 to 8 servings.

Baked Celery

2 bunches celery
1-1/4 cups dry white
    wine
3 tablespoons freshly
    chopped mixed herbs,
    such as parsley, basil
    and thyme
Salt and pepper to taste
1/4 cup butter, softened
1/4 cup fine dry bread
    crumbs

---

1. Wash celery under
cold running water; trim
ends and cut stalks into
equal-sized pieces.
2. Blanch celery in
lightly salted boiling
water 5 minutes, pages
124-125.
3. Remove celery with a
slotted spoon; drain
well.
4. Preheat oven to 400F
(200C).
5. Pour wine into
heatproof casserole or
baking dish. Add herbs
and celery. Season with
salt and pepper.
6. Work butter and
bread crumbs together
until well blended.
Spoon or spread over
celery.
7. Bake in preheated
oven 15 to 20 minutes or
until celery is tender.
Makes 4 to 6 servings.

Vegetable Bake

1/2 lb. spiral noodles
1/3 lb. edible pea pods
3 large ripe tomatoes,
    peeled, seeded,
    coarsely chopped or 1
    (16-oz.) can whole
    peeled tomatoes,
    chopped
2 onions, chopped
1 (7-oz.) can
    vacuum-packed
    whole-kernel corn,
    drained
Salt and pepper to taste
3 eggs
1-1/4 cups half and half
1 tablespoon freshly
    chopped basil
1/4 cup grated Parmesan
    cheese

---

1. Cook spirals in
lightly salted boiling
water until al dente or
tender but firm to the
bite. Drain and rinse
under cold running
water. Set aside.
2. Trim ends of peas;
blanch in lightly salted
boiling water 3 minutes.
Drain and rinse under
cold running water.
3. Preheat oven to 375F
(190C); grease a 1-1/2- to
2-quart casserole or
baking dish.
4. Combine pasta, pea
pods, tomatoes, onions
and corn in prepared
dish; season with salt
and pepper.
5. Beat eggs and cream
until well blended. Stir
in basil. Pour over
pasta-vegetable mixture;
sprinkle with Parmesan
cheese.
6. Bake in preheated
oven 35 to 45 minutes or
until top is golden
brown.
Makes 4 to 6 servings.

Baked Endive

8 Belgian endive
2 tablespoons butter
3/4 cup dry white wine
8 thin slices boiled ham
8 slices Swiss or
    Gruyère cheese
Salt and pepper to taste

---

1. Rinse endive under
cold running water; trim
root ends.
2. Melt butter in a large
skillet. Add endive; turn
gently to coat. Pour in
wine; bring to a boil.
Cover; reduce heat and
simmer 10 minutes.
Remove endive with a
slotted spoon; drain
well, reserving cooking
liquid.
3. Preheat oven to 400F
(200C). Grease a shallow
baking dish.
4. Wrap each endive
with 1 ham slice and 1
cheese slice. Arrange
wrapped endive in a
single layer in prepared
dish. Season with salt
and pepper; pour 1/4
cup reserved cooking
liquid over.
5. Bake in preheated
oven 10 to 15 minutes or
until cheese is golden
brown.
Makes 4 servings.

Soups: Delicious Beginnings

The increase in the quality and variety of canned and packaged soup has brought about a decrease in the preparation of homemade soup. But, if you make a big pot of homemade stock when time permits, and store the stock in the freezer, making soup at home can be a quick and easy task. It will also have the added advantage of being more nutritious and economical than commercial-made soup. With stock on hand, you are ready to make almost any kind of soup with whatever other ingredients you may have available. Soup can be anything from a light, elegant clear consommé to a thick creamy treat topped with puff pastry, or a soup so filled with pieces of meat and fresh vegetables that it really is a whole meal in a bowl. And there is almost nothing you can serve on a cold wintery night that is more welcome than a bowl of steaming hot homemade soup.

Basic Stock

There is no trick to making stock. The technique involves nothing more than filling a very big pot with water and a variety of flavorful ingredients. Then allowing the pot to simmer almost unattended for several hours. Finally you strain the liquid. It will keep for six months in the freezer, ready to use at any time to make a wide range of delicious dishes, made all the more delicious because the liquid used for cooking is stock instead of water.

Beef Stock

1 large onion
2 lbs. beef shank cross-cuts
2 lbs. beef marrow bones
2 lbs. soup vegetables, such as carrots, parsnips, celery, turnips or leeks
1/2 bunch parsley
Salt and pepper to taste
Water

1. Cut onion in half crosswise; place, cut-side down, in a large stock pot. Cook over high heat until browned.

3. Bring to a boil over medium heat; skim foam from surface until surface is clear.

2. Add remaining ingredients. Pour in 4 to 5 quarts cold water or enough to cover.

4. Reduce heat and simmer, partially covered, at least 2 hours. Add more water, if necessary.

5. Remove vegetables and meat with a slotted spoon. Cut into serving-size pieces to use in soup, if desired.

6. Remove bones; strain and degrease stock. Cool and freeze stock. Or combine stock with cooked meat and vegetables and serve as soup. Makes about 3 quarts.

Hints for Making Stock

The most important ingredient in stock is bones. Bones can be uncooked or leftover from something like a turkey or rib roast. If the bones have a lot of meat on them, so much the better. But stock can be made from bones with only a small amount of meat. A beef stock must be made with beef bones and a chicken stock with chicken or turkey bones. Veal bones can be added to either beef or chicken stock and are ideal to use for a light all-purpose stock that is not intended to have a very strong flavor or dark color. Lamb and pork bones, as well as fish trimmings, should only be used when making stock for lamb, pork or fish dishes because stock made with these bones will have a strong distinctive flavor. One method that can be used to add a rich dark color to stock is to brown the bones in the oven before adding them to the cold water.

Vegetables that are added to stock can be from a package of soup vegetables or simply some of the vegetables you are likely to have on hand. Onions and firm root vegetables with modest flavor are ideal to use along with celery stalks and leaves. Don't add potatoes because they will disintegrate in the stock. When parsley is added, the stems should be included because parsley stems have lots of flavor.

Unless you are on a salt-free diet, add salt to bring out the flavor of the other ingredients. Be careful not to add too much salt because the stock may be used in a dish that has additional salt in it. It is always possible to add more salt.

The best way to add additional seasoning to stock is to make a *bouquet garni.* Cut a double thickness 4- or 5-inch square of cheesecloth. Place a garlic clove, bay leaf, several peppercorns, parsley, celery leaves and other herbs or spices in small amounts in the center of the cheesecloth. Pull the corners of the cheesecloth to the center and tie them firmly with string. Place the cheesecloth bag in the stock pot along with the bones and vegetables. When the stock is cooked, remove the bag and throw it away.

As stock begins to cook, foam and fat will rise to the surface. This should be removed with a skimmer or spoon. Once all the foam has been removed, you can ignore the stock as it simmers, partially covered. Check it occasionally to see if more water should be added.

When stock has simmered for several hours, most of the flavor and nutrients from the vegetables and meat will have cooked out. Discard the overcooked vegetables but, if you have added meat, you may want to dice it and use it in soup.

More About Stock

Once stock has been made, there are many ways it can be used after the finishing touches have been added.

To Finish Stock

When stock is fully cooked, line a large fine strainer with a double thickness of cheesecloth; strain stock into a bowl. If time permits, cover stock and place it in the refrigerator. Fat that remains in the stock will rise to the surface and solidify. It can be easily removed with a spoon. If stock must be used immediately, skim off any fat with a spoon. Use a paper towel to absorb any excess fat that may still be floating on the surface.

Uses for Stock

To make soup, gravy, sauces, aspic, savory molds and glazes, and as cooking liquid for vegetables, rice, stews and casseroles.

Consommé

Consommé is a special clear, elegant soup made from fat-free beef stock or chicken stock. It can be served plain, lightly garnished or chilled and served as jellied consommé. No mater how it is served, stock must be enriched and clarified first.

How to Store Stock

If you plan to use stock within a few days, cover and refrigerate it. Allow the fat to solidify on surface, but do not remove fat. The covering of fat will keep stock fresh. Remove fat before using.

If stock is to be stored in the freezer, cover and refrigerate. Remove solidified fat; then heat stock so it can be poured and measured. Divide into usable quantities of 2 or 4 cups and place in rigid freezer containers, leaving enough head space for expansion. Cover and store in freezer up to 6 months.

Fat-free stock can also be poured into ice-cube trays and frozen. Place frozen cubes in a plastic bag; use a few cubes at a time to add a touch of special flavor to vegetables or other foods.

Both stock and consommé must be strained. Line a large fine strainer or chinois with a double thickness of cheesecloth. Ladle stock or consommé into strainer. When consommé is strained, do not press residue in strainer to release extra liquid.

The best way to skim off fat is to allow liquid to cool so fat can rise to the surface and solidify. If stock or consommé is to be used immediately, skim off as much fat as possible with a spoon; remove any remaining fat by sliding the edge of a paper towel across the surface of hot liquid.

Beef Consommé

3 qts. beef stock
1 carrot
1 leek, green top included
1 celery stalk
2 lbs. lean ground beef
Salt and pepper to taste
3 egg whites
3 egg shells, crushed

1. Place stock in a large stock pot; bring to a boil. Reduce heat and simmer until reduced to 8 or 9 cups.
2. Place carrot, leek and celery in a food processor fitted with a metal blade; process until finely chopped.
3. Combine chopped vegetables with ground beef; season with salt and pepper. Add to stock.
4. Beat egg whites until frothy. Add to stock along with egg shells. Simmer, DO NOT boil, 2 hours without stirring.
5. Push crusty foam that forms to side of pot. Strain liquid through a large fine strainer lined with a double thickness of cheesecloth. Skim off fat and adjust seasoning. Reheat before serving. Makes 6 servings.

Special Sauces Used to Flavor Soup

The flavor of some kinds of soup is enhanced by the addition of special sauces. *Aioli* is a French sauce often added to fish soup or spread on bread. *Pesto* is an Italian sauce sometimes added to soup or pasta.

Aioli

4 garlic cloves, minced
2 egg yolks
1/4 teaspoon salt
2 to 3 tablespoons
  lemon juice
About 1 cup olive oil

1. Place garlic in a mortar; pound with pestle to make a smooth paste.
2. Place in a small bowl; add egg yolks and salt. Beat until thickened.
3. Add a little oil, drop by drop, beating until mixture is thickened and consistency of whipping cream. Gradually add remaining oil, beating constantly.
4. Beat in lemon juice. Makes about 1-1/4 cups.

Pesto

1-1/2 cups fresh basil
  leave
2 garlic cloves
2 to 3 tablespoons pine
  nuts
1/4 cup butter, softened
1/4 cup olive oil
1/2 cup grated Parmesan
  cheese
Salt to taste

1. Place all ingredients in a blender or food processor fitted with a metal blade.
2. Process until pureed, scraping mixture down as necessary.
Makes about 1-1/2 cups.

30 Quick Garnishes & Additions to Soup

Soup, more than almost any other dish, provides cooks with an opportunity to use their imagination along with whatever food may be on hand. A simple soup benefits from an attractive and flavorful garnish, and just about anything can be used. Soup that already has lots of ingredients in it can be varied or changed by a substitution of ingredients. Try some of our suggestions or raid your refrigerator or cupboard and create your own variations.

1. Beef marrow, sliced, cooked and heated in soup 5 minutes.

2. Lettuce, shredded and added to soup just before serving.

3. Vermicelli, added to soup and cooked 10 minutes.

4. Tomatoes, diced and used to garnish soup with fresh basil leaves.

5. Mushrooms, sliced; tomatoes, diced; cooked pasta and diced apple; heated in soup.

6. Celeriac, peeled, cut into julienne strips and heated in soup 5 minutes.

7. Tomatoes, peeled, seeded, cut into thin strips and heated in soup 5 minutes.

8. Celery and leeks, cut into julienne strips and simmered in soup 6 minutes.

9. Frankfurters, thinly sliced and heated in soup with shredded red cabbage.

10. Peas, cooked in soup 15 to 20 minutes.

11. Beets, cooked, diced and sprinkled over soup.

12. Mushrooms, sliced and added to soup with minced chives.

13. Small pasta shapes, cooked in soup 10 minutes.

14. Peas, asparagus tips, thinly sliced cooked carrots, diced onion and diced green pepper; heated in soup.

15. Gruyère cheese, shredded and sprinkled on soup just before serving.

16. Rice, cooked and added to soup, about 1 tablespoon per serving.

17. Boiled ham, cut into julienne strips and heated in soup 5 minutes.

18. Carrot, celeriac or other vegetables, diced and simmered in soup until cooked.

19. Red and green strips of pepper, added to soup with cooked rice.

20. Chives and tiny sorrel leaves used to garnish soup.

21. Dairy sour cream, spooned onto soup, about 1 tablespoon per serving.

22. Carrots, sliced, cut into attractive shapes and simmered in soup 8 minutes.

23. Asparagus tips, cooked and heated in soup.

24. Crepe, cooked with herbs and thinly sliced, used to garnish soup.

25. Leeks, thinly sliced and cooked in soup 10 minutes.

26. Saffron threads, sprinkled over soup and simmered 10 minutes.

27. Cauliflowerets, cooked and simmered in soup 5 minutes.

28. Herbs, freshly chopped and sprinkled on soup.

29. Tortellini, page 89, simmered in soup 15 minutes.

30. Egg Vermicelli, page 150, heated in soup.

Special Additions for Soup

All kinds of soup, homemade or canned, can be dressed up. Egg Flan, Egg Vermicelli, dumplings, quenelles, grated or shredded cheese, small slices of seasoned toast and even puff pastry are some of the things that can be used.

Egg Flan

2 eggs
1/2 cup milk, warmed
Salt to taste

1. Beat eggs in a bowl until foamy.
2. Add hot milk and salt; beat until well blended.
3. Place in a heatproof au gratin dish or pie plate over, not in, pan of simmering water. Pour egg mixture into dish.
4. Cover and cook over medium heat 30 to 40 minutes or until flan is firm.
5. Run the tip of a sharp knife around inside edge of dish, then invert flan onto work surface.
6. Cut flan into strips, then into small pieces.

Variations
Add 1 or more of the following ingredients to egg mixture before cooking:
● chopped spinach
● chopped pistachio nuts or almonds
● finely chopped herbs
● chopped mushrooms
● paprika or curry powder

Egg Vermicelli

1 egg
2 tablespoons all-purpose flour
Salt to taste
1/8 teaspoon grated nutmeg

1. Beat egg until foamy.
2. Add flour; beat until blended. Season with salt and nutmeg.
3. Press egg mixture through strainer into hot simmering soup. Cook 5 minutes.

Marrow Balls

1/2 cup beef marrow
1 cup fresh white bread
  crumbs
2 tablespoons freshly
  chopped parsley
2 eggs
Salt and pepper to taste
All-purpose flour

1. Finely chop beef
marrow; place in a
medium bowl.
2. Add bread crumbs,
parsley and eggs.
3. Stir until well mixed.
Season with salt and
pepper.
4. Sprinkle work surface
with flour. Spoon
mixture onto work
surface; shape into a
long thin roll. If mixture
is too loose, work in a
little flour.
5. Cut roll into small
pieces; shape each piece
into tiny ball.
6. Drop marrow balls
into hot simmering soup
or water; cook 12 to 15
minutes. Balls will rise
to top of soup when
cooked.

Veal Quenelles

1/4 lb. boneless lean
  veal shoulder
1/3 to 1/2 cup whipping
  cream
Salt and pepper to taste

1. Cut veal into thin
strips and place in a
bowl. Add 2
tablespoons cream; stir
to coat.
2. Place in a blender or
food processor fitted
with a metal blade.
3. Process until smooth.
4. Place veal in bowl;
stir in remaining cream
until thoroughly
blended.
5. Shape teaspoonfuls
of mixture into small
oval balls.
6. Drop balls, a few at a
time, into lightly salted
simmering water or
stock; cook 6 to 8
minutes. Do not
overcrowd pan.

Croutons

3 slices white bread
2 tablespoons butter
Salt to taste

1. Remove crusts from
bread; cut bread into
small cubes.
2. Melt butter in a
skillet over medium
heat. Add bread cubes;
toss to coat.
3. Cook over medium
heat, shaking skillet
constantly, until cubes
are lightly browned on
all sides. Season with
salt.

Variation
● Add 1 garlic clove to
butter in skillet.

Cheese Topping for Soup

Spoon soup into heatproof bowls or
crocks. Sprinkle grated or thinly sliced
Gruyère, Swiss, mozzarella or Parmesan cheese over soup. Place bowls on a
baking sheet; broil until cheese is
melted and golden brown.

Puff-Pastry Topping for Soup

Preheat oven to 425F (225C). Roll out
1 or 2 sheets of puff pastry. Cut circles of
puff pastry slightly larger than rims of
soup bowls. Brush rim of each filled
bowl with beaten egg yolk; place a pastry circle over a bowl, pressing pastry
edge down against rim of bowl. Repeat
for each bowl. Brush pastry edges with
beaten egg yolk. Bake in preheated
oven 20 to 25 minutes or until pastry is
golden brown.

Cream Soup: Thick, Smooth & Flavorful

It does not seem likely the famous chef Escoffier gave a moment of thought to calories as he perfected his own versions of veloutes or "velvet soups." These are not dishes for the faint of heart or for substitutions.

What makes cream soups delicious is rich whipping cream and real butter. If you are limited to the use of skim milk and margarine, these soups are not for you!

Cream of Cauliflower Soup

1/2 head cauliflower
1 cup chicken stock or
  bouillon
3 tablespoons butter
3 tablespoons
  all-purpose flour
1-1/2 cups milk
1 cup whipping cream
Salt and white pepper
  to taste
Chervil sprigs

1. Break cauliflower into small flowerets.
2. Bring stock to a boil in a large saucepan. Add cauliflower; cook 5 to 8 minutes or until tender.
3. Set aside a few flowerets to garnish. Pour remaining mixture into a blender or food processor fitted with a metal blade; process until pureed. Set aside.
4. Melt butter in a large saucepan. Add flour; cook 1 minute, stirring constantly. Add milk slowly, stirring, until mixture thickens.
5. Stir in cream and pureed cauliflower mixture; cook until heated through. Season with salt and pepper.
6. Ladle into small bowls; top each serving with reserved flowerets and sprigs of chervil.
Makes 4 servings

Cream of Mushroom Soup

1 lb. mushrooms
1/4 cup butter
1 small onion, finely
　chopped
1/4 cup all-purpose
　flour
3-1/2 cups chicken stock
　or bouillon
Salt and white pepper
　to taste
1 cup whipping cream
Thyme leaves

1. Set aside a few
mushrooms for garnish.
Finely chop remaining
mushrooms.
2. Melt butter in a large
saucepan. Add chopped
mushrooms and onion;
cook until mushrooms
are limp, 5 to 7 minutes.
3. Sprinkle flour over
mushrooms; cook 1
minute, stirring
constantly.
4. Add stock to
mushrooms gradually,
stirring until mixture
comes to a boil and
thickens.
5. Pour half the soup
into a blender or food
processor fitted with a
metal blade; process
until pureed. Stir
pureed soup back into
remaining soup. Season
with salt and pepper.
6. Add cream; cook
over medium heat,
stirring, until heated
through.
7. Slice reserved
mushrooms. Ladle soup
into small bowls; top
each serving with sliced
mushrooms and thyme
leaves.
Makes 4 to 6 servings.

Tomato Soup

3 to 4 large ripe
　tomatoes
2 tablespoons butter
1 onion, finely chopped
1 carrot, finely chopped
2 tablespoons
　all-purpose flour
2 cups chicken stock or
　bouillon
1 tablespoon brown
　sugar
1/8 teaspoon grated
　nutmeg
Salt and pepper to taste
1 cup whipping cream
　plus cream to garnish
Basil leaves

1. Blanch tomatoes,
then peel. Cut in half
and gently squeeze each
half into strainer placed
over bowl to remove
seeds. Chop flesh;
combine with juice in
bowl. Set aside.
2. Melt butter in a large
saucepan. Add onion
and carrot; sauté until
onion is transparent.
Sprinkle flour over
onion; cook, stirring, 1
minute.
3. Add reserved
tomatoes with juice,
stock, sugar, nutmeg,
salt and pepper. Stir
well; bring to a boil,
stirring constantly.
Reduce heat and
simmer, uncovered,
about 25 minutes.
4. Pour into a blender
or food processor fitted
with a metal blade;
process until pureed.
5. Wipe out saucepan to
remove any stray seeds.
Pour pureed soup back
into saucepan through
strainer. Stir in cream;
reheat gently.
6. Ladle into small
bowls; spoon 1
tablespoon cream
carefully onto surface of
soup. Garnish with basil
leaves.
Makes 4 to 6 servings.

Thickening with Egg Yolks & Cream

Soups thickened with egg yolks are
rich and delicious. The procedure is not
complicated, but it must be done carefully. Use 1 egg yolk and 1 tablespoon
whipping cream for each cup of soup to
be thickened. Place egg yolk in a small
bowl; beat gently. Beat in cream. Slowly
pour a little hot soup into egg mixture,
beating constantly. Add enough soup
to make egg-yolk mixture very warm.
Pour mixture back into remaining soup
slowly, stirring constantly. Cook over
low heat until soup is thickened. Do not
allow soup to come to a boil because
eggs will curdle. Use same method to
thicken sauces.

Thickening with Flour & Butter

There is an easy foolproof, lump-free
way to thicken soups and sauces with
flour and butter. Combine equal
amounts of softened butter and flour
and make a mixture called a *beurre manie.* Use 1 tablespoon butter and 1 tablespoon flour to thicken 2 cups of soup.
Place softened butter on a piece of
waxed paper; add flour and work them
together with your fingers until thoroughly combined. Form into a cylinder
shape; wrap in plastic wrap and keep in
the refrigerator or freezer until ready to
use. When ready to use, break off small
pieces and add to hot soup or sauce. Stir
until dissolved; cook until thickened.

Improving Packaged Soup

Most canned and packaged soups call
for the addition of water or milk, and
nothing more. If you want to improve
these products, you can do so easily.
Here are a few suggestions.
1. Substitute stock for water.
2. Substitute cream for milk.
3. Reduce liquid called for by 1/4 cup
and add dry vermouth, dry sherry or
maderia.
4. Add leftover pasta, diced vegetables
or diced meat. Thicken cream soup with
egg yolk or *beurre manie,* above. Top
with croutons.
5. Add fresh herbs.

The Nouvelle Cuisine Way

In addition to traditional cream soups there are non-fattening thick soups, filling and good to eat. The basic ingredients used are simply pureed vegetables and stock. Nouvelle cuisine has renewed interest in these soups, which appear on restaurant menus with increasing frequency. Of course you can always add cream to enhance the flavor, but it is by no means essential!

Pureed Soup

1 lb. vegetables
2-1/2 cups beef stock or
  chicken stock
Salt and pepper to taste

1. Wash, trim and chop vegetables.
2. Bring 2/3 cup stock to a boil in a medium saucepan. Add vegetables; cover and cook until tender.
3. Pour into a blender or food processor fitted with a metal blade; process until pureed.

4. Return to saucepan; add remaining stock. Stir well; cook over medium heat until heated through. Season with salt and pepper. Makes 4 servings.

Variation
● Stir in freshly chopped herbs, whipping cream, dairy sour cream or *beurre manie,* page 153. Top with croutons.

Note: If vegetables used to make soup have seeds or bits of skin in puree, strain before final heating.

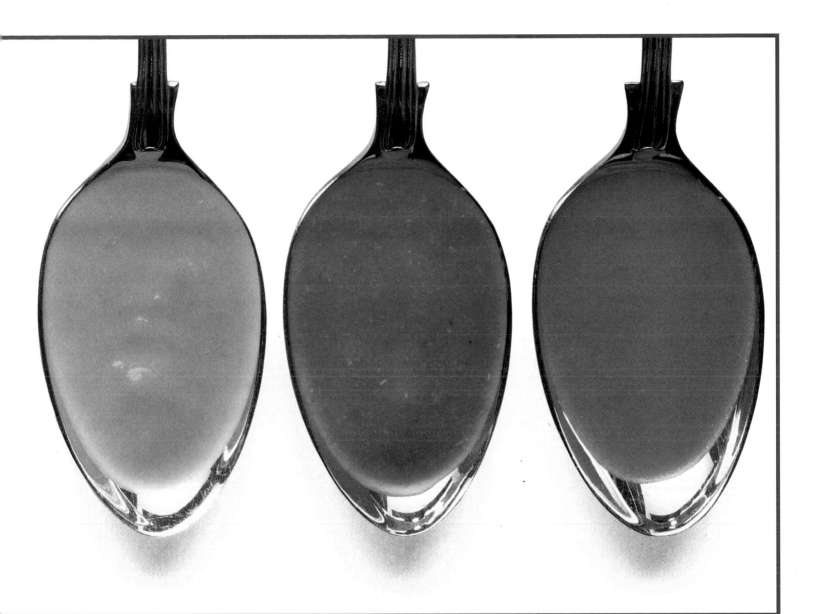

Pureed Fruit Soup

Many kinds of fruit can be used instead of vegetables. Fruit soup is particularly delicious when it is thickened, chilled and served cold.

Replace vegetables with fruit. Replace stock with water or a combination of water and wine. Omit salt and pepper. Add sugar to taste; simmer until fruit is tender. Puree in blender or food processor fitted with a metal blade; press through strainer to remove seeds and skin. Thin with milk or cream, if necessary. Adjust seasoning to taste. Serve hot or cold.

Colorful Purees

(left to right)
Pale green—pureed fresh peas cooked with fresh mint.
White—pureed cauliflower seasoned with fresh nutmeg.
Red—pureed beets seasoned with lemon juice to add tartness.
Orange—pureed carrots and oranges for an unusual taste treat.
Dark green—pureed broccoli and green herbs.

Pink—pureed, strained raspberries mixed with milk or cream.

The Pride of Italian Cooking

Just about every country has its own version of vegetable soup, but few are more popular than Italian Minestrone. In some parts of Italy, pasta is always added to the soup. In other parts of Italy, rice is used instead.

Minestrone Soup

3/4 cup dried white or
  pinto beans
2 oz. lean salt pork,
  diced
2 onions, diced
2 carrots, diced
2 celery stalks, diced
2 medium zucchini,
  diced
2 medium tomatoes,
  peeled, seeded,
  chopped
2 cups shredded savoy
  cabbage
1/4 lb. green beans, cut
  in 1-inch pieces
1 cup green peas
1 potato, peeled, diced
1 leek, diced
1 garlic clove, minced
1/2 bunch parsley,
  chopped
2 tablespoons freshly
  chopped basil
2 tablespoons butter
3 tablespoons olive oil
6 cups Beef Stock,
  pages 144-146
3/4 cup short-grain rice
  or 1 cup small pasta
Salt and pepper to taste
About 1/2 cup grated
  Parmesan cheese

1. Sort beans; rinse well. Soak beans in water to cover overnight. Drain and place in a large saucepan. Add 6 cups water and salt pork. Cook over medium heat 1 hour or until tender. Drain and set aside.

2. Prepare vegetables and herbs, setting onions and garlic aside.

3. Heat butter and oil in a large deep pan.

4. Add onions and garlic; sauté until transparent.

5. Add remaining vegetables, parsley, basil and reserved beans.

6. Cook about 10 minutes, stirring occasionally.

7. Add stock; bring to a boil over medium heat. Reduce heat and simmer, uncovered, about 1 hour.

8. Add rice or pasta; cook until tender. Season to taste. Ladle into bowls; sprinkle with Parmesan cheese. Makes 6 to 8 servings.

A Meal in a Pot

A filling soup, made from flavorful stock, meat and vegetables, can be a meal in itself, particularly when it is accompanied by a fresh green salad and crisp French bread or rolls, fresh and hot from the oven. The wonderful thing about this kind of soup is that almost any combination of meat and vegetables will work. The vegetables used can be fresh produce in season, or fresh, frozen or canned vegetables on hand. The meat can be purchased to make the soup or leftovers. Dried beans, rice, pasta and any herb or seasoning that compliments the other ingredients can be added. Filling soups are mix-and-match creations, genuine catch-alls, and one of the best ways to use leftovers. Whether you start from scratch, use leftovers, or use some of each, you can make wonderful soup. The only problem you may face is that this kind of soup often is difficult to duplicate unless you keep track of exactly what ingredients you use. Try some of our suggestions or use our recipes as guidelines and create your own meal in a pot.

Winter Soup

3 tablespoons vegetable oil
1 garlic clove, minced
1 onion, chopped
1 red-bell pepper, seeded, chopped
1/2 lb. pepperoni or other hot sausage, casing removed, sliced
2 tomatoes, peeled, seeded, chopped
1 zucchini, chopped
1 small eggplant, peeled, chopped
6 to 8 cups Beef Stock, pages 144-146
1-1/2 cups diced cooked beef
1 tablespoon tomato paste
Freshly chopped herbs
Salt and pepper to taste

1. Heat oil in a large stock pot. Add garlic, onion, red pepper and pepperoni; sauté 10 minutes. Add tomatoes, zucchini and eggplant; cook 5 minutes.
2. Add stock, diced beef, tomato paste and herbs; stir well. Bring to a boil over medium heat. Reduce heat; simmer 20 to 30 minutes or until vegetables are tender. Season to taste. Makes 6 servings.

Lentil-Vegetable Soup

6 to 8 cups Beef Stock, pages 144-146
1-1/2 cups dried lentils
2 tablespoons vegetable oil
4 carrots, chopped
2 onions, chopped
1 leek, chopped
4 small potatoes, peeled, diced
1-1/2 cups diced cooked beef or ham
Salt and pepper to taste
Freshly chopped parsley

1. Pour stock into a large stock pot; add lentils. Cover and cook over low heat 1-1/2 hours.
2. Heat oil in a medium skillet. Add carrots, onions and leek; sauté 10 minutes.

3. Add cooked vegetables, potatoes and meat to stock pot; simmer 30 minutes or until lentils and vegetables are tender. Season to taste; sprinkle with parsley.
Makes 6 to 8 servings.

Springtime Soup

3 tablespoons vegetable oil
2 to 3 carrots, chopped
1 kohlrabi, peeled, julienned
1 small cauliflower, broken into flowerets
6 to 8 cups Beef Stock, pages 144-146
2 cups diced cooked veal

1 cup green peas
Salt and pepper to taste
Freshly chopped parsley and chives

1. Heat oil in a large stock pot. Add carrots, kohlrabi and cauliflower; sauté 10 minutes, stirring occasionally.
2. Add stock and veal; bring to a boil. Reduce heat and simmer 30 minutes. Add peas, salt and pepper. Simmer 10 minutes or until vegetables are tender. Sprinkle with parsley and chives.
Makes 6 servings.

Cabbage Soup

3 tablespoons vegetable oil
1-1/2 cups shredded Savoy cabbage
1-1/2 cups shredded white cabbage
1/3 lb. green beans, cut into 1-inch pieces
6 to 8 cups Beef Stock, pages 144-146
2 cups diced cooked ham
3 to 4 potatoes, peeled, diced
1 teaspoon caraway seeds
Salt and pepper to taste

1. Heat oil in a large stock pot. Add cabbage and beans; cook 10 minutes, stirring occasionally.

2. Add stock, ham, potatoes and caraway seeds. Bring to a boil over medium heat. Reduce heat and simmer 20 to 30 minutes or until vegetables are tender. Season to taste.
Makes 6 servings.

Vichyssoise

2 cups peeled, diced
  potatoes
1 bunch leeks, sliced,
  white part only
2 cups chicken stock or
  bouillon
1 cup milk
Salt and white pepper
  to taste
1 cup whipping cream
Snipped chives

1. Place potatoes and
leeks in a medium
saucepan. Add enough
water to cover; bring to
a boil over medium
heat. Reduce heat; cover
and simmer 20 minutes
or until potatoes are
tender.
2. Drain well; place in a
blender or food
processor fitted with a
metal blade. Process
until pureed.
3. Heat stock and milk
in a large saucepan.
Add pureed potato
mixture; stir well.
Simmer 3 to 4 minutes,
stirring occasionally.
Pour into a bowl; cool to
room temperature.
4. Add cream, salt and
white pepper; stir until
thoroughly blended.
Refrigerate 3 to 4 hours
or until well-chilled.
Sprinkle with chives just
before serving.
Makes 4 to 6 servings.

Mulligatawny Soup

3 tablespoons vegetable
  oil
1 cup chopped onion
1/2 cup diced celery
1 tart apple, peeled,
  diced
3 tablespoons
  all-purpose flour
1 tablespoon curry
  powder
3 whole cloves
6 cups chicken stock or
  bouillon
Salt and pepper to taste
1-1/2 cups diced cooked
  chicken
1-1/2 cups cooked rice

1. Heat oil in a large
saucepan. Add onion,
celery and apple; sauté
until onion is
transparent.
2. Blend flour and curry
powder. Sprinkle over
vegetables; cook,
stirring, 3 minutes or
until deep golden
brown.
3. Add cloves and
chicken stock; stir well.
Bring to a boil over
medium heat. Reduce
heat; cover and simmer
30 minutes.
4. Remove and discard
cloves. Season with salt
and pepper. Add
chicken and rice;
simmer 10 to 15
minutes.
Makes 6 servings.

Zuppa Pavese

1/4 cup butter
2 tablespoons olive oil
6 slices Italian or white
  bread
6 cups Beef Stock,
  pages 144-146
Salt and white pepper
  to taste
6 egg yolks
6 tablespoons grated
  Parmesan cheese

1. Heat butter and oil in
a large skillet. Add
bread; fry on both sides.
Remove from skillet;
drain on paper towels.
2. Heat stock until
simmering. Season with
salt and pepper; ladle
into soup bowls.
3. Carefully slide 1 egg
yolk into each bowl of
soup.
4. Cut bread slices in
half; place 2 halves on
sides of each egg yolk.
Sprinkle bread with
Parmesan cheese. Serve
hot.
Makes 6 servings.

Hot Borscht

1 lb. beef brisket or
  boneless chuck,
  trimmed, cut into
  cubes
2 carrots, chopped
1 large onion, chopped
1 bay leaf
Salt and pepper to taste
6 to 8 beets, peeled,
  sliced
2 tomatoes, peeled,
  chopped
2 potatoes, peeled,
  chopped
1/2 lb. kielbasa, sliced,
  if desired
1 tablespoon lemon
  juice
1 tablespoon brown
  sugar
Freshly chopped parsley
  or dill
Dairy sour cream

1. Place beef, carrots,
onion, bay leaf, salt and
pepper in a large
saucepan; add 8 cups
water.
2. Bring to a boil over
medium heat. Skim
foam from surface until
surface is clear; reduce
heat. Cover and simmer
1 hour. Skim surface of
soup to remove fat, if
necessary.
3. Remove and discard
bay leaf. Add beets,
tomatoes, potatoes,
kielbasa, lemon juice
and sugar; stir well.
Add water, if necessary,
to cover.
4. Cover and simmer 45
minutes to 1 hour or
until meat and
vegetables are tender.
5. Ladle into bowls;
sprinkle with parsley.
Top each serving with a
dollop of sour cream.
Makes 6 to 8 servings

Gazpacho

2 large tomatoes,
  peeled, seeded, finely
  chopped
1 large red-bell pepper,
  seeded, chopped
1 medium onion, finely
  chopped
1 cucumber, peeled,
  seeded, finely
  chopped
2 garlic cloves, crushed
1/3 cup olive oil
2 tablespoons red-wine
  vinegar
1 teaspoon ground
  cumin
Hot-pepper sauce to
  taste
Salt and pepper to taste
4 cups iced water
2 cups fresh bread
  crumbs
Freshly chopped
  parsley, bread cubes
  or croutons

1. Set aside 2
tablespoons each
tomato, red pepper,
onion and cucumber to
garnish.
2. Place remaining
tomato, red pepper,
onion and cucumber in
a blender or food
processor fitted with a
metal blade. Add garlic;
process until smooth.
3. Add oil, vinegar,
cumin, hot pepper
sauce, salt and pepper;
process until blended.
4. Add iced water, 1
cup at a time,
processing until smooth.
5. Pour into a large
bowl; add bread
crumbs. Stir until
blended. Refrigerate
until well chilled.
6. Ladle into soup
bowls; garnish with
reserved vegetables.
Sprinkle with parsley
and bread cubes.
Makes 6 to 8 servings.

Onion Soup

2 tablespoons butter
2 tablespoons olive oil
5 large onions, thinly
  sliced
2 teaspoons brown
  sugar
Salt and pepper to taste
3 tablespoons
  all-purpose flour
8 cups Beef Stock,
  pages 144-146
1 cup dry vermouth or
  dry white wine
1 teaspoon browning
  sauce
6 to 8 thick slices
  French bread, toasted
1 cup grated Gruyère,
  Swiss or Parmesan
  cheese

1. Heat butter and oil in
a large saucepan. Add
onions; stir well. Cover
and cook over low heat
15 minutes, stirring
occasionally.
2. Add brown sugar,
salt and pepper; stir
well. Cook over medium
heat until onions are
browned.
3. Sprinkle flour over
onions; cook, stirring, 2
minutes.
4. Add stock and wine;
bring to a boil. Stir in
browning sauce. Reduce
heat and simmer 20 to
30 minutes.
5. Ladle soup into
heatproof bowls or
crocks. Place 1 slice
bread on top of soup;
sprinkle with grated
cheese.
6. Place under
preheated broiler; broil
until cheese is melted
and golden brown.
Makes 6 to 8 servings.

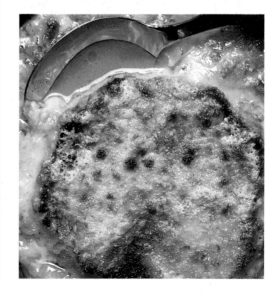

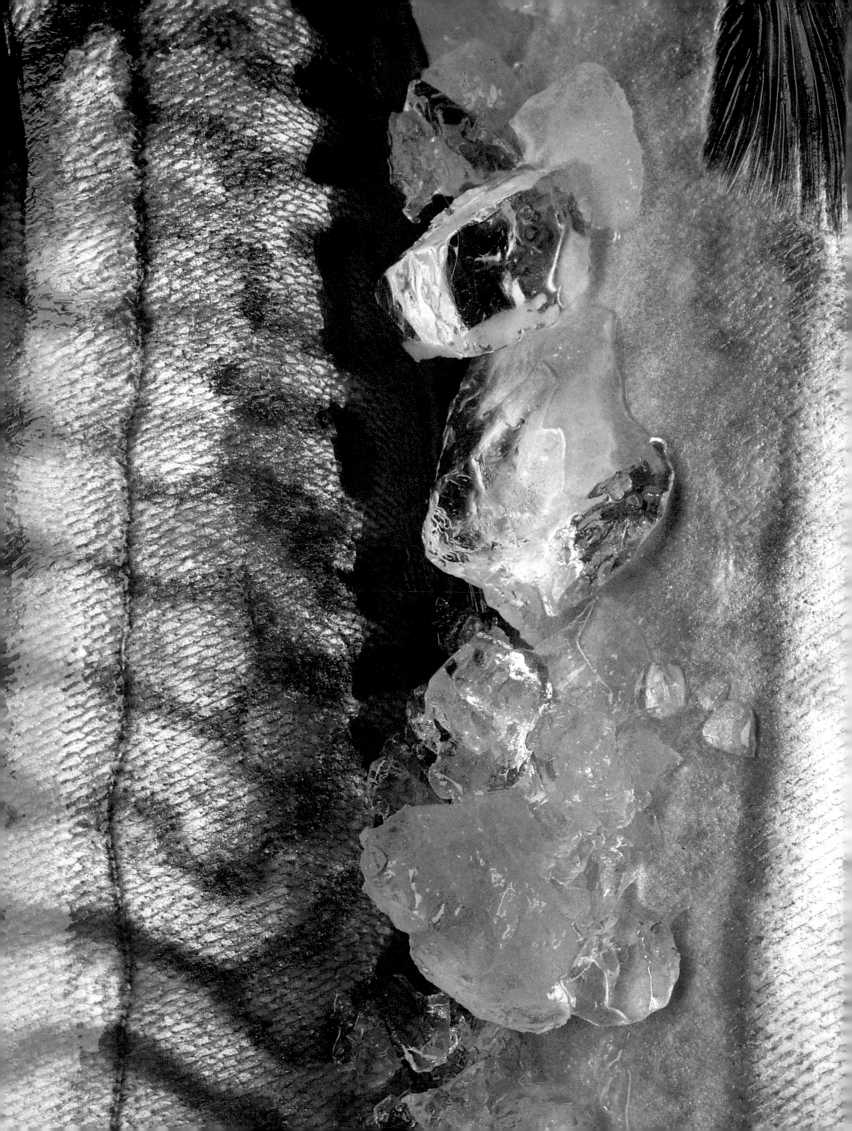

Fish: Special Gifts from Water

It seems like only yesterday that fish was thought of as a kind of second-class citizen. There certainly were many people who rarely, if ever, ate fish. And there were many who ate fish for religious reasons or because it was inexpensive. Times have certainly changed. Fish is no longer inexpensive and many religious requirements for eating fish have been eliminated. Nonetheless, fish has grown enormously in popularity as people have recognized the importance of reducing the amount of red meat in their diet, and as new and different varieties of fish have become available. The growth of the frozen-food industry has made it possible to buy many kinds of fish in all parts of the country at almost any time of year. And with the increase in travel, many people have discovered fish they never had an opportunity to eat before. Fish cookery has moved a long way from the mid-week tuna casserole of old. A well-prepared fish dinner often is the menu of choice at the most elegant company dinner.

How To Cook Fish

In addition to the cooking methods shown here, fish can be cooked in many other ways: baked, broiled, barbecued, deep-fat fried, steamed, smoked or microwaved. Some fish can also be marinated and served without cooking. No matter how you prepare it, you should start with very fresh fish or fish that has been properly frozen. When available, fresh fish is always preferable to frozen. The flavor of good-quality fish can be enhanced by herbs and spices, light sauces, or simply a little butter and lemon juice. But the too-strong flavor and unpleasant odor of fish that is not fresh cannot be enhanced by anything.

Buying Fish

Most fish markets get their fish fresh very early every morning. Supermarkets are not always able to do this. However, supermarkets are an excellent source for a wide variety of frozen fish. Fresh fish will be almost free of odor, have firm flesh, clear eyes, red or pink gills, and shiny scales that are not loose. The skin should not feel sticky or slippery. Once you have made your selection, the fishman will clean, gut, scale and fillet the fish for you if you ask him. And, if you are planning to make a fish stock, ask him to give you some fish heads and bones.

When You Bring Fish Home

Ideally, fresh fish should be cooked and served the same day it is purchased. It will not remain fresh in the refrigerator for more than 1 or 2 days. If you have to keep fresh fish longer than that, store it in the freezer in a container filled with water. It can be kept in the freezer at 0F (-20C) or lower for about 6 months. Wrap fish carefully before you place it in the refrigerator to keep it from drying out and from absorbing the odors of other food. When you are ready to cook the fish, rinse under cold running water and pat dry with paper towels. Place wrapped frozen fish on a plate in the refrigerator and allow it to defrost in the refrigerator overnight. Rinse and pat dry before cooking.

Poaching in Water

Juice of 1 lemon
Salt to taste
1 onion, sliced
1 bay leaf
6 peppercorns
1/2 cup dry vermouth, if desired
Fish steak

1. Pour about 4 cups water in a medium saucepan; place over medium heat.

2. Add juice of 1 lemon.

Poaching in Stock

1 carrot, sliced
1 onion, quartered
1 leek, sliced
1 garlic clove
5 parsley sprigs
2 lemon slices
6 peppercorns
Salt to taste
Fish steak

1. Pour about 4 cups water in a saucepan. Add remaining ingredients except fish.

2. Place over medium heat; bring water to a boil. Cook 10 minutes.

Braising over Vegetables

1 carrot, julienned
1 celery stalk, julienned
1 small leek, julienned
1 cup dry white wine
1 tablespoon butter
Salt and pepper to taste
Fish steak

1. Arrange vegetables in a small baking dish.

2. Pour wine over vegetables.

Oven Poaching

Fish steak
2-1/2 cups dry white wine or dry vermouth

1. Place fish on a rack in a fish poacher.

2. Pour in 2-1/2 cups dry white wine. Add enough water to cover fish.

Pan-frying or Sautéing

Salt and pepper to taste
All-purpose flour
1 tablespoon vegetable oil
1 tablespoon butter
Fish steak

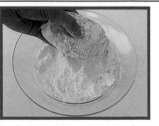

1. Season fish with salt and pepper; dredge in flour. Shake off any excess flour.

2. Heat oil and butter in a medium skillet.

3. Add salt and remaining ingredients except fish; bring water just to a boil.

4. Reduce heat; lower fish gently into simmering water.

5. Poach 10 minutes or until fish flakes easily. Remove fish with a slotted spoon.

3. Reduce heat; lower fish gently into simmering stock.

4. Poach fish in simmering stock 10 minutes or until fish flakes easily.

3. Dot vegetables with butter.

4. Place fish over vegetables; season to taste.

5. Cover and bake in 425F (220C) oven 10 minutes per inch of thickness or until fish flakes easily.

3. Cover pan tightly.

4. Bake in 425F (220C) oven 10 minutes per inch of thickness or until fish flakes.

3. Lower fish into hot fat.

4. Cook 5 minutes on each side, turning fish over once.

5. Remove from skillet; drain on paper towels.

Fish: Any Way You Choose

One of the nicest things about fish is that it is flexible in more ways than one. Many fish can be cooked by the same method; many sauces that are appropriate to serve with fish can be served with several kinds of fish; and, although there are some seasonings that have a particular affinity for certain fish, you can use just about any seasoning you like. A recipe that works well with a light-colored fish will work for most light-colored fish, and the same is true for dark-colored fish. You can take fish out of the refrigerator and decide on the spur of the moment how you want to cook it and how you want to sauce or season it. If, as you start to prepare fish, you discover you are missing some ingredients called for in a particular recipe, just pick another recipe. A little butter and lemon juice often are all you really need to fix a delicious fish dinner.

Categories of Fish

The two main categories of fish are round fish and flat fish. Fish can be further divided by where they come from, fresh or salt water, and divided once again by their fat content. Fish with light-colored flesh are usually low in fat; fish with firm, dark flesh are usually higher in fat content.

How Much Fish to Buy

Estimate 1/3 to 1/2 pound per person for filleted fish. Estimate 1 pound per person for whole fish, head and tail included.

The Nutritional Value of Fish

Fish is highly nutritious, low in calories and sodium, and high in protein, B-complex vitamins and many minerals. Most of the fat is polyunsaturated. There is no question that the high nutritional value of fish has contributed to its growth in popularity in this age of growing consciousness about what we should eat.

Cooking Time for Fish

Several years ago The Canadian Department of Fisheries conducted a research project on the best methods for cooking fish. The result of their research provides a good rule of thumb for estimating how long fish should be cooked. The principle they developed is to measure fish at its thickest point and, no matter what cooking method is used, cook 10 minutes per inch. When cooking a rolled fillet, measure the fillet after it has been rolled. But 10 minutes per inch is maximum cooking time. Sometimes fish cooks more quickly, so check carefully.

Frozen fish will take longer to cook, and fish cooked in a microwave oven will take less time. Be careful not to overcook fish. Overcooking will make fish tough and dry, and will destroy the delicate flavor.

Cod & Spinach with Mustard Sauce

Mustard Sauce, page 254
2 lbs. fresh spinach, stems removed
1/4 cup butter
1/4 teaspoon grated nutmeg
Salt and pepper to taste
4 cod steaks, about 1 inch thick
1 lemon, sliced
Dill sprigs

1. Prepare Mustard Sauce; set aside and keep warm.
2. Rinse spinach several times in cold water. Place in a large saucepan; cook over high heat 2 minutes or until limp. Drain well; press out excess liquid with back of a spoon.
3. Melt butter in saucepan; add spinach. Stir to coat spinach; cook until heated through. Season with nutmeg, salt and pepper; keep mixture warm.
4. Poach fish according to directions for any poaching method, pages 164-165.
5. Serve fish with spinach and Mustard Sauce. Garnish with halved lemon slices and dill sprigs.
Makes 4 servings.

Flounder with Herb Sauce

Herb Cream Sauce, page 256
1-1/2 lbs. fillet of flounder
2 tablespoons butter
1 lb. fresh mushrooms, sliced
Salt and pepper to taste
Sprigs of parsley, basil and tarragon

1. Prepare Herb Sauce; set aside and keep warm.
2. Poach fillets according to directions for any poaching method, pages 164-165.
3. Melt butter in a skillet over high heat. Add mushrooms; sauté until limp. Season with salt and pepper.

Serving Fish

Fish that is supposed to be served warm, should be cooked at the last possible minute because fish will dry out if kept warm in the oven while you prepare a sauce or other food. Most sauces can be kept warm in the top of a double boiler over barely simmering water, or reheated gently just before serving.

Although all fish benefit from an attractive garnish, white fish in particular should have some color added to it for eye appeal. Lemon and lime juice enhance the flavor of most fish, and slices of either fruit make a beautiful garnish. Sprigs of fresh green herbs are always appropriate. Choose herbs that compliment the seasoning in the fish sauce or other foods served with the fish. If the flavor of the fish is not too delicate, a light sprinkling of paprika can provide a nice touch of color. Use a paprika with a mild flavor.

Eye appeal is often a clue to the nutritional balance of foods served together. White-fish fillets served with mashed potatoes and cauliflower will look bland and unappetizing and will also have a poor nutritional balance. But the same fish served with parsley potatoes and a bright-green vegetable will have both eye appeal and greater nutritional value. Properly seasoned rice is always good with fish. However, if you serve a sauce for the fish, don't serve a sauced starch or vegetable too. Keep the food that accompanies the fish simple.

Most people prefer to drink a dry white wine with fish. The delicate flavor of fish is likely to be overwhelmed by the strong flavor of a full-bodied red wine. However, a light red or rosé can be served with dark fish or a strongly flavored fish or stew. Beer is usually the drink of choice at a New England Clam Bake and chilled champagne can be served at any time.

4. Serve fish and mushrooms with Herb Sauce. Garnish with sprigs of parsley, basil and tarragon. Serve with hot cooked rice or buttered potatoes. Makes 4 servings.

Sole with Saffron Sauce & Shrimp

Saffron Cream Sauce, page 257
1 lb. lemon sole fillets
2 tablespoons butter
1/2 lb. small shrimp, peeled, deveined
Salt and pepper to taste
Chervil sprigs

1. Prepare Saffron Sauce; set aside and keep warm.
2. Starting at wide end, roll each fillet, jelly-roll style; secure with wooden picks.
3. Poach fillets according to directions for any poaching method, pages 164-165.
4. Melt butter in a medium skillet; add shrimp. Cook over medium heat 3 to 4 minutes or until shrimp turn pink, stirring constantly. Season with salt and pepper.
5. Serve sole turbans and shrimp with Saffron Sauce. Garnish with chervil sprigs. Makes 4 servings.

Salmon & Vegetables with Butter Sauce

Simple Butter Sauce, page 251
4 carrots, julienned
2 leeks, julienned
2 tablespoons butter, melted
Salt and pepper to taste
1-1/2 lbs. salmon fillets
Tarragon sprigs

1. Prepare Butter Sauce; set aside and keep warm.
2. Cook carrots and leeks separately in boiling water until just tender. Drain well; toss with melted butter. Season with salt and pepper; keep warm.
3. Poach salmon according to directions for any poaching method, pages 164-165.
4. Serve salmon with julienned vegetables and Butter Sauce. Garnish with tarragon. Makes 4 servings.

Cooking Whole Fish

A dinner of whole fish can be anything from a small lake trout sautéed over an open fire, to a large salmon cooked in a fish poacher or a stuffed red snapper baked in the oven. In most parts of the world, whole fish are cooked with heads and tail still attached. However, if you are bothered by the feeling that the fish is looking at you somewhat reproachfully, as many Americans are, you can remove the head before cooking.

Poaching Whole Fish

If you want to poach whole fish often, invest in a fish poacher. The rack that fits in the poacher has handles at each end that make it very easy to lift the fish out of the poaching liquid.

Rinse gutted fish under cold running water; pat dry with paper towels. Season inside of fish; stuff with fresh herbs, sliced onions or leeks and strips of carrot. Tie fish with kitchen string or blanched strips of leek, shown above. Be sure poaching liquid covers fish completely to ensure even cooking. Cover and cook gently in simmering liquid.

Poached Whole Fish in Vegetable Stock

3 cups water
3 cups dry white wine
2 carrots, cut in chunks
1 onion, cut in chunks
1 garlic clove
1 celery stalk, cut in chunks
1 lemon, sliced
2 bay leaves
8 peppercorns
4 dill sprigs
4 parsley sprigs
1 teaspoon salt
1 whole medium fish, prepared according to directions on left
1 cup whipping cream
1 to 2 tablespoons brandy, if desired
Lemon wedges

1. Place water and all ingredients except fish, cream, brandy and lemon wedges in a fish poacher.

2. Cover poacher; bring liquid to a boil. Reduce heat and simmer 10 minutes.

3. Place fish on a rack; lower carefully into simmering liquid. Add more water or wine, if necessary, to cover fish completely.

4. Cover and simmer 20 to 30 minutes or until fish flakes easily.

5. Remove fish; set aside and keep warm.

6. Strain stock, discarding vegetables and seasonings. Return stock to poacher. Cook over high heat until reduced by half.

7. Add cream; cook over medium heat until thickened, stirring constantly. Stir in brandy, if desired. Adjust seasoning; then pour into a gravy boat.

8. Remove string from fish; place fish on a serving platter. Season with salt and pepper. Garnish with lemon wedges. Serve sauce separately.

Makes 6 to 8 servings.

Stock Variations
● To make coconut stock, replace part of water or wine with canned coconut milk. Add 1 teaspoon freshly grated ginger and juice of 1 lemon.
● To make red-wine stock, substitute dry red wine for white wine.
● Omit vegetables; poach fish in chicken stock.

Court Bouillon

1 lb. fish bones and
   heads
4 to 6 cups water
3 to 4 cups dry white or
   red wine
1 large onion, cut in
   large chunks
2 carrots, cut in large
   chunks
2 garlic cloves
1 bay leaf
1 or 2 fresh thyme or
   parsley sprigs
Salt and pepper to taste

1. Place fish bones and
heads in a large
stockpot. Add water;
bring to a boil over
medium heat. Cover
and simmer 30 minutes.
2. Strain stock through
cheesecloth; discard
bones and heads.
3. Return fish stock to
pot. Add wine, onion,
carrots, garlic, bay leaf,
thyme, salt and pepper,
bring to a boil.
4. Reduce heat; simmer
20 minutes.
5. Add desired
shellfish; cook for time
indicated on the right.
6. Remove shellfish
with a slotted spoon;
serve immediately.

The Shellfish Family

Shellfish are divided into two categories: crustaceans and mollusks. Lobster, langoustine, crayfish, shrimp and crab are crustaceans. The Latin derivation of crustacean is *crusta* or *rind*, which is a good description of the jointed shell that covers the bodies of these shellfish. Mussels, clams, cockles, periwinkles, snails, scallops, oysters and squid are mollusks with soft, edible bodies enclosed partly or entirely in a hard shell.

Shellfish can be purchased in or out of the shell, but most shellfish in the shell must be alive when cooked. Keep shellfish in the refrigerator until you are ready to cook it. But, don't make the mistake of putting live shellfish in fresh water. It will kill the fish.

Maine, Spiny & Rock Lobster
Cook in Court Bouillon 15 to 20 minutes, depending on size.

Langoustine or Mediterranean Prawns
Cook in Court Bouillon 5 to 7 minutes. Allow 6 to 8 per person.

Crayfish or Crawfish
Cook in Court Bouillon 5 to 8 minutes, depending on size. Allow 12 to 15 crayfish per person.

Jumbo Shrimp
Cook in Court Bouillon 3 to 5 minutes.

Tiny Shrimp
Cook in Court Bouillon 2 to 5 minutes.

Mussels, Clams & Cockles
Cook in Court Bouillon until shells open. Discard any that do not open. Allow 8 to 10 per person.

Snails & Periwinkles
Require careful and thorough washing before cooking about 3 hours in Court Bouillon.

Fish: Delicious in a Bowl

Fish soup is a wonderful way to start a meal or, when chock-full of all kinds of wonderful ingredients, a delicious meal in itself. Although Court Bouillon and Fish Stock are not served as soup, they are often used as a base for making bisques and chowders, or to make soup that is more like stew, such as Cioppino, Bouillabaisse or Gumbo. Passions can run very high about the correct way to make a regional fish soup and, if you are lucky enough to eat a bowl of Bouillabaisse in a small town in France, you may never be able to find out exactly how it was made. The story that the good citizens of Colonial Massachusetts were so upset about the addition of tomatoes to their beloved New England Clam Chowder that they passed a law prohibiting what has come to be known as Manhattan Clam Chowder is probably apocryphal. Even if you are not privy to some special secret recipe, there are many wonderful ways you can use fish and shellfish in soup.

Fish Stock

3 tablespoons butter
2 garlic cloves, minced
1 onion, diced
1 carrot, chopped
3 small leeks, chopped
1 celery stalk, chopped
About 1-1/2 lbs. fish trimmings
4 cups water
4 cups dry white wine
1-1/2 teaspoons salt
8 to 10 peppercorns
4 parsley sprigs
2 bay leaves

Fish trimmings are heads, bones and fins. Use trimmings from any white fish, such as flounder, haddock, turbot or cod to make fish stock. Do not use trimmings from oily or fatty fish, such as mackerel.
1. Melt butter in a large stock pot. Add garlic, onion, carrot, leeks and celery; sauté over medium heat until onion is transparent. Stir in fish trimmings.
2. Add water, wine, salt, peppercorns, parsley and bay leaves; bring to a boil. Reduce heat and simmer, uncovered, 30 minutes. Do not stir.
3. Strain stock through a double thickness of cheesecloth. Discard vegetables, fish trimmings and seasonings. Use stock to make fish soup, sauces and gravies.
Makes about 1-1/2 quarts.

Tips:
● Don't stir fish stock while it is cooking. Stirring will make it cloudy.
● Don't cook stock longer than 30 minutes because flavor will become too strong.
● Fish stock can be stored in refrigerator up to 1 week or frozen up to 3 months.

Light Seafood Soup

2 tablespoons butter
1 garlic clove, crushed
1 onion, minced
1 carrot, diced
2 leeks, diced
1 cup dry white wine
6 cups Fish Stock
1 bay leaf
1/2 teaspoon dried leaf thyme
1/4 teaspoon ground saffron or several saffron threads
Salt and pepper to taste
1 lb. thick, white-fish fillets, cut in chunks
1/2 lb. shrimp, peeled, deveined
1 lb. mussels, scrubbed
12 littleneck clams, scrubbed
Pesto or Aioli, page 147

1. Melt butter in a large saucepan. Add garlic, onion, carrot and leeks; sauté until onion is transparent.
2. Add wine, stock, bay leaf, thyme, saffron, salt and pepper; bring to a boil.
3. Add fish chunks; simmer 10 minutes. Add shrimp, mussels and clams. Cover and simmer until shellfish open and shrimp turn pink.
4. Ladle into soup bowls; serve with Pesto or Aioli Sauce and crusty French bread. Makes 6 servings.

Variations
Add 1 or more of the following ingredients to soup:
● Peeled diced tomatoes
● Diced fennel
● Diced cooked chili peppers

Flounder or Sole?

Fish markets and restaurants often sell sole, and they usually charge more for it than flounder. But the only "real" sole available in the United States is frozen sole imported from France or England. Many varieties of flounder are called *sole*, but no matter what name you give this fish, it is one of the most popular available. Whether you use real sole or one of the many varieties of flounder, recipes for these fish are interchangeable. And one of the nicest ways to prepare flounder is to fry it whole, shown here.

Pan-fried Flounder

4 medium flounder
All-purpose flour
1/2 cup butter
2 to 3 tablespoons
vegetable oil
Salt and pepper to taste
Juice of 1 lemon
Diced cooked bacon

1. Rinse fish under cold running water; pat dry with paper towels.
2. Cut a lengthwise slit down dark side of each fish for easy removal of bone after cooking.
3. Dredge fish in flour; shake off excess.
4. Heat butter and oil in a large skillet until bubbly.
5. Fry fish, 1 or 2 at a time, until golden brown on bottom. Turn and season with salt and pepper.
6. Fry until golden brown. Remove fish to a serving platter; season second side. Sprinkle with lemon juice and bacon.
7. Repeat with remaining fish. Serve immediately.
Makes 4 servings.

Variations
● Garnish with sautéed diced shrimp.
● Cook 2 to 3 tablespoons butter in skillet until lightly browned; pour over cooked fish. Sprinkle with lemon juice and freshly chopped parsley.
● Rub fish with Worcestershire sauce before dredging in flour. Sauté sliced almonds in butter until golden brown. Drain on paper towels. Sprinkle over cooked fish.
● Serve with buttered new potatoes and a cucumber-dill salad or tossed green salad.

Our Trout Septet

Schubert immortalized the trout in his song "Die Forelle," The Trout, and again in his beautiful Trout Quintet. If you close your eyes while you listen to the music, you can almost see the rippling stream filled with trout running past a picturesque farmhouse. We have gone beyond Schubert's quintet to bring to a septet of ways to prepare this popular fish. Next time you serve trout, light some candles and put on the record. It will provide the perfect setting for a meal you will long remember.

Trout Wrapped in Lettuce

Wrap cleaned, dressed trout in blanched lettuce, spinach or Chinese cabbage leaves. Braise over vegetables, poach in oven or cook in a smoker oven.

Bleu Trout

Bring 3 cups water, 1 cup white vinegar, juice of 1 lemon, 6 peppercorns and 1 teaspoon salt to a boil in a large saucepan. Plunge live trout into boiling liquid. Reduce heat immediately; poach trout 10 minutes per inch. Don't allow liquid to boil. Clean trout; serve with melted butter. It is the vinegar in the recipe that causes the skin to turn blue.

Trout en Papillote

Season cavity of cleaned dressed trout with salt and pepper to taste. Stuff cavity with sliced green onions, herbs, such as basil, tarragon and parsley, and crushed garlic. Wrap trout tightly in foil; place in a shallow baking dish. Bake in preheated 400F (250C) oven 15 to 20 minutes or until fish flakes easily.

Charcoal Broiled Trout

Make several slashes on each side of cleaned dressed trout. Sprinkle with freshly chopped herbs, such as dill, tarragon and thyme. Brush rack of grill with oil or place greased foil on rack. Place rack over hot coals. Place fish on oiled rack or foil; grill several inches from heat, 5 minutes on each side. Alternatively, place prepared trout in oiled grill basket. This will prevent fish from breaking on grill.

Trout Amandine

Dredge cleaned dressed trout in all-purpose flour; shake off excess. Heat 3 to 4 tablespoons butter and 1 tablespoon oil in a skillet. Add sliced almonds and trout; sauté 5 minutes or until trout is golden brown. Spoon almonds over fish. Turn trout over; season with salt and pepper. Cook 5 minutes. Place on a serving platter; season second side. Spoon almonds and butter over.

Trout Meuniere

Dredge cleaned dressed trout in all-purpose flour; shake off excess. Heat 3 to 4 tablespoons butter and 1 tablespoon oil in a skillet; sauté trout 5 minutes or until golden brown. Turn trout over; season with salt and pepper. Cook 5 minutes. Place on a serving platter; season second side. Sprinkle with lemon juice. Garnish with lemon slices.

Swedish Salmon Trout

Line a shallow dish with dill. Combine 1 teaspoon coarsely ground pepper, 2 to 3 teaspoons chopped dill, 1 tablespoon sugar and 4 tablespoons coarse salt. Rub on dressed, boned salmon trout. Place fish on top of dill; sprinkle with 2 tablespoons white vinegar. Cover tightly with plastic wrap. Weight down with a plate and can. Refrigerate 18 to 24 hours. Thinly slice; serve with pumpernickel bread and hot mustard.

Poultry: A Favorite Around the World

Herbert Hoover is often given credit for having been the first to express the hope that there would be a chicken in every pot on Sundays. But that wish did not originate with him. It was said a lot earlier by Henry IV, the Bourbon king of France, at his coronation in 1589. A chicken in every pot may have seemed far-fetched at the time, but today chicken is surely one of the more economical ways to feed a family. Although the popularity and availability of chicken exceeds that of other kinds of poultry, turkey, Cornish hen, duck and goose are welcome additions at most tables for holiday meals and throughout the year.

All About Poultry

Poultry should be wrapped, stored in the refrigerator and used within 2 days of purchase. If you don't plan to use it within 2 days, store it in the freezer. Properly wrapped poultry can be kept safely in the freezer at 0F (-20C) for as long as 10 months. Thaw wrapped poultry in the refrigerator overnight, longer for large turkeys, or follow manufacturers' instructions and defrost in a microwave oven.

When you are ready to cook poultry, rinse it under cold running water, then thoroughly pat dry with paper towels. Giblets are usually packed inside whole birds and should be removed before rinsing. Trim excess fat from poultry, then season according to recipe.

Safety Precautions

It is important to note that special precautions must be taken in the preparation of any raw poultry. This is to avoid contamination of any work surface or cutting utensils. Knives and cutting surfaces, particularly porous wood surfaces, must be washed thoroughly to remove any bacteria before they can be used again. Hands must be washed before handling other foods. In addition, the cavity of a whole bird provides an excellent place for the growth of bacteria. Therefore, it is absolutely vital to remember that poultry should not be stuffed until just before it is placed in the oven. It is equally important to remove leftover stuffing and store it in a separate bowl in the refrigerator. Do not leave stuffing inside cooked poultry.

Timing

Properly cooked poultry will be 180F (80C) when checked with a meat thermometer. The tip of the thermometer should be inserted into the thickest part of the thigh and should not touch bone. If you don't own a meat thermometer, pierce the inner thigh with a fork. If the juices run clear and the leg moves easily, the poultry is cooked. Let roasted poultry stand, covered, 10 to 15 minutes at room temperature before carving to allow the juices to settle and the meat to "set." The internal temperature of stuffing must be 165F (75C) before it is safe to eat.

Trussing

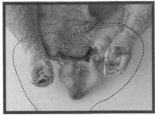

1. Place poultry, breast-side up, on a work surface. Wrap string around tail and cross over legs.

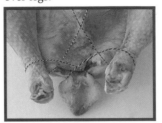

2. Wind string around legs; pull string toward center; cross ends of string.

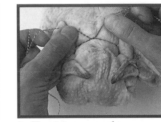

3. Pull string tightly to pull legs together. Tie string.

4. Pull ends of string up from legs along each side of breast.

5. Turn bird over; grasp ends of string.

6. Tuck wing-tips under; pull string over wings.

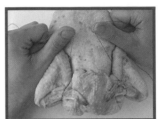

7. Pull string tightly around wings.

8. Tie string securely.

9. Cut off ends of string.

10. Turn bird breast-side up.

How Much To Buy

When buying whole poultry estimate about 3/4 pound per person. Estimate about 1/3 pound per person for boneless cuts. A 5-pound roaster will yield about 5 cups diced, cooked meat.

Trussing

Trussing, left, will help poultry retain its shape during roasting. Both stuffed and unstuffed poultry should be trussed. If you use the method shown, string should be twice the length of the bird. Poultry skewers can also be used to close the cavity of poultry. If skewers are used, it is still important to tuck wings under and tie legs together.

Sauces & Gravies

Roast poultry should be served with a sauce or gravy. See pages 258-259 for hints on making gravy and pages 252-257 for sauces.

Roasting

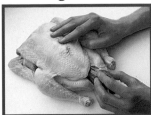

1. Remove giblets from cavity of chicken.

2. Brush skin lightly with vegetable oil or melted butter.

3. Season chicken all over with salt and paprika.

4. Place chicken, breast-side up, on a rack in a roasting pan.

5. Baste chicken several times during cooking.

6. Place cooked chicken on a carving board.

7. Cut leg from chicken with a sharp knife.

8. Cut through joint between breast and wing to remove wing.

9. Cut through hip joint to separate drumstick from thigh.

10. Cut breast meat in diagonal slices.

Roasting & Carving

Place washed and dried poultry, breast-side up, on a work surface. Season inside cavity with salt. If bird is to be cooked unstuffed, add an onion, a few sprigs of parsley and half a lemon to cavity. If bird is to be stuffed, prepare 1/2 cup stuffing per pound of poultry; fill cavity lightly. Allow room for expansion of stuffing during cooking. Close cavity; brush skin of stuffed or unstuffed bird lightly with vegetable oil or melted butter or margarine. Season all over with salt and paprika. Truss according to directions. Place, breast-side up, on a rack in a roasting pan. Roast in preheated 350F (175C) oven 2 to 3-1/2 hours, depending on size, or until internal temperature reaches 180F (80C), basting often. Remove to a carving board. Cover loosely and let stand 10 to 15 minutes before carving.

Choose a small carving board if you are carving a small bird so it will not look lost and give the impression there may not be enough to eat. A smooth china platter is difficult to carve on because the poultry is likely to slide around. Don't surround uncarved poultry with vegetables and garnishes that will get in the way when you start to carve. Remove the trussing or skewers. Spoon the stuffing into a serving bowl.

Now you are ready to carve. You will need a long-handled fork and a very sharp carving knife. If you use a knife that is not sharp, you will tear the poultry rather than carve it. Hold the bird firmly in place with the fork and insert the knife between the thigh and the breast. Cut the skin and bend the thigh outward. Slice through the hip joint and remove the leg. Remove the second leg. Place the legs on a separate serving dish; slice dark meat off thighs and drumsticks. Slice diagonally down between breast and wing. Cut through joint and remove wing. Remove second wing. Place fork on the side of the breast to be carved; slice diagonally down from breast bone to carving board. Lift off each slice and place on serving dish with dark meat and wings.

Poultry Family

When poultry is roasted, the method for trussing and some of the basic rules for roasting apply no matter what kind of poultry is cooked. There are, however, some differences. The fat content of the bird must be taken into account. Lean game birds require extra fat. Very fatty birds, such as duck and goose, require special treatment to reduce the amount of fat that remains in the cooked bird.

Cooking Fatty Birds

Duck and goose have a very thick layer of fat beneath the skin. In order to provide a way for this fat to drain off during cooking, it is necessary to prick the skin all over before roasting. During roasting, the fat drips out through the prick holes and accumulates in the roasting pan. Some of the fat that accumulates can be used for basting and a small amount of fat can be used to make gravy or a special sauce. The remainder of the fat should be drained off during cooking.

Barding Lean Birds

Game birds are very lean. If they are cooked without additional fat, they will be dry. The process of adding fat is called *barding*. Place bacon strips over the breast of the bird and, if desired, tie in place. Remove bacon 15 to 20 minutes before roasting is finished to allow the skin to become crisp.

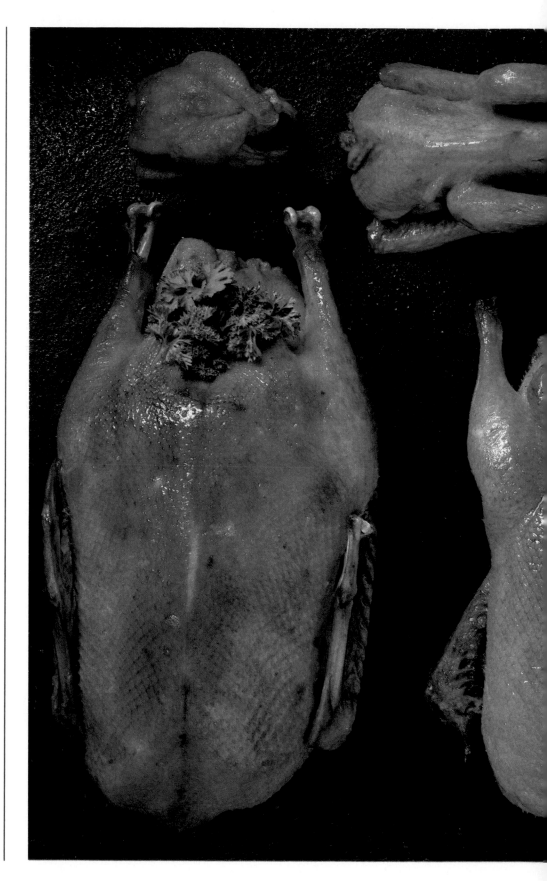

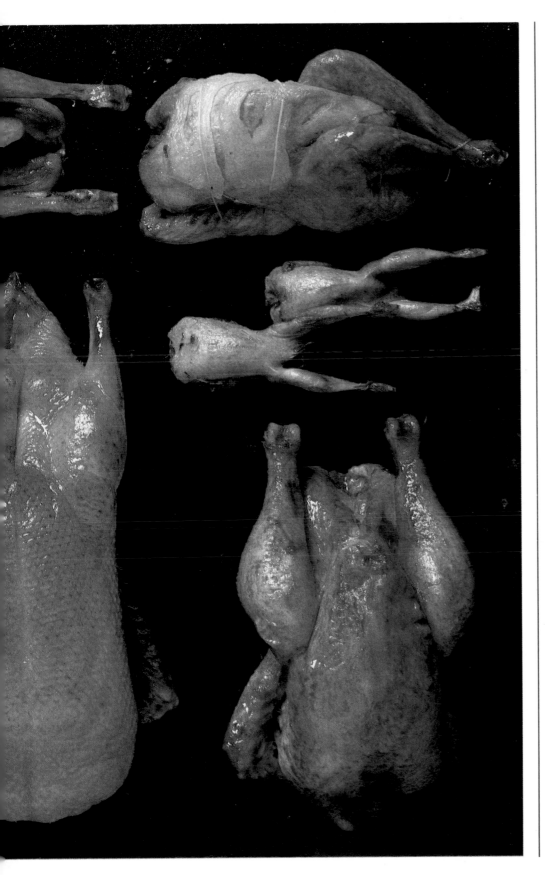

Types of Poultry

Cornish Game Hen (top left)
Available fresh or frozen; 3/4 to 1-1/2 pounds. Roast on a rack in a preheated 400F (200C) oven 45 minutes to 1 hour, basting frequently.

Guinea Fowl (top center)
Available frozen or fresh in limited supply at specialty markets; 2 to 4 pounds. Roast on a rack in a preheated 350F (175C) oven 1-1/2 to 2-1/2 hours, basting frequently.

Pheasant (top right)
Available frozen; 2 to 3-1/2 pounds. Bard with strips of bacon. Roast on a rack in a preheated 350F (175C) oven 1-1/2 to 2 hours, basting frequently.

Goose (bottom left)
Available fresh or frozen; 6 to 14 pounds. Prick skin all over before roasting. Roast on a rack in a preheated 325F (170C) oven, basting frequently.
6 to 8 pound goose—cook 3 to 3-1/2 hours
8 to 14 pound goose—cook 3-1/2 to 5 hours

Duck or Duckling (bottom center)
Available fresh or frozen; 4 to 6 pounds. Prick skin all over before roasting. Roast on a rack in a preheated 350F (175C) oven 2-1/2 to 3 hours, basting frequently.

Roasting Chicken (bottom right)
Available fresh; 3-1/2 to 7 pounds. Roast on a rack in a preheated 350F (175C) oven 2 to 3-1/2 hours, basting frequently. Reduce time by 15 minutes for unstuffed bird.

Capons
Available fresh or frozen; 4 to 7 pounds. Roast on a rack in a preheated 350F (175C) oven 2-1/2 to 3-1/2 hours, basting frequently.

Quail (right center)
Available frozen, fresh and smoked; 1/2 to 1 pound. Roast on a rack in a preheated 350F (175C) oven 40 to 60 minutes, basting frequently.

Turkey
Available fresh or frozen; 6 to 24 pounds. Roast on a rack in a preheated 325F (170C) oven 20 minutes per pound, basting often.

Duck

Although there are more than 60 species of duck, the most popular duck in the United States is Long Island duck. These domesticated birds are direct descendants of the Chinese ducks first imported to the United States in about 1870. Any list of truly famous ethnic dishes would certainly include Peking Duck from China and Duck à l'Orange from France. Most people think of oranges as the ideal fruit to serve with duck, but there are other fruits that equally compliment its rather strong flavor. Try our recipe for Duck à l'Orange or prepare some of the variations that follow instead. There are very few dishes you can serve to company that will be appreciated more.

Duck Stock

Rinse duck giblets; place in a medium saucepan. Add 2-1/2 cups water, 1 parsley sprig, 1 small onion, 1 small celery stalk, 1 small carrot and salt to taste. Bring to a boil over medium heat. Reduce heat; cover and simmer 30 to 45 minutes or until giblets are fork tender. Remove giblets; set aside. Strain stock through a double thickness of cheesecloth into a bowl. Let cool; skim off fat. Use stock to make gravy or sauce. Finely chop giblets; add to gravy, if desired.

Duck à l'Orange

1 (4- to 6-lb.)
  oven-ready duck
Salt and pepper to taste

Sauce:
Finely slivered peel of 2
  large oranges
2 tablespoons
  all-purpose flour
1/2 cup duck stock or
  chicken stock
1/2 cup orange juice
1/2 cup dry red wine
2 to 3 tablespoons sugar
2 tablespoons lemon
  juice
2 tablespoons
  orange-flavored
  liqueur
Basil sprigs
Orange slices

---

1. Preheat oven to 350F (175C).
2. Remove giblets; set aside. Rinse duck under cold running water; pat dry with paper towels. Remove and discard excess fat. Prick skin all over with a large fork. Rub skin with salt and pepper.
3. Place duck, breast-side up, on a rack in a shallow roasting pan. Roast in preheated oven 2 to 2-1/2 hours or until internal temperature registers 185F (85C) on a meat thermometer inserted in thickest part of thigh. Remove duck from roasting pan; keep warm. Drain drippings into bowl; skim off fat, reserving drippings and 2 tablespoons fat.
4. To make sauce, blanch orange peel in 1 cup boiling water 3 minutes. Remove peel with a slotted spoon; drain on paper towels. Set aside.
5. Heat reserved duck fat in a medium saucepan. Stir in flour; cook 1 minute. Add reserved drippings, stock, orange juice, wine and sugar; stir well. Cook, stirring constantly, until mixture thickens and comes to a boil. Add reserved orange peel and lemon juice. Cook over medium heat 3 minutes. Stir in liqueur. Adjust seasoning to taste.
6. Cut duck in half lengthwise. Place, skin-side up, on a serving platter. Spoon sauce over duck. Pour remaining sauce into a gravy boat; serve separately. Garnish with basil sprigs and orange slices.
Makes 2 servings.

Variations

Duck with Raspberry Sauce
1. Prepare duck according to directions on page 184 through step 3.
2. Drain and mash 1 (10-ounce) package thawed frozen raspberries. Place in a medium saucepan. Add 1/4 cup sugar, 1 tablespoon cornstarch, 1/2 cup dry white wine and 2 tablespoons lemon juice; stir well.
3. Bring to a boil, stirring constantly. Cook until sauce is thickened.
4. Spoon sauce over duck. Garnish with parsley sprigs.

Duck with Cherry Sauce
1. Prepare duck according to directions on page 184 through step 3.
2. Drain 1 (16-ounce) can pitted dark sweet cherries, reserving juice. Set cherries aside; place juice in a medium saucepan. Add reserved drippings and 2 tablespoons cherry jam. Stir well; cook over low heat, stirring constantly, until jam is melted.
3. Blend 2 teaspoons cornstarch, 1/2 cup dry red wine and 1/4 cup duck stock or water in a small bowl. Add to saucepan; cook over low heat, stirring constantly, until mixture is thickened.

4. Add reserved cherries, 1 teaspoon lemon juice and 1 tablespoon butter. Simmer 1 to 2 minutes.
5. Spoon sauce over duck. Garnish with watercress.

Stuffing: A Special Bonus Inside Poultry

Whole birds can be cooked stuffed or unstuffed. Many different kinds of ingredients are suitable to use in stuffing. They range from the more usual bread or rice base to exotic stuffings, such as oysters or chestnuts. Poultry juices, as well as fat, add flavor to the stuffing as it cooks, which is a major advantage to cooking stuffing inside poultry. However, stuffing can also be placed in a casserole and baked separately in the oven. When stuffing is cooked separately, it's a good idea to add a small amount of extra liquid and cover the casserole during cooking in order to keep the stuffing moist. No matter how you cook stuffing, you can increase or decrease liquid by a small amount, depending on whether you want stuffing that is moist or dry. The addition of seasoning and extra ingredients is a matter of taste. Almost anything goes. Don't forget to add 1 or 2 lightly beaten eggs to bread or rice stuffing in order to bind the ingredients together. And remember to follow the precautions given on page 180 to be sure your stuffing is safe to eat. When making stuffing, estimate 1/2 cup stuffing for each pound of poultry.

Basic Bread Stuffing

1 cup chicken stock or broth
1/2 cup butter
4 cups herb-seasoned stuffing mix or corn-bread stuffing mix
2 eggs, lightly beaten
Salt and pepper to taste

1. Place stock and butter in a small saucepan; bring to a boil. Cook until butter is melted.
2. Pour over stuffing mix; toss with a fork until well blended. Add eggs; mix until blended. Season with salt and pepper.

Variations
Add 1 or more of the following ingredients to bread stuffing:
● Sautéed chopped onion
● Sautéed sliced mushrooms
● Cooked sausage meat
● Diced cooked giblets
● Slivered almonds
● Sliced water chestnuts
● Chopped celery
● Freshly chopped parsley

Basic Rice Stuffing

3 tablespoons butter
1 onion, chopped
1 cup long-grain rice
2-1/4 cups chicken stock or broth
1 teaspoon poultry seasoning

1. Melt butter in a medium saucepan. Add onion; sauté until transparent. Add rice; stir to coat. Add stock and poultry seasoning; stir well.
2. Bring to a boil over medium heat. Reduce heat, cover and simmer 18 to 20 minutes or until liquid has been absorbed.

Variations
Add 1 or more of the following ingredients to rice stuffing:
● 1 egg, lightly beaten
● Sautéed chopped red- or green-bell pepper
● Sautéed sliced mushrooms
● Diced cooked giblets
● Chopped celery
● Slivered almonds
● Soaked raisins

Giblet & Vegetable-Herb Stuffing

Add 1 or more of the following ingredients to bread stuffing:
- Chopped cooked giblets
- Minced garlic
- Sliced green onions
- Sautéed chopped onion
- Sautéed sliced mushrooms
- Diced cooked ham
- Freshly chopped sage, marjoram, thyme and parsley

Dried-Fruit Stuffing

Pour hot water over dried fruit, such as apricots, prunes, figs, apples, dates or raisins. Let stand 30 minutes. Drain well; chop fruit. Add to rice stuffing along with chopped peanuts, pecans, cashews, walnuts, almonds, hazelnuts, pine nuts or pistachios.

Fresh-Fruit Stuffing

Fresh fruit can be added to bread stuffing or rice stuffing. Add 1 or more of the following ingredients:
- Seedless grape halves
- Chopped apples
- Peeled, seeded, chopped orange sections
- Coarsely chopped cranberries

Chicken Breasts

Chicken breasts are often used to make the best and most elegant dishes. When you look at the price per pound for boned, skinned chicken breasts or chicken cutlets, you may feel they are expensive or even extravagant. However, since there is no waste and since a large whole chicken breast will feed 2 people, it is economical to serve. Chicken breasts take very little time to cook. They can be served with a variety of sauces and inventive garnishes. When a recipe for soup, salad or casserole calls for diced or cubed cooked chicken, chicken breasts are the perfect answer. They can be poached quickly in simmering liquid and used in any number of different ways. One whole breast will make 1 cup of diced cooked chicken. Be careful not to overcook. Overcooking will make the chicken dry and tough.

Sautéed Chicken Breasts 6 Ways

2 tablespoons butter
1 tablespoon vegetable oil
1 whole chicken breast, boned, skinned, cut in half
Salt and pepper to taste
Paprika

Heat butter and oil in a medium skillet until bubbly. Season chicken with salt, pepper and paprika. Place in skillet; sauté 3 to 5 minutes on each side. Serve with one of the ideas on the next page.
Makes 2 servings.

1. Melt 2 tablespoons butter in a small skillet. Add 2 tablespoons sugar; stir until dissolved. Cook until syrup is light golden in color. Add 4 canned chestnuts; cook until syrup is caramel in color. Remove chestnuts; set aside. Add 12 to 14 peeled seedless grapes; sauté until golden. Remove and set aside. Add 2 to 3 tablespoons whole berry cranberry sauce to skillet; cook until melted. Spoon cranberry sauce over chicken; top with chestnuts and grapes. Garnish with sage sprigs.

2. Peel and slice 1 banana. Dip slices in a lightly beaten egg. Drain off excess egg; dip in shredded coconut. Heat 2 inches vegetable oil in a deep saucepan; deep-fry coated banana slices in hot oil. Remove with a slotted spoon; drain on paper towels. Melt 1 tablespoon butter in a small skillet; sauté 2 apricot halves in skillet. Heat 1/2 cup Curry Sauce, page 255; spoon over chicken. Top with apricot halves and banana slices. Sprinkle with shredded coconut. Garnish with maraschino cherries and mint sprigs.

3. Cut 1 carrot and 1 leek into julienne strips. Melt 2 tablespoons butter in a medium skillet. Add vegetables; sauté 3 to 4 minutes. Spoon vegetables over chicken; garnish with basil sprigs.

4. Melt 3 tablespoons butter in a medium skillet. Cut 2 canned artichoke hearts in half; add to skillet along with 1 cup sliced mushrooms and 2 sliced green onions. Sauté until mushrooms are limp. Spoon over chicken and garnish with fresh herbs.

5. Melt 2 tablespoons butter in a small skillet; sauté 1/4 pound small peeled shrimp 3 to 4 minutes or until pink. Season with salt and pepper. Spoon shrimp over chicken; garnish with lemon wedges and chervil sprigs.

6. Heat 1 (8-ounce) can whole-kernel corn in a small saucepan. Drain; set aside. Cook 6 to 8 broccoli flowerets and 6 to 8 carrot balls in lightly salted water until fork tender. Arrange vegetables over chicken.

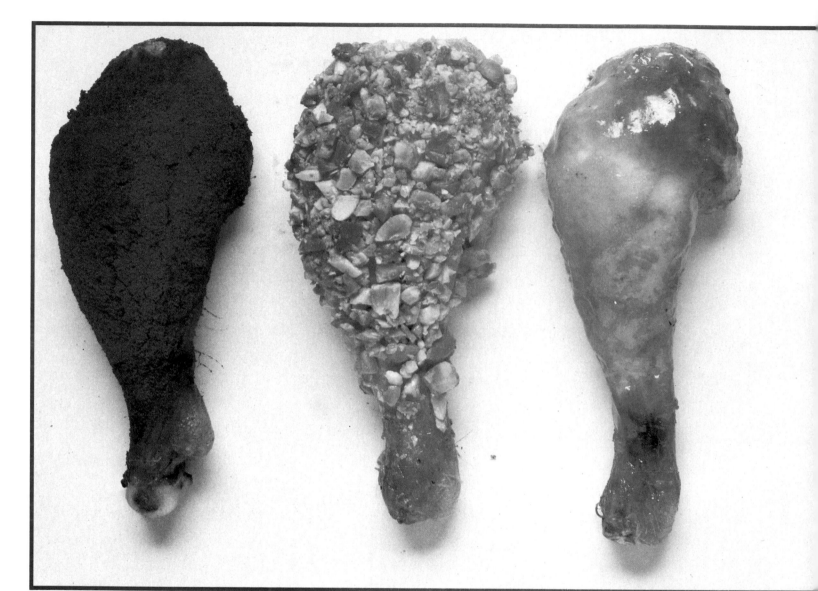

Chicken Legs: Great Finger Food

Chicken legs or drumsticks are popular with children and adults. They are the perfect food to serve at a picnic or buffet. We have prepared them with different coatings, some crisp and some not. Try any of these variations for a quick and easy family meal, or make them all and arrange them on a big platter for colorful, different company fare. Remember, chicken legs are dark meat and take longer to cook than chicken breasts. Don't forget to provide lots of napkins to go with this special finger food.

Paprika Coating

Sprinkle drumsticks with salt; dredge in sweet paprika. Place on a rack in a shallow roasting pan. Bake in a preheated 400F (200C) oven 25 to 35 minutes.

Peanut Coating

Finely chop unsalted peanuts. Sprinkle drumsticks with salt; dip in beaten egg. Drain off excess egg; roll drumsticks in chopped peanuts. Place on a rack in a shallow roasting pan. Bake in a preheated 400F (200C) oven 25 to 35 minutes.

Apricot Coating

Sprinkle drumsticks with salt; brush with vegetable oil. Place on a rack in a shallow roasting pan. Bake in a preheated 400F (200C) oven 15 minutes. Melt apricot jam in a small saucepan; brush on both sides of drumsticks. Bake 10 to 20 minutes longer, brushing with additional jam once or twice during baking.

Cranberry Coating

Sprinkle drumsticks with salt; brush with vegetable oil. Place on a rack in a shallow roasting pan. Bake in a preheated 400F (200C) oven 15 minutes. Heat whole-berry cranberry sauce in a small saucepan; brush or spoon on both sides of drumsticks. Bake 10 to 20 minutes longer.

Crumb Coating

Sprinkle drumsticks with salt; dredge in all-purpose flour. Shake off excess flour; dip in beaten egg. Drain off excess egg; roll in plain or seasoned bread crumbs or cracker crumbs. Place on a rack in a shallow roasting pan. Bake in a preheated 400F (200C) oven 25 to 35 minutes. Garnish with freshly chopped parsley.

Coconut Coating

Sprinkle drumsticks with salt; dip in beaten egg. Drain off excess egg; roll in flaked coconut. Place on a rack in a shallow roasting pan. Bake in a preheated 400F (200C) oven 25 to 35 minutes. Garnish with additional flaked coconut.

Coq au Vin

1/2 lb. salt pork, diced
2 broiler-fryer chickens,
  cut in serving pieces
All-purpose flour
2 garlic cloves, minced
1 large onion, diced
2 carrots, coarsely
  chopped
1 lb. small button
  mushrooms
1 lb. small onions
2 cups dry red wine
1/2 cup chicken stock
1 bay leaf
Salt and pepper to taste
Freshly chopped parsley

1. Cook salt pork in a
large skillet until
browned. Discard pork;
drain off all but 4
tablespoons fat.
2. Dredge chicken in
flour. Add chicken to
skillet; brown on all
sides. Remove with a
slotted spoon; set aside.
3. Add garlic and diced
onion to skillet; sauté
until transparent. Add
carrots, mushrooms and
small onions; sauté until
onions are golden.
Sprinkle 1/4 cup
all-purpose flour over
vegetables; cook 1
minute, stirring
constantly.
4. Gradually add wine
and stock to skillet.
Cook, stirring, until
mixture comes to a boil.
Add bay leaf, salt and
pepper.
5. Return chicken to
skillet. Reduce heat;
cover and simmer 30 to
35 minutes or until
chicken is tender.
6. Discard bay leaf.
Place chicken and
vegetables on a serving
platter. Pour sauce over.
Sprinkle with parsley.
Makes 6 to 8 servings.

Sweet & Sour Duck

1 (5- to 6-lb.) duck, cut
  in serving pieces
3 cups orange juice
Salt and pepper to taste
3 tablespoons
  all-purpose flour
3 to 4 tablespoons
  vegetable oil

Sauce:
2 tablespoons vegetable
  oil
1 onion, cut in rings
1 bunch green onions,
  sliced
1 teaspoon freshly
  grated ginger
1-1/4 cups dry sherry
3 tablespoons brown
  sugar
2 tablespoons cider
  vinegar
1/2 cup soy sauce
2 teaspoons cornstarch
Hot cooked rice

1. Prick duck all over
with a large fork.
2. Place orange juice in
a deep skillet; bring to a
boil. Add duck; reduce
heat, cover and cook 20
minutes.
3. Remove duck; pat
dry with paper towels.
Season with salt and
pepper; dredge with
flour.
4. Discard orange juice;
wipe out skillet. Heat 3
to 4 tablespoons oil in
skillet; add duck. Cook
until well-browned.
Remove; set aside.
Discard fat; wipe out
skillet.
5. To make sauce, heat
oil in skillet. Add onion
rings, green onions and
ginger; sauté until
transparent.
6. Combine sherry,
sugar, vinegar, soy
sauce and cornstarch.
Add to skillet; stir well.
Bring to a boil. Cook,
stirring, until sugar is
completely dissolved.
Cook until slightly
reduced.
7. Return duck to
skillet; warm over low
heat.
8. Arrange duck over
rice. Spoon sauce over
duck. Pour remaining
sauce into a gravy boat.
Makes 2 to 3 servings.

Chicken à la Provencale

1 broiler-fryer chicken,
  cut in serving pieces
Salt and pepper to taste
About 1/2 cup olive oil
2 large onions, sliced
2 red-bell peppers, cut
  in strips
2 garlic cloves, minced
1/2 cup chicken stock or
  broth
1 (16-oz.) can whole
  peeled tomatoes,
  chopped
1 zucchini, sliced
1 small eggplant, sliced
All-purpose flour
Freshly chopped parsley

1. Season chicken with
salt and pepper. Heat 2
to 3 tablespoons oil in a
large skillet. Add
chicken to skillet; cook
until browned on all
sides. Remove with a
slotted spoon; set aside.
2. Add onions, peppers
and garlic to skillet;
sauté until onions are
transparent, adding
more oil if necessary.
Add stock and tomatoes
with their juice. Stir
well; bring to a boil.
Return chicken to skillet;
reduce heat, cover and
simmer 25 to 35
minutes.
3. Dredge zucchini and
eggplant slices with
flour. Heat 4
tablespoons oil in a
separate skillet. Add
zucchini and eggplant to
skillet. Cook until lightly
browned on all sides,
adding more oil to
skillet if necessary.
Remove with a slotted
spoon; drain on paper
towels.
4. Arrange chicken,
zucchini and eggplant
on a serving dish. Pour
sauce over. Sprinkle
with parsley.
Makes 4 servings.

Chicken Curry

1 broiler-fryer chicken,
  cut in small pieces
Salt and pepper to taste
3 to 4 tablespoons
  vegetable oil
2 garlic cloves, minced
2 medium onions, diced
2 tart apples, peeled,
  diced
1 tablespoon tomato
  paste
1 tablespoon
  all-purpose flour
1 to 2 tablespoons curry
  powder
2-1/2 cups coconut milk
Hot cooked rice

1. Season chicken with
salt and pepper. Heat
oil in a skillet. Add
chicken; cook until
golden brown on all
sides. Remove with a
slotted spoon; set aside.
2. Drain off all but 2
tablespoons fat from
skillet. Add garlic,
onions and apples; sauté
until onion is
transparent. Stir in
tomato paste, flour and
curry powder; cook 1
minute.
3. Gradually add
coconut milk; cook,
stirring constantly, until
mixture thickens and
comes to a boil. Return
chicken to skillet. Cover,
reduce heat and simmer
25 to 30 minutes or until
chicken is tender. Serve
over hot cooked rice.
Makes 4 servings.

Chicken Pot Pie

5 tablespoons butter
1 onion, chopped
1/4 lb. mushrooms,
  sliced
1/2 cup chopped celery
3 tablespoons
  all-purpose flour
1-1/2 cups half and half
1 cup dry white wine or
  chicken stock
Salt and pepper to taste
1/2 teaspoon dried-leaf
  thyme
1 tablespoon freshly
  chopped parsley
2 cups diced cooked
  potatoes
2 cups diced cooked
  chicken or turkey
4 slices cooked ham,
  diced
1 sheet (1/2 of 17-1/4 oz.
  pkg.) frozen puff
  pastry, thawed
1 egg beaten with 1
  tablespoon milk

1. Melt 2 tablespoons
butter in a skillet. Add
onion, mushrooms and
celery; sauté until onion
is transparent. Spoon
into a bowl.
2. Melt 3 tablespoons
butter in a saucepan.
Stir in flour; cook 1
minute. Gradually add
cream and wine; cook,
stirring, until mixture
thickens and boils.
Season with salt and
pepper. Remove from
heat; stir in thyme and
parsley.
3. Add potatoes,
chicken and ham to
vegetable mixture. Stir
sauce into chicken
mixture. Spoon into a
deep 9-inch pie plate or
2-quart casserole.
Preheat oven to 400F
(200C).
4. Roll out pastry to
1-1/2 inches larger than
dish. Brush edge of dish
with water; place pastry
over filling. Press edges
down on rim. Brush
pastry with egg mixture;
prick twice. Bake 20
minutes or until golden.
Cool 10 minutes before
serving.
Makes 6 servings.

Chicken Fricassee

1 (4-lb.) stewing
  chicken, quartered
Salt and pepper to taste
3 tablespoons vegetable
  oil
4 cups water
1 carrot, cut in chunks
2 celery stalks
1 large onion, quartered
2 to 3 parsley sprigs
1 bay leaf
2 tablespoons butter
1/2 lb. mushrooms,
  sliced
3 to 4 canned artichoke
  hearts, quartered

Sauce:
3 tablespoons butter
3 tablespoons
  all-purpose flour
Reserved stock
2 egg yolks
1/2 cup whipping cream
2 teaspoons dill weed
2 tablespoons lemon
  juice
Lemon wedges
Chopped parsley

1. Season chicken with
salt and pepper. Heat
oil in a Dutch oven.
Add chicken; cook until
browned. Add water,
carrot, celery, onion,
parsley, bay leaf, salt
and pepper. Bring to a
boil; cover and simmer 1
hour.
2. Remove chicken.
Strain stock.
3. Melt butter in a
skillet. Add mushrooms
and artichokes; sauté 5
minutes.
4. Skin and bone
chicken; cut up meat.
5. Melt butter in a
saucepan. Stir in flour;
cook 1 minute. Add
stock and enough water
to make 2-1/2 cups.
Cook, stirring, until
thickened and boiling.
6. Beat egg yolks and
cream. Slowly add 1/2
cup sauce to mixture.
Pour egg-yolk mixture
into hot sauce; stir well.
Add mushroom
mixture, chicken, dill
and lemon juice. Cook
over low heat until hot.
Garnish with lemon
wedges and parsley.
Makes 4 servings.

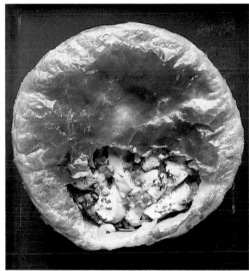

Steaks, Chops & Cutlets

A great many people feel there is nothing that can replace the satisfaction of eating a piece of tender meat, carefully seasoned and properly cooked. The wonderful aroma of meat as it cooks can be a great appetite enhancer. Steaks, chops and cutlets are the special cuts of meat—tender, delicious and easy to cook.

Steak Know-How

Traditionally, steak is cooked quickly by dry heat—broiling, grilling, pan-frying or pan-broiling. When meat is cooked by dry heat, it is not tenderized during cooking. Therefore, it is important to buy a tender cut of meat to begin with, or to tenderize meat in a marinade before it is cooked by dry heat. There are two major factors that determine whether or not a retail cut of meat is likely to be tender: the grade of the meat and the wholesale or primal cut. Follow the guidelines on the right to be sure the steak you serve will be tender, juicy and flavorful.

What Meat Grades Mean

The grading of meat is a service provided to meat packers by the federal government. Meat packers must pay to have their meat graded and their participation is voluntary. Therefore, it is reasonable to assume that if a meat packer does not think he has a top grade of meat, he will not pay to have the government confirm this.

Grading is based on a uniform method of identifying those characteristics of meat that affect flavor and tenderness, and therefore the value of the meat. The top grade is *USDA Prime*, sold mostly to fine restaurants and butcher shops and almost never available in supermarkets. The next grade of meat is *USDA Choice* which is readily available in most supermarkets. The grade below Choice is *USDA Good*, rarely identified on meat packages because it is not a very good grade. When there is no indication of grade on a package of meat, in all likelihood it means the grade is USDA Good or the meat has not been graded. Ungraded meat is generally known as a *house brand* and usually is equivalent to Good grade.

If you are going to cook meat by dry heat, you should not buy any grade below USDA Choice because it probably will not be very tender. One added word of caution. When a package of meat is labeled with the grade, the grade is always preceded by the letters "USDA." When the words "choice" or "prime" appear on a package without the letters "USDA," these words are simply meaningless adjectives the butcher is using to persuade you to buy the meat. They do not indicate grade.

What Cut of Meat to Buy

Retail cuts of meat are identified by names such as steak, chop, cutlet or roast. In most parts of the country, the cut must be further identified by the wholesale cut or section a cut comes from. It is identification of the wholesale cut that provides a clue to the potential tenderness of a steak. The most tender and most expensive steaks come from the loin. These include top loin, porterhouse and sirloin steaks. Steaks from the round, including top round, eye round, bottom round and tip steaks, are not as tender as loin steaks and often have to be marinated before they can be cooked by dry heat. Steaks from the chuck, such as arm, shoulder and blade steaks, are not suitable for cooking by dry heat. If there is no indication of the wholesale cut on a package of meat, ask the butcher. Don't buy a cut of meat that is simply marked "steak."

Tournedos with Herb Butter

Herb Butter:
1/2 cup butter
Juice of 1/2 lemon
1 garlic clove, crushed
1/4 cup freshly chopped mixed herbs
Red (cayenne) pepper to taste, if desired

Tournedos:
8 (6- to 8-oz.) beef loin tenderloin steaks
1/4 cup butter
2 tablespoons vegetable oil
Salt and pepper to taste

1. Assemble ingredients for herb butter. Allow butter to come to room temperature.

2. Place ingredients in a bowl; blend thoroughly with a wooden spoon.

3. Spoon butter mixture onto a sheet of waxed paper.

4. Shape butter mixture into a log about 1-1/2 inches thick.

5. Twist ends of waxed paper tightly to enclose butter. Freeze until ready to use.

6. Assemble ingredients for tournedos. Allow meat to come to room temperature.

7. Season meat on both sides with freshly ground pepper.

8. Heat butter and oil in a heavy skillet.

9. When butter foams, add meat to pan.

10. Cook over medium heat until bottom is browned; turn meat over.

11. Season with salt; cook meat to desired doneness.

12. Remove butter from freezer. Unwrap and cut into 1/2-inch-thick slices.

13. Place steaks on a serving platter; top each with a slice of herb butter.

How Much Steak to Buy

The amount of steak to buy can depend on many factors. You must take into consideration appetites, how much food will be served with the steak, whether or not the steak is boneless or bone-in and how well trimmed the steak is. An average portion of boneless meat is about 3 ounces. Leftover steak can be used to make steak sandwiches or it can be cut up and used in a casserole or as hash. Buy enough steak to provide second helpings. If you have bought a good-quality steak, and cooked it properly, you are likely to need more than one 3-ounce portion per person.

Hints for Cooking Steak

● Choose steaks that have little flecks fat, known as *marbling* throughout the meat. This fat will melt during cooking and provide both juiciness and flavor.
● In order to serve steak rare or medium-rare, buy steak that is about 2 inches thick. Be sure the steak is cut evenly so one end is not 2 inches thick and the other end only 1 inch thick.
● Trim excess fat from steaks before cooking.
● Don't salt steak before it is cooked. Salt will draw juices to the surface of the meat and make it less tender and less juicy.
● When steak is broiled, it should be placed on a broiler rack 2 to 3 inches from source of heat.
● Serve steak immediately. Although a roast should stand 15 to 20 minutes before it is carved, steak is ready to eat as soon as it is cooked.

From Rare to Well-Done

Most people are very specific about how they want their steak cooked. In order to cook a steak to desired doneness, you must take into account the temperature of the steak to be cooked, the thickness of the steak, the weight of the pan and the degree of heat used. The guidelines on the right are for steaks at room temperature, about 2 inches thick, cooked in a heavy pan over medium-high heat.

Rare

Brown outer crust, deep-red interior and juicy. Cook 3 to 4 minutes per side.

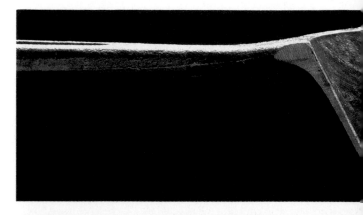

Medium-Rare

Brown outer crust, pink inside and red center. Cook 5 to 6 minutes per side.

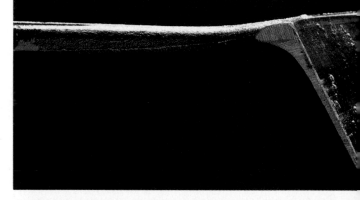

Medium-Well

Brown outer crust and pink through center. Cook 7 to 8 minutes per side.

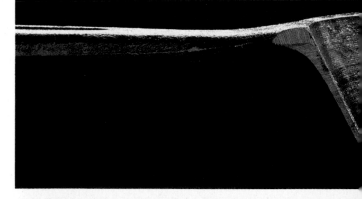

Well-Done

Brown outer crust, completely cooked through and grey throughout. Not recommended for beef loin tenderloin steaks.

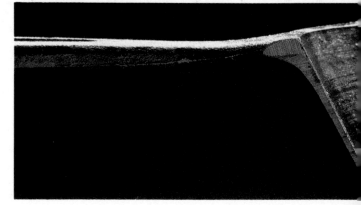

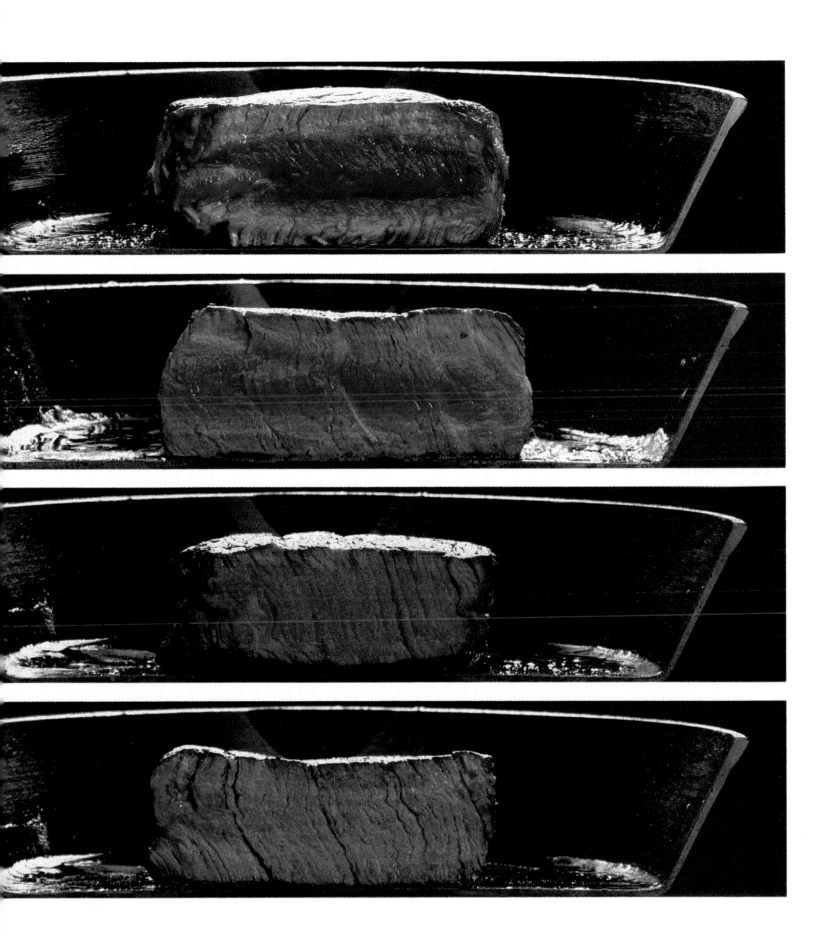

Garnishing Tournedos

Tournedos can be served plain or garnished in a variety of ways. Try some of the toppings or make up your own. Suggestions provide enough to top 4 tournedos.

1. Tomato & Fried-Parsley Topping
Peel 1 large tomato. Cut into 8 wedges; remove seeds. Remove leaves from 8 parsley sprigs. Melt 3 tablespoons butter in a skillet. Add parsley; sauté 1 minute until shriveled. Remove from skillet. Place tomato wedges in skillet; toss quickly in remaining melted butter. Arrange 2 tomato wedges on each steak; garnish with parsley.

2. Marrow & Chive Topping
Wrap 2 to 3 marrow bones separately in cheesecloth. Cook in lightly salted simmering water 30 minutes. Remove; let cool. Unwrap bones; push marrow out of bones. Cut into thin slices. Add marrow slices to skillet in which steak was cooked. Cook over low heat 1 minute heat through. Arrange on steaks; sprinkle with chives.

3. Artichoke Bottom & Pea Topping
Drain 1 (8-ounce) can green peas; heat in 2 tablespoons butter with 4 canned artichoke bottoms. Sprinkle with sugar and salt. Arrange artichoke bottoms on steaks. Spoon peas into artichoke bottoms.

4. Hearts of Palm Topping
Cut 2 canned hearts of palm in half. Cut each piece in half lengthwise. Melt 2 tablespoons butter in a skillet. Add 1 tablespoon lemon juice and hearts of palm. Cook 1 minute; season. Place 2 pieces of hearts of palm on top of each steak. Garnish with a lemon slice and lemon balm.

5. Fried-Onion Topping
Slice 4 medium onions; separate into rings. Combine 2 tablespoons all-purpose flour and 1 to 2 tablespoons paprika. Dredge onions in flour mixture. Heat 3 tablespoons butter or in a skillet. Add coated onion rings; fry until golden brown. Arrange rings on top of steaks.

6. Peppercorn & Watercress Topping
Drain 3 tablespoons green peppercorns. Add to skillet in which steak was cooked; cook 1 minute. Spoon over steaks; garnish with watercress.

7. Pear & Blue-Cheese Topping
Preheat oven to 400F (200C). Place 4 canned pear halves, cut-side up, in a greased baking dish. Spoon 1 tablespoon crumbled blue cheese into cavity of each pear half. Bake 4 minutes or until cheese is lightly browned. Top steaks with pear halves.

8. Braised-Celery Topping
Slice 2 celery stalks on an angle. Braise 8 minutes in 1 tablespoon butter, 2 tablespoons white wine and 1 tablespoon lemon juice. Season with salt. Spoon celery on steaks; garnish with celery leaves.

9. Herb-Butter & Lemon Topping
Prepare 1/2 recipe Herb Butter, pages 196-197. Top steaks with a lemon slice; pipe Herb Butter onto lemon. Garnish with chervil.

10. Corn & Red-Pepper Topping
Cut 1 red-bell pepper into strips. Blanch strips in boiling water 2 minutes; drain. Drain 1 (8-ounce) can whole-kernel corn; add to skillet in which steak was cooked. Add blanched pepper strips; cook 2 minutes until heated through. Spoon over steaks.

11. Anchovy & Olive Topping
Arrange 4 anchovy fillets in a crisscross pattern on steaks; top with olives.

12. Mango Topping
Peel and pit 2 mangoes. Cut in 12 thin wedges. Melt 1 tablespoon butter in a skillet. Add mango wedges; cook 1 minute. Arrange 3 wedges on each steak; garnish with chervil.

13. Bacon & Watercress Topping
Cook 4 bacon slices until crisp; drain. Place 1 bacon slice on each steak; garnish with watercress.

14. White-Asparagus Topping
Wash and trim 24 white asparagus spears. Cut into 3-inch tips. Cook tips in lightly salted water until crisp-tender; drain well. Melt 2 tablespoons butter in a skillet. Add asparagus; toss quickly to coat. Arrange over steaks; sprinkle with chopped parsley.

15. Pickled-Vegetable Topping
Arrange 2 pickled ears of baby corn on each steak. Add pickled carrot slices and a gherkin. Garnish with chervil.

16. Sprout & Mushroom Topping
Slice 1/4 pound mushrooms; place in a bowl. Add 1 cup bean sprouts and 3 tablespoons Vinaigrette Dressing, page 139. Toss; spoon over steaks. Garnish with thyme.

201

Marinating Steaks

Steaks cut from the round, such as beef eye-round steak shown on the right, should be marinated before cooking by dry heat. This makes them more tender and flavorful. Ingredients in a marinade can be varied, but it is important to use wine, vinegar, lemon juice or some acidic liquid to break down the connective tissues. This process will make the steak more tender. Remaining marinade ingredients add flavor.

Marinade

1 cup olive oil
1/2 cup sherry vinegar,
   red or white wine or
   1/4 cup lemon juice
2 tablespoons soy sauce
2 garlic cloves, sliced
Coarsely ground pepper
2 tablespoons freshly
   chopped herbs
1 teaspoon Italian
   seasoning
Red peppercorns, if
   desired
1 tablespoon
   Worcestershire sauce
1 teaspoon sugar

Use a good-quality olive oil or walnut oil; add good-quality wine or vinegar and a combination of fresh and dried herbs, seasonings, garlic and soy sauce to make a flavorful marinade.
1. Place all ingredients in glass screw-top jar; shake vigorously. Arrange meat in shallow glass dish; pierce with a fork. Pour marinade over meat; turn to coat. Cover and refrigerate several hours or overnight, turning meat occasionally.
2. Remove meat from marinade; pat dry. Remove any pieces of spices or herbs that may stick to meat.

Pointers for Cooking Steaks

Barding
Wrap a bacon slice around edge of beef loin tenderloin or marinated eye-round steaks; secure with string or wooden picks. Bacon will keep the meat moist during cooking. Remove string or pick before serving.

Irregular Shapes
Irregular pieces of beef loin tenderloin can be tied with kitchen string to make a nice round shape. Remove string before serving.

Pan Juices
Pan juices can be deglazed by adding a little stock, wine or water. Bring to a boil; cook until slightly reduced. Juices can be thickened and served as gravy by adding 2 tablespoons whipping cream or a little beurre manie, page 153.

Flambé
To flambé steaks, add a high-percentage alcohol, such as brandy, to pan juices; ignite carefully. Serve steaks directly from pan as soon as flame dies out.

Sauces
There are a wide variety of prepared sauces that can be served with steak, such as steak sauce, barbecue sauce, chili sauce, soy sauce and flavored mustards.

Grilling
Add mesquite or hickory chips to a charcoal fire when cooking steak on a barbecue grill. It will add marvelous flavor to the meat.

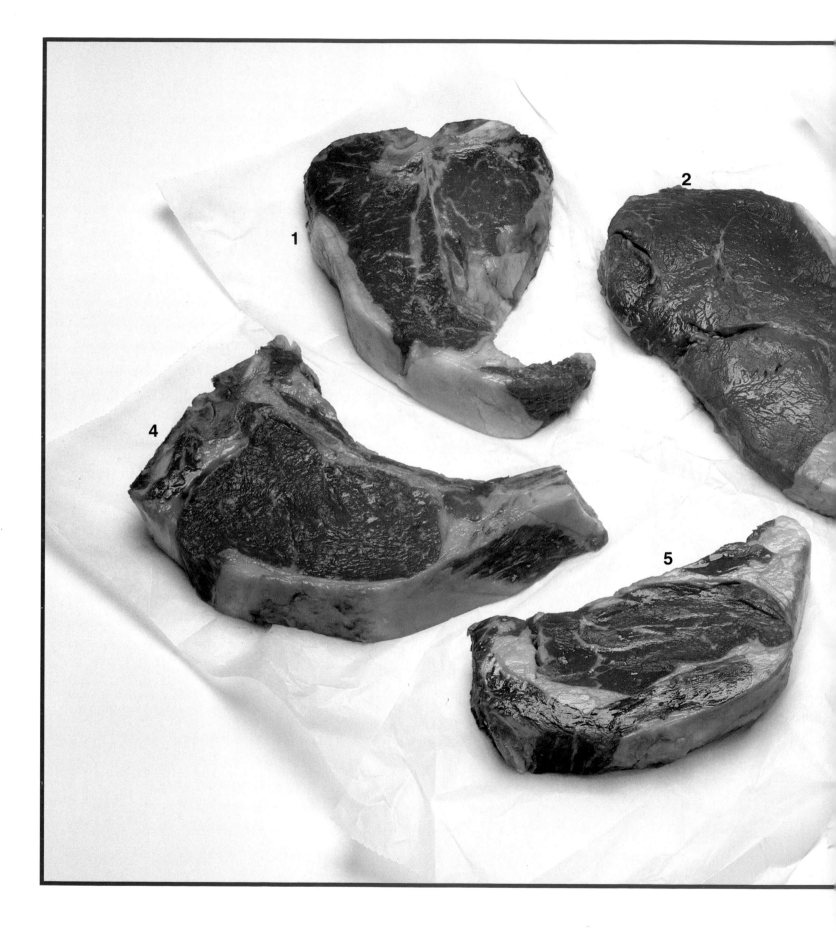

Beef Cuts

There are many different ways of cutting beef. It varies not only from country to country, but also region to region. Below are some of the basic cuts of beef used in the United States.

1. Beef Loin Porterhouse Steak. Also known as a Porterhouse steak. It contains top loin, tenderloin, backbone and fingerbone. It is similar to a T-Bone steak, but the tenderloin is larger. Suggested cooking methods include broiling, pan-broiling and pan-frying.

2. Beef Loin Top Sirloin Steak Boneless. Also known as a Top Sirloin Steak. This is the same as a Beef Loin Sirloin Steak, bones and tenderloin removed. Suggested cooking methods include broiling, pan-broiling and pan-frying.

3. Beef Loin Tenderloin Roast & Steak. Other names include Tenderloin Tip Roast, Filet Mignon Roast, Chateaubriand, Filet Mignon, Fillet Steak and Tender Steak. Cut from tenderloin muscle. Elongated with rounded large end, gradually tapering to thin, flat end. Boneless, with little if any fat covering, Very tender. Steaks are cut across grain from beef loin tenderloin roast. Suggested cooking methods include broiling, pan-broiling and pan-frying.

4. Beef Loin Top Loin Steak. Also known as Shell Steak, Strip Steak and Club Steak. Contains top loin muscle and backbone running length of cut. Tenderloin muscle has been removed. Has an outside fat covering, with or without tail. Suggested cooking methods include broiling, pan-broiling and pan-frying.

5. Beef Rib Steak Boneless. Sometimes known as a Spencer Steak. Cut from rib section. Contains rib-eye muscle. Suggested cooking methods include broiling, pan-broiling and pan-frying.

6. Beef Loin Top Loin Steak Boneless. Also known as Strip Steak, Kansas City Steak and New York Strip Steak. Same as #4, with bone removed. Suggested cooking methods include broiling, pan-broiling and pan-frying.

Beyond Beef Steaks

There are other kinds of steaks, as well as chops and cutlets, that can be cooked by dry heat in a skillet or under a broiler. Although beef is usually implied when the word "steak" is used alone, ham, pork, lamb, veal and game steaks or fillets are also available. All of the suggestions on the right are for dishes that can be cooked quickly in a skillet or under the broiler.

Venison Steak

Venison steaks, cut from the round or sirloin, are usually 1 to 1-1/2 inches thick and brownish red in color. They can be broiled or pan-fried over high heat until medium-rare and somewhat pink inside. Serve with cranberries, sautéed apples, horseradish sauce, a brown sauce, cracked pepper, wild mushrooms, Brussels sprouts, red cabbage, potato croquettes or spatzle.
Shown:
Venison steak with chestnuts and cranberry-filled pear half, garnished with fresh thyme.

Lamb Chops

Lamb chops are cut from the shoulder, loin or rib section. They can be broiled, pan-broiled, pan-fried or braised. Trim off excess fat, then cook until just pink inside.
Frenched chops are rib chops that have had the meat and fat trimmed away from both sides of the end of the bone. Serve with mint jelly, mint sauce, rosemary, garlic, onions, roast potatoes, broiled tomatoes or curry sauce.
Shown:
Frenched chops with mint jelly, garnished with fresh mint leaves.

Pork Chops

Pork chops are cut from all parts of the loin and are available fresh or smoked. They can be breaded or stuffed and broiled, pan-broiled, pan-fried or braised. Fresh pork must be thoroughly cooked until light grey in color throughout.
Serve with applesauce, sweet potatoes, broiled tomatoes or warmed fruit, such as peaches, prunes, plums or apricots.
Shown:
Center-cut pork chop with sautéed peppers, garnished with parsley.

Veal Cutlets

Veal cutlets are cut from the leg and are available thinly sliced or cut as thick as 1/2 inch.
To make breaded veal cutlets, place veal on a flat surface; cover with plastic wrap. Pound with meat mallet until slightly flattened. Dredge in seasoned flour. Add a few drops of vegetable oil to a beaten egg; dip floured cutlets in egg. Drain off excess egg. Dip in seasoned bread crumbs or cracker meal. Heat 2 tablespoons butter and 1 tablespoon olive oil in a heavy skillet. When foamy, add breaded veal cutlet; cook 2 to 3 minutes on each side over medium-high heat until golden. Drain. Serve with spatzle, red cabbage, potato dumplings, artichoke hearts, broiled tomatoes or asparagus.
Shown:
Breaded veal cutlet garnished with lemon slices, anchovies and capers.

Liver

Calves' liver is the most tender and popular cut of beef liver. Beef liver is also popular and easily available. Pork and lamb liver are available in some areas. Liver can be sautéed, braised, broiled or grilled.
To cook liver, rinse well, then pat dry. Dredge in seasoned flour; shake off excess. Heat 2 tablespoons butter and 1 tablespoon vegetable oil in a heavy skillet. When butter is foamy, add liver; cook 3 to 3-1/2 minutes per side over medium heat until browned on both sides and still pink inside. Do not overcook because liver will be tough and dry. Season with salt and pepper to taste. Serve with sautéed onions, crisp-cooked bacon, a mustard sauce or broiled avocado slices.
Shown:
Calves' liver with sautéed apple slices and onions.

Swiss Veal Strips

1 lb. thick-sliced veal
  cutlets
2 tablespoons olive oil
1 tablespoon butter
1 onion, finely chopped
2 tablespoons
  all-purpose flour
1/4 cup dry white wine
1 cup whipping cream
Salt and pepper to taste
Freshly chopped parsley

1. Cut veal into thin strips. Heat oil and butter in a heavy skillet. Add veal strips; stir-fry over medium-high heat 3 to 4 minutes or until lightly browned. Remove with a slotted spoon; set aside.
2. Add onion to skillet; sauté until transparent. Sprinkle flour over onion; cook, stirring, 1 minute.
3. Slowly add wine and cream; cook, stirring constantly, until sauce is thickened.
4. Return meat to skillet; cook 1 minute. Season with salt and pepper and sprinkle with parsley.
Makes 3 to 4 servings.

Is Veal Really Too Expensive to Buy?

As the price of veal has risen, fewer and fewer people have bought it. As a result, good veal has become harder and harder to find in supermarkets and even butcher shops. But is it really too expensive? Veal cutlets are boneless cuts of meat without fat. There is absolutely no waste. All you need is about 1/4 pound per person. If you were to serve pork back ribs, you would need to buy 1-1/2 pounds per person. Even if veal is as high as $10.00 per pound, it will cost only $2.50 per portion, which is less than many other cuts of meat cost. Learning to judge the cost of meat per portion is the only way to determine whether or not meat is affordable.

Veal Cutlets: An Italian Specialty

Cooking a veal cutlet quickly in a skillet is a simple procedure. It is the sauce and other ingredients that makes the difference. Italians have made a fine art of cooking veal cutlets, all variations on the same simple theme.

Veal Marsala

6 thin-sliced veal cutlets, about 1-1/2 lbs.
All-purpose flour
Salt and pepper to taste
1/4 cup olive oil
3 tablespoons butter
1/2 cup Marsala wine
1/4 cup chicken stock

1. Place veal on a flat surface. Pound until slightly flattened. Cut cutlets in half.
2. Season flour with salt and pepper; dredge cutlets.
3. Heat 2 tablespoons oil in a skillet. Add 3 veal pieces; cook over medium heat 2 minutes on each side or until browned. Remove from skillet; keep warm.
4. Add remaining 2 tablespoons oil; cook remaining veal. Drain oil from skillet.
5. Place butter in skillet; heat until foamy. Add Marsala and stock; boil until slightly reduced.
6. Return veal to skillet; cook 1 minute.
7. Arrange veal on a platter; spoon sauce over.
Makes 6 servings.

Veal with Sage

6 thin-sliced veal cutlets, about 1-1/2 lbs.
Pepper to taste
6 thin slices prosciutto or Parma Ham
2 tablespoons freshly chopped sage
2 tablespoons butter
2 tablespoons olive oil
1/2 cup dry white wine
Salt to taste
12 sage leaves

1. Place veal on a flat surface. Pound until slightly flattened. Sprinkle cutlets on 1 side with pepper.
2. Place 1 slice prosciutto on each cutlet; sprinkle with chopped sage. Fold cutlets in half; secure with a wooden pick.
3. Heat butter and 1 tablespoon olive oil in a skillet until foamy. Add a few pieces of veal; cook over medium-high heat 2 minutes on each side or until browned. Remove from skillet; keep warm.
4. Add remaining 1 tablespoon oil to skillet; cook remaining veal.
5. Add wine to skillet; bring to a boil. Boil until reduced by half. Season with salt and pepper.
6. Remove wooden picks; arrange veal on a platter. Spoon sauce over. Garnish with sage. Makes 6 servings.

Veal Piccata

6 thin-sliced veal
  cutlets, about 1-1/2
  lbs.
All-purpose flour
Salt and pepper to taste
1/4 cup olive oil
2 tablespoons butter
1/2 cup dry white wine
  or vermouth
Juice of 1 lemon
Lemon slices
Lemon-balm sprigs

1. Place veal on a flat
surface. Pound until
slightly flattened. Cut
cutlets in half. Season
flour with salt and
pepper; dredge cutlets.
2. Heat 2 tablespoons
oil in a skillet. Add a
few pieces of veal; cook
over medium-high heat
2 minutes on each side
or until browned.
Remove from skillet;
keep warm.

3. Add remaining 2
tablespoons oil to skillet;
cook remaining veal.
Drain oil from skillet.
4. Place butter in skillet;
heat until foamy. Add
wine and lemon juice;
bring to a boil. Cook,
stirring, until slightly
reduced.
5. Return veal to skillet;
cook 1 minute.
6. Arrange veal on a
platter; spoon sauce
over. Garnish with
lemon slices and lemon
balm.
Makes 6 servings.

Veal with Tarragon

6 thin-sliced veal
  cutlets, about 1-1/2
  lbs.
1/4 cup olive oil
1/2 cup dry white wine
1 cup whipping cream
Salt and pepper to taste
2 tablespoons freshly
  chopped tarragon
Fresh tarragon sprigs

1. Place veal on a flat
surface. Pound until
slightly flattened. Cut
cutlets in half.
2. Heat 2 tablespoons
oil in a skillet. Add a
few pieces of veal; cook
over medium-high heat
2 minutes on each side
or until browned.
Remove from skillet;
keep warm.
3. Add remaining 2
tablespoons oil to skillet;
cook remaining veal.

4. Add wine to skillet;
bring to a boil. Add
cream slowly; cook until
slightly reduced. Season
to taste. Stir in chopped
tarragon.
5. Arrange veal on a
platter; spoon sauce
over. Garnish with
tarragon.
Makes 6 servings.

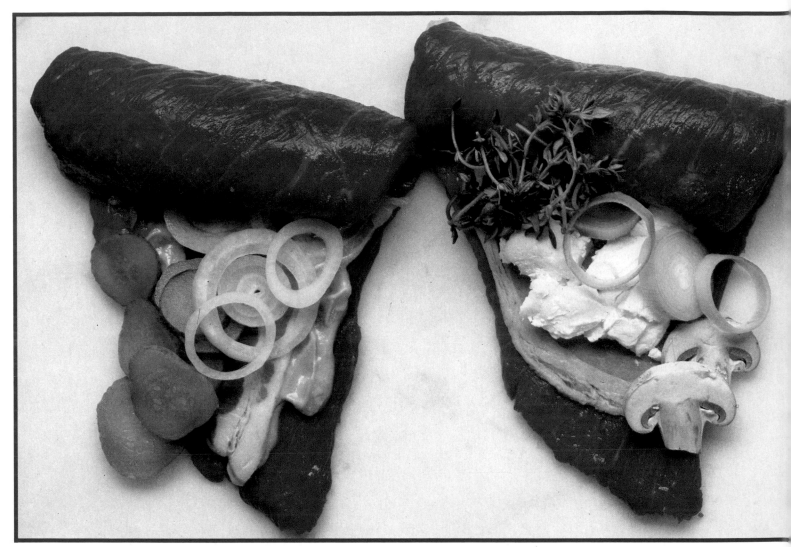

Rolled Meat Parcels

Large thin slices of meat can be filled, rolled and braised in a flavorful liquid to make delicious main dishes. Depending on the origin of the recipe, they are called *Roulades, Braciole, Paupiettes* or simply *Beef* or *Veal Rolls*. When beef is used, it should be top round or flank. When veal is used, a cutlet from the leg is best. Fillings can vary according to taste and imagination.

Beef Roulades

1 lb. beef top round or
  flank steak, cut into 4
  (1/4-inch-thick) slices
Dijon-style mustard
4 bacon slices, partially
  cooked
1 onion, thinly sliced
4 gherkins, sliced
Salt and pepper to taste
3 tablespoons butter
1 tablespoon olive oil
1/4 cup beef broth
1/2 cup dry red wine

1. Place meat on flat surface, cover with plastic wrap. Pound with a meat mallet until slightly flattened.
2. Spread mustard on 1 side of each slice; place bacon slice over mustard. Arrange onion and gherkin slices on top of bacon.
3. Roll meat, jelly-roll style, starting at narrow end. Tie rolls lengthwise and crosswise with string or secure with wooden picks. Season all over with salt and pepper.
4. Heat butter and oil in a heavy skillet. Add beef rolls; brown on both sides over medium heat.
5. Add beef broth and wine; bring to a boil over high heat. Reduce heat; cover and simmer 15 to 20 minutes, turning rolls over at least once. Remove rolls from pan; keep warm.
6. Reduce liquid in pan over high heat or thicken with beurre manie, page 153.
Makes 4 servings.

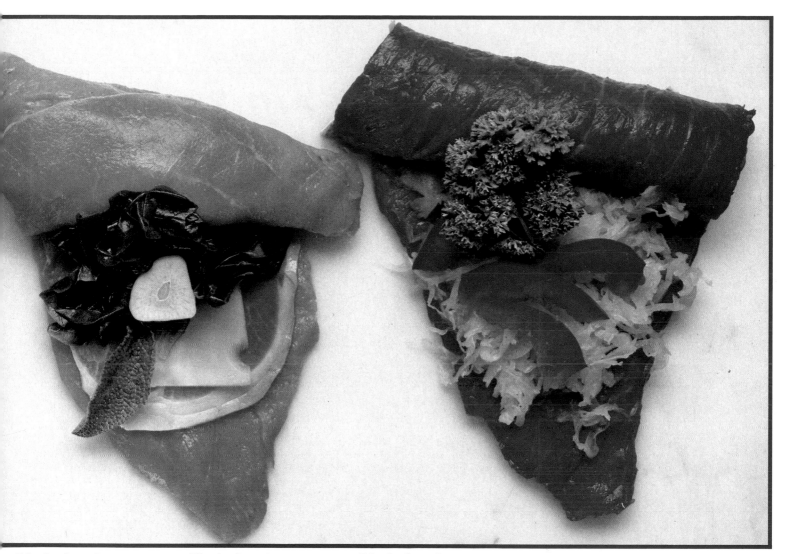

Variation 1

1 lb. beef top round or
    flank steak, cut into 4
    (1/4-inch-thick) slices
4 boiled-ham slices
Whipped cream cheese
4 mushrooms, sliced
1 leek, sliced
4 small thyme sprigs
Salt and pepper to taste
3 tablespoons butter
1 tablespoon olive oil
1/4 cup beef broth
1/2 cup dry red wine

1. Prepare according to
directions for Beef
Roulades, using
ingredients listed above.
Makes 4 servings.

Variation 2

4 large veal cutlets
4 prosciutto slices
4 Swiss-cheese slices
8 large spinach leaves,
    blanched
1 garlic clove, sliced
4 sage leaves
Salt and pepper to taste
3 tablespoons butter
1 tablespoon olive oil
1/4 cup chicken broth
1/2 cup dry white wine
    or sherry

1. Prepare according to
directions for Beef
Roulades through step
4, cooking veal rolls
about 2 minutes on each
side. Add broth and
wine; bring to a boil.
Cook 3 to 5 minutes or
until liquid is reduced
by half.
Makes 4 servings.

Variation 3

1 lb. beef top round or
    flank steak, cut into 4
    (1/4-inch-thick) slices
1/4 cup drained
    sauerkraut
1/2 red-bell pepper, cut
    in thin strips
4 teaspoons freshly
    chopped parsley
Salt and pepper to taste
3 tablespoons butter
1 tablespoon olive oil
1/4 cup beef broth
1/2 cup beer

1. Prepare according to
directions for Beef
Roulades, using
ingredients listed above.
Makes 4 servings.

Ground Meat: Burgers & Beyond

Freshly ground meat, combined with all kinds of wonderful seasoning, as well as onion and—for those who like it—garlic, can be the basis of wonderful meals. Hamburgers, meatballs, meat loaves, meat pies, casseroles and ethnic dishes, such as stuffed cabbage and egg rolls, can all be made with ground meat. Although ground meat is usually thought of as family fare, it can be used to make lots of delicious company dishes as well.

Hamburgers: Always Popular

There are very few foods as popular and well-known throughout the world as the hamburger. Although there is some disagreement about its origin, everyone agrees it is an odd name for a food that contains no ham and never has. The hamburger was introduced, pretty much as we know it today, at the St. Louis World's Fair in 1903, where it was an immediate success. And much of the success of the fast-food industry is due to the popularity of the hamburger. But you don't have to go to a restaurant or fast-food store to get really good hamburgers. They can be easily made at home in a variety of ways, welcome food at almost any kind of informal meal.

How to Buy Ground Beef

There is more confusion about what kind of ground beef to buy than about almost any other kind of meat. Most of the time meat shoppers are concerned about buying meat as lean as possible for health reasons. However, very lean ground beef will make dry, flavorless hamburgers. It is the fat, mixed with the lean in ground beef, that will melt as the hamburger cooks and make a hamburger juicy and full of flavor. Although meat from the chuck is not as tender as meat from the round, and therefore not recommended for most dishes cooked by dry heat, the process of grinding meat tenderizes it, making ground chuck as tender as ground round or ground sirloin.

The important thing for a shopper to determine, as much as possible, is the fat content of ground meat rather than the wholesale cut. Some supermarkets mark the lean to fat ratio on packages of ground beef. The range is from 70% lean, the minimum amount required by law, to 90% lean. If you want to make a good juicy hamburger, buy ground beef that is about 80% lean. If the lean to fat ratio is not marked on a package, ask the butcher. And remember, you can save money by buying chuck instead of round because grinding will make chuck just as tender as round.

Buy lean ground beef for use in casseroles or combination dishes to minimize waste. Brown the meat and pour off any drippings before blending it with other ingredients.

Hamburgers

1 lb. ground beef
1 onion, finely chopped
Salt and pepper to taste
1 teaspoon Worcestershire sauce, if desired
1 to 2 tablespoons butter or vegetable oil

1. Assemble ingredients.

2. Place meat in a bowl. Add onion, Worcestershire sauce, salt and pepper.

3. Blend ingredients thoroughly.

4. Shape mixture into 3 or 4 plump, round, slightly flattened patties.

5. Heat butter or oil in a skillet. Cook hamburgers to desired doneness.

Cooking Methods for Hamburgers

Broiling

Place hamburgers on a rack in a broiler pan. Broil 3 inches from source of heat 5 to 6 minutes per side for rare, 7 minutes per side for medium, and 8 to 9 minutes per side for well-done.

Charcoal grilling

Place hamburgers on a grill over a moderately hot fire. Grill about 4 inches from source of heat about 4 to 5 minutes per side for rare, 6 minutes per side for medium, and 7 to 8 minutes per side for well-done.

Pan-broiling

Sprinkle salt in a heavy skillet; place over high heat 1 minute. Add hamburgers; cook about 5 minutes per side for rare, 6 minutes per side for medium, and 7 minutes per side for well done.

Pan-frying

Heat 1 to 2 tablespoons butter or oil in a heavy skillet over medium-high heat. Add hamburgers; cook 5 minutes per side for rare, 6 minutes per side for medium, and 7 minutes per side for well-done.

1. Assemble ingredients.

2. Place all ingredients except oil in a bowl and blend thoroughly.

3. Wet hands under cold running water.

4. Shape meat mixture between palms to make small balls.

5. Heat oil in a heavy skillet. Cook meatballs until brown and crusty.

Meatballs

1 lb. lean ground beef
1 onion, finely chopped
1 egg, beaten
1/4 cup fine dry bread crumbs
1/4 cup grated Parmesan cheese
Salt and pepper to taste
2 tablespoons freshly chopped parsley
2 tablespoons vegetable oil

Other Kinds of Ground Meat

Beef is clearly the most often used ground meat, but lamb, veal and pork are also available ground and can be used to make many interesting dishes.

Lamb

Ground lamb can be seasoned and formed into patties or kabobs, then broiled, pan-broiled, pan-fried or charcoal grilled. It is used successfully in casseroles, but it is not usually combined with other ground meat because lamb has a strong flavor and would overwhelm the flavor of other meats. Ground lamb tends to have a high fat content and can be cooked without additional fat.

Veal

Ground veal is very lean and not suitable for cooking as a hamburger. However, it is delicious when combined with beef and pork to make a meat loaf or when used alone to make meat loaf, pâtés, casseroles or dumplings.

Pork

Ground fresh pork can be combined with beef and veal to make meat loaf. It can also be used alone or combined with smoked ground pork (ham) for an interesting flavor combination in casseroles. Although neither fresh or smoked ground pork are used to make hamburgers, they can be used to make unusual meatballs. Cook fresh pork thoroughly and serve well-done at all times.

Cold Ground Meat

Cold hamburgers are not very appetizing but meat loaf and pâtés are delicious when served cold. They can be cooked in advance and frozen, ready to take along on a picnic or serve to unexpected company.

Hamburgers Plus .....

A properly cooked plump hamburger, served on a warm crisp roll with ketchup and mustard, is heavenly food all by itself. But you can make it even better by adding some of the toppings shown here, or by trying some of the variations suggested on pages 218-219. You can even try some of the toppings suggested for small steaks, pages 200-201.

Toppings for Hamburgers

1. Peeled orange sections or drained mandarin oranges, garnished with tarragon leaves.
2. Thinly sliced onion rings, garnished with a parsley sprig.
3. Sliced pickled beets, garnished with a chervil sprig.
4. Sliced radishes and mushrooms, marinated in oil and vinegar; garnished with watercress.
5. Strips or rings of sweet red- and green-bell peppers.
6. Hamburger on a pineapple ring, topped with a slice of processed cheese; garnished with maraschino cherries.
7. Sliced cherry tomatoes, garnished with basil leaves.
8. Fried egg, garnished with paprika.
9. Mild or hot ketchup, garnished with snipped chives.
10. Shredded cabbage, marinated in oil, vinegar, pepper and sugar.
11. Sliced dill pickles, garnished with dill sprigs.
12. Shredded Monterey jack cheese, garnished with cilantro.

Burgers Galore

Of all the many ways a hamburger can be served, few ways are more popular than the hamburger shown here.

Super Burgers

1 recipe Hamburgers,
  page 214
3 sesame-seed rolls
Lettuce leaves
Mayonnaise
Sliced pickles
3 Cheddar-cheese slices
6 tomato slices
Ketchup

---

1. Prepare hamburgers; cook to desired doneness.
2. Cut rolls in half crosswise; place under broiler or on a grill until cut side of roll is lightly browned.
3. Spread mayonnaise on rolls; arrange lettuce leaves on bottom of rolls.
4. Top each roll with sliced pickles, hamburger, cheese slice and tomato slices. Spread ketchup on tomato slices.
5. Top each with remaining half of roll. Makes 3 servings.

Burger Variations

Pizza Burger
Add 1 teaspoon Italian seasoning to hamburger mixture before cooking. Top hamburger with pizza sauce and mozzarella cheese.

Mexican Taco Burger
Add 1 tablespoon taco-seasoning mix and 2 teaspoons chili powder to hamburger mixture before cooking. Top hamburger with chili sauce, shredded Monterey Jack cheese and chopped onion.

Cheese & Bacon Burger
Top hamburgers with crisp-cooked bacon and sliced American or Cheddar cheese.

Oriental Burger
Add 2 tablespoons soy sauce, 2 tablespoons dry sherry, 1 minced garlic clove and 1/2 teaspoon ground ginger to hamburger mixture before cooking. Top hamburger with sautéed mushrooms, bean sprouts and teriyaki sauce.

Greek Burger
Add 2 tablespoons dry white wine to hamburger mixture before cooking. Top hamburger with sliced red onion, feta cheese and chopped, pitted black Greek olives.

California Burger
Add 1/2 cup alfalfa sprouts to hamburger mixture before cooking. Top hamburger with guacamole, chopped tomatoes and hot chili sauce.

Shaping Ground Meat

One of the advantages of using ground meat in a recipe is that it can be used in so many ways. Shape it any way you choose, traditionally or imaginatively. Use hamburger or meatball mixture, pages 214-215 for these ideas.

Meat-Loaf Ring

Pack meat mixture into a 5-cup ring mold. Bake in 375F (190C) oven 40 to 60 minutes. Drain off fat; invert onto a serving plate. Fill center with mashed potatoes; top potatoes with peas.

Stuffed Cabbage

Blanch Savoy cabbage leaves in boiling water 3 minutes; drain well. Spoon 2 to 3 tablespoons meat mixture onto center of each cabbage leaf. Fold cabbage, envelope-style, over mixture; secure with wooden picks. Simmer in Fresh Tomato Sauce, page 82, about 1 hour.

Meat Rolls

Shape meat mixture into rolls about 1 inch thick and 4 inches long. Pan-fry or pan-broil. Use in meatball recipes.

Meatballs

Shape meat mixture into meatballs. Pan-fry, pan-broil or cook in sauce. Serve as appetizers on small skewers or in a sauce, or use for a main course.

Round Meat Loaf

Pack meat mixture into a 1- to 1-1/2-quart round casserole. Bake in 375F (190C) oven 40 to 60 minutes. Drain off fat. Serve with Fresh Tomato Sauce, page 82.

Chop Shape

Shape meat mixture into a pork-chop shape. Broil, pan-broil or pan-fry.

Pastry Appetizers

Brown meat mixture in a skillet, seasoning as desired. Drain off fat; set aside. Thaw 1 (17-1/4-oz.) package frozen puff pastry. Roll out each sheet of pastry on a lightly floured surface to a 12-inch square. Cut each sheet into 16 (3-inch) squares. Spoon 1 to 2 teaspoons cooked hamburger mixture onto center of each square. Brush pastry edges with water; fold pastry over meat mixture, envelope-style. Brush parcels with beaten egg. Place on ungreased baking sheets; bake in 400F (200C) oven 15 to 20 minutes or until puffed and golden brown. Remove from baking sheets; cool on racks.

Ground Meat for Sauces & Casseroles

Place meat mixture in a skillet. Cook over medium heat, stirring occasionally, until no longer pink. Drain off fat. Add to sauce or use in casseroles.

Make-Ahead Meat Loaf

Line an 8'' x 4'' loaf pan with foil, extending foil 4 to 5 inches above pan. Pack meat mixture in foil-lined pan. Fold foil over and seal. Freeze until firm. Remove from pan; return wrapped, frozen loaf to freezer. To cook, unwrap and return to loaf pan. Bake in 350F (175C) oven 1-1/2 hours. Drain off fat. Serve.

Seasoning Ground Meat

Ground meat can be seasoned any way you choose, although good-quality meat can be served with almost no seasoning. Salt will bring out the natural flavor of the meat. Other seasonings, used in excess, will mask the flavor of meat. Don't use too many seasonings at one time because flavors will cancel out each other.

In addition to spices and herbs, other ingredients can be added to ground meat to make a variety of dishes. Chopped vegetables, fruit and nuts are often added in ethnic recipes. Use the examples on the right with 1 pound of lean ground meat. Place meat in a bowl; add additional ingredients; blend well. Shape as desired before cooking.

Mid-Eastern Mixture

1 lb. lean ground lamb
  or beef
1 small red-bell pepper,
  seeded and diced
2 to 3 tablespoons
  chopped dried
  apricots and prunes
2 tablespoons pine nuts
1 to 2 tablespoons
  pistachios
1/4 teaspoon ground
  allspice
4 to 6 saffron threads or
  1/8 teaspoon ground
  saffron
1 tablespoon freshly
  chopped mint

Scandinavian Mixture

1 lb. lean ground beef
  or veal
2 tablespoons chopped
  cooked beets
2 tablespoons diced or
  grated carrot
1 leek, finely chopped
1 tablespoon drained
  capers
1 tablespoon diced
  anchovies
1 to 2 tablespoons dairy
  sour cream
2 tablespoons freshly
  chopped parsley

South American Mixture

1 lb. lean ground beef
1 small tomato, peeled,
  seeded, diced
2 tablespoons drained
  whole-kernel corn
1 tablespoon chopped
  pitted black olives
1 chili pepper, seeded,
  diced
1/2 cup diced apple
1 garlic clove, minced
1 to 2 tablespoons
  golden or dark raisins
2 tablespoons chopped
  almonds
Coarsely ground pepper

Indian Mixture

1 lb. lean ground lamb
1 pineapple slice, diced
2 apricots, peeled, diced
1 to 2 hot chilies,
  seeded, diced
2 to 3 teaspoons paprika
1 tablespoon curry
  powder
1/2 teaspoon caraway
  seeds
1 teaspoon drained
  green peppercorns,
  crushed
1/4 teaspoon ground
  nutmeg

Stuffed Tomatoes

**4 large firm ripe
tomatoes
Salt and pepper to taste
1 recipe hamburger
mixture, page 214
Seasoning as desired**

1. Cut lids from tops of
tomatoes; set aside.
Scoop out pulp and
seeds; discard seeds and
chop pulp. Season
inside of tomato shells;
turn upside down on
paper towels to drain.
2. Combine hamburger
mixture, seasoning and
tomato pulp in a skillet;
cook until meat is no
longer pink. Drain off
fat.
3. Fill shells with
mixture; replace tops.
Place, in a greased
baking dish. Bake in
375F (190C) oven 25
minutes or until tender.
Makes 4 servings.

Stuffed Kohlrabi

**6 to 8 kohlrabi
Salt and pepper to taste
1 recipe hamburger
mixture, page 214
Seasoning as desired**

1. Peel kohlrabi; cut lids
from tops of bulbs. Set
tops aside; hollow out
bulbs. Dice flesh.
2. Place diced kohlrabi
in salted boiling water;
simmer 15 minutes or
until tender. Remove
with a slotted spoon; set
aside. Place shells in
boiling water; cook 10
minutes. Drain well.
Season inside shells.
3. Cook hamburger
mixture and diced
kohlrabi in skillet until
meat is no longer pink;
drain off fat.
4. Fill shells with
mixture; replace tops.
Place, in a greased
baking dish. Pour 1 cup
boiling water into
bottom of dish. Bake in
375F (190C) oven 35
minutes or until tender.
Makes 4 to 6 servings.

Stuffed Peppers

4 large yellow-, green-
or red-bell peppers
Salt and pepper to taste
1 recipe hamburger
mixture, page 214
Seasoning as desired
1/2 cup cooked rice, if
desired

1. Cut lids from tops of peppers; set aside. Remove seeds; season inside peppers.
2. Cook hamburger mixture in a skillet until meat is no longer pink; drain off excess fat. Stir in rice, if desired.
3. Fill peppers with meat mixture; replace tops. Place, in a shallow baking dish. Bake in 375F (190C) oven 30 to 40 minutes or until tender.
Makes 4 servings.

Ground Meat as Stuffing for Vegetables

Well-seasoned cooked ground meat, stuffed into a colorful vegetable and baked can make a filling and delicious main dish. Cooked rice can be mixed with the ground meat to make the dish even more filling, and almost any kind of seasoning can be used. If desired, the top of the meat can be sprinkled with cheese and browned quickly under the broiler, or a sauce can be spooned over the meat. The amount of stuffing required depends entirely on the size and number of vegetables to be stuffed.

Vegetables Suitable for Stuffing

Bell peppers
Tomatoes—large tomatoes for a main dish, cherry tomatoes as an appetizer
Kohlrabi
Eggplant boats
Zucchini boats
Cucumber boats
Onions—large onions for a main dish, pearl onions for an appetizer
Large mushroom caps—for a main dish or an appetizer
Small turnips

Scoop out vegetables and discard seeds. If desired, chop the vegetable pulp; add it to the meat mixture. Be sure to leave a 1/2-inch-thick shell to hold the stuffing.

Meat-Loaf Surprise

1 lb. lean ground beef
1/2 lb. ground veal
1/2 lb. lean ground
  pork
1 large onion, chopped
1/2 cup seasoned dry
  bread crumbs
2 eggs
2 to 3 tablespoons
  freshly chopped
  parsley
2 teaspoons Italian
  seasoning
2 teaspoons
  Worcestershire sauce
1/4 cup ketchup
Salt and pepper to taste
2 hard-cooked eggs,
  peeled
Basil leaves

1. Preheat oven to 350F
(175C).
2. Place all ingredients
except hard-cooked eggs
and basil in a large
bowl; mix thoroughly.
3. Shape meat into a
loaf. Make 2
indentations in top of
meat; push eggs into
holes. Cover eggs with
meat mixture; smooth
top.
4. Place meat loaf on a
rack in a shallow
roasting pan; bake 80 to
90 minutes. Place on a
serving dish; slice.
Makes 6 to 8 servings.

Stuffed Cabbage

1 small head cabbage
1 recipe hamburger
  mixture, page 214
Seasoning as desired
1 cup cooked long-grain
  rice
3 tablespoons freshly
  chopped parsley
2 cups beef stock
2 tablespoons vinegar
2 teaspoons sugar
1/4 lb. bacon, diced
2 to 3 onions, chopped

1. Remove core of
cabbage; discard. Place
whole cabbage in a large
saucepan of lightly
salted simmering water;
cook 4 to 6 minutes or
until leaves are pliable.
Remove cabbage; drain
well.
2. Combine hamburger
mixture, additional
seasoning, rice and
parsley; blend well.
3. Remove 12 large
outer leaves of cabbage;
lay leaves flat. Spoon a
small amount of meat
mixture onto center of
each leaf. Fold sides in
over meat completely.
Tie filled cabbage leaves
with string.
4. Coarsely chop
remaining cabbage;
place in a Dutch oven.
Add broth, vinegar and
sugar; stir well. Place
filled cabbage leaves
over chopped cabbage.
Bring to a boil over
medium heat. Reduce
heat; cover and simmer
50 to 60 minutes or until
cabbage is tender.
5. Cook bacon in a
skillet until crisp.
Remove with a slotted
spoon; drain on paper
towels. Drain off all but
drippings. Add onions
to 3 tablespoons
drippings; sauté until
transparent.
6. Arrange stuffed
cabbage on a plate;
sprinkle with bacon and
onions. Serve chopped
cabbage separately or
use in soup.
Makes 6 servings.

Bolognese Sauce

2 tablespoons butter
1/4 lb. pancetta or lean
  salt pork, diced
1 large onion, diced
1 carrot, finely chopped
1/2 cup finely chopped
  celery
1/2 lb. lean ground beef
1/2 lb. ground veal
1 cup dry red wine
1 bay leaf
1 teaspoon dried leaf
  oregano
1 teaspoon dried leaf
  basil
Salt and pepper to taste
1 (28-oz.) can crushed
  tomatoes
1 cup beef broth
1/2 cup half and half or
  milk, if desired

1. Melt butter in a large
saucepan. Add
pancetta, onion, carrot
and celery. Cook until
onion is transparent.
Add ground beef and
veal; cook, stirring until
meat is no longer pink.
Drain off excess fat.
2. Add wine, bay leaf,
oregano, basil, salt and
pepper; stir well. Cook
over low heat until most
of wine has evaporated.
3. Add tomatoes and
broth; stir well. Simmer
over low heat 1 to 1-1/2
hours or until sauce is
thickened.
4. Stir in cream; simmer
10 minutes. Remove and
discard bay leaf. Serve
over hot cooked pasta.
Makes about 3 cups
sauce.

Cevapcici

1/2 lb. lean ground beef
1/4 lb. ground veal
1/4 lb. lean ground pork
1/4 lb. lean ground
   lamb
3 garlic cloves, minced
1 egg
Salt and pepper to taste
Chopped onion

1. Place beef, veal, pork, lamb, garlic, egg, salt and pepper in a bowl; blend thoroughly.
2. Shape mixture into logs about 1 inch thick and 4 inches long.
3. Place on a rack in a broiler pan; broil 5 to 6 minutes on each side or cook over charcoal grill, about 4 inches from source of heat.
4. Serve with chopped onion.
Makes 6 to 8 servings.

Swedish Meatballs

Meatballs:
1 lb. lean ground beef
1/4 lb. lean ground
   pork
1 medium onion,
   minced
2 tablespoons freshly
   chopped parsley
1/3 cup fine dry bread
   crumbs
1/4 cup milk
1 egg
1/4 teaspoon grated
   nutmeg
Salt and pepper to taste
2 tablespoons butter or
   vegetable oil

Sauce:
3 tablespoons butter
3 tablespoons
   all-purpose flour
1/2 cup beef broth
1 cup half and half
Salt and white pepper
   to taste
1 to 2 tablespoons
   drained capers
Parsley sprigs

1. Combine beef, pork, onion, parsley, bread crumbs, milk, egg, nutmeg, salt and pepper in a bowl; blend.
2. Shape mixture into 1-inch balls. Melt butter in a skillet; add meatballs, a few at a time. Cook until browned on all sides. Remove from skillet with a slotted spoon; drain on paper towels. Drain fat from skillet; wipe with paper towels.
3. To make sauce, melt butter in skillet. Add flour; cook 1 minute, stirring constantly. Gradually add broth and cream and cook, stirring constantly, until mixture thickens. Add salt, white pepper and capers; stir well.
4. Return meatballs to skillet; simmer 3 to 4 minutes or until heated through. Garnish with parsley sprigs.
Makes 6 servings.

Shanghai Spring Rolls

20 egg-roll or won-ton
   skins
2 teaspoons cornstarch
1 tablespoon soy sauce
1 tablespoon rice
   vinegar or dry sherry
1/2 lb. lean ground pork
Vegetable oil
1/2 cup shredded
   bamboo shoots
1 cup fresh bean
   sprouts
1 bunch green onions,
   finely chopped
1 teaspoon sugar
Salt and white pepper
   to taste
1 egg white, lightly
   beaten

1. Remove egg-roll or won-ton skins from package and cover with a damp towel to keep moist.
2. Stir together cornstarch, soy sauce and vinegar or sherry in a small bowl until smooth. Add ground pork; stir well. Cover and let stand 20 minutes.
3. Heat 2 tablespoons oil in a skillet until hot. Add pork mixture; cook until meat is no longer pink, stirring frequently. Remove from skillet with a slotted spoon; set aside.
4. Add bamboo shoots, bean sprouts and green onions to skillet; stir-fry 1 minute. Add sugar, salt and pepper; stir well. Stir in pork. Remove from heat; let cool.
5. Spoon 1 to 2 tablespoons pork filling onto bottom corner of egg roll or won-ton skin. Fold lower corner of skin over filling. Brush sides and upper edge of skin with beaten egg white. Fold in sides and roll to make a tight parcel. Repeat with remaining skins and filling. Keep filled skins covered with a damp towel.
6. Heat 4 to 5 inches oil in a deep-fat fryer. Add spring rolls, a few at a time; deep-fry until golden brown and crisp. Remove with a slotted spoon; drain on paper towels. Serve with hot Chinese mustard and duck sauce.
Makes 20 spring rolls.

Roasts & Casseroles

Steaks, chops, cutlets and ground meat, discussed in previous chapters, are fine for feeding just a few people. But when there will be several people for dinner, a roast, stew or casserole is an ideal food to serve. It can be an elegant dinner at which you serve an expensive roast, cooked by dry heat, or a more economical meal at which you serve pot roast or stew. Whichever menu you choose, you will be able to sit comfortably with your guests while the food cooks, almost unattended.

Pot Roasts

Large cuts of meat from the chuck or shoulder and sometimes the round can be tenderized by long, slow cooking in liquid. When meat is cooked this way, it usually is referred to as a *pot roast*, no matter what species of meat is used. Seasoning is rubbed onto the surface of the meat and the meat is browned on all sides to help retain juices and give it a nice brown color. There are two ways to brown the meat. It can be placed on a broiler rack and browned under the broiler, or it can be placed in a large heavy saucepan or Dutch oven and browned in a small amount of hot oil. The meat should be turned so it is browned all over. When meat is browned in hot oil, the oil should be removed from the pan before cooking liquid is added in order to eliminate as much fat as possible from the final sauce. Many liquids, or combination of liquids, can be used. Stock, water, dry red or white wine and tomato juice or crushed tomatoes are all appropriate, depending on the flavor desired. Meat should be covered during cooking and turned periodically. Vegetables can be added to the cooking liquid about 45 minutes to an hour before the meat is finished cooking. Additional liquid can be added to the meat during cooking, if necessary.

Oven Pot Roast

5 tablespoons butter
1 tablespoon vegetable oil
6 tablespoons all-purpose flour
1 (5- to 6-lb.) beef rump roast
2 cups beef broth
2 cups water
2 garlic cloves, pressed
3 small bay leaves
1 teaspoon Italian seasoning
1/2 teaspoon black pepper
1/2 teaspoon dried-leaf thyme
1 turnip
10 medium carrots
1 medium celeriac
6 red or white thin-skinned potatoes
1 lb. small onions, peeled

1. Assemble all ingredients,

6. Remove fat from drippings.

2. Pat 2 tablespoons flour into beef roast.

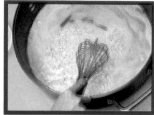
7. Add flour to hot butter. Blend together with a whisk, stirring until bubbly.

3. Brown roast on all sides in hot butter and oil.

8. Gradually pour in drippings, stirring constantly.

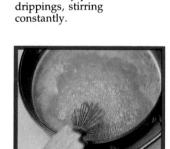
4. Add vegetables to roast. Return to oven.

9. Cook, stirring constantly until desired consistency and flour has lost its raw taste.

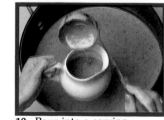
5. Remove roast and vegetables from pan. Place on a platter; keep warm.

10. Pour into a serving container. Serve with roast and vegetables.

1. In a large dutch oven, heat 1 tablespoon butter and oil over medium-high heat. Pat 2 tablespoons flour over all meat surfaces. When butter mixture foams, add floured meat; brown on all sides.
2. Add broth, water, garlic, bay leaves, Italian seasoning, pepper and thyme; bring to a boil. Cover and bake in a 350F (175C) oven 1-1/2

hours or until meat is nearly tender.

3. Meanwhile, peel turnip; cut into eighths. Cut off root and top of celeriac. Peel and cut in half. Then cut each half into eighths. Cut potatoes in half. Remove pan from oven. Add vegetables.

4. Return pot roast to oven. Cover and bake 45 minutes or until vegetables and meat are tender.

5. Remove meat and vegetables to a platter; keep warm. Pour pan drippings into a 2-quart measure.

6. Spoon off fat; add water, if necessary, to make 4 cups.

7. Wipe out roasting pan. Melt remaining 1/4 cup butter in pan over medium-high heat. When butter foams, add remaining 1/4 cup flour.

Blend together with a whisk, stirring constantly until bubbling.

8. Gradually pour in drippings, stirring constantly. Continue cooking and stirring until desired consistency.

9. Pour into a serving container. Serve with roast and vegetables. Makes 5 to 6 servings.

Many Ways to Cook Large Pieces of Meat

Although a large cut of meat often is referred to as a roast, there are more ways to cook it than by roasting it in the oven. In addition to roasting by dry heat, large cuts of meat can also be braised or cooked in liquid, also known as *pot roasting*. One clue to the best cooking method is in the potential tenderness of the cut of meat. Tender cuts, such as beef rib roast, leg of lamb or ham, are cooked by dry heat. Cuts from the shoulder in any species should be cooked by moist heat to make them tender. But, with many other cuts, you can choose whichever cooking method you like.

Roast Veal

1 (5- to 6-lb.) boneless veal loin with kidney attached
Salt and pepper to taste
2 tablespoons vegetable oil
1 onion, chopped
2 celery stalks with leaves, chopped
2 Italian parsley sprigs
2 tarragon sprigs
1 cup dry white wine
Additional fresh parsley and tarragon

1. Cut kidney from loin; remove and discard fat. Spread veal flat, skin-side down; sprinkle with salt and pepper. 2. Cut kidney in half lengthwise; arrange down center of meat. Roll meat to enclose kidney; tie with string. Sprinkle meat with salt and pepper. 3. Preheat oven to 400F (200C). Brush meat with oil; place in a large roasting pan. Bake 25 minutes. 4. Scatter onion, celery, parsley and tarragon around roast; pour wine over meat. Reduce oven to 375F (190C); cook 1-1/2 to 2 hours or until internal temperature of meat registers 170F (75C) on a meat thermometer. Baste with drippings several times during cooking. 5. Place meat on a platter; garnish with parsley and tarragon. Strain juices, discarding vegetables and herbs; skim off fat. Serve pan juices with meat or prepare gravy, pages 258-259.
Makes 8 to 10 servings.

Pot Roasted Beef Brisket

1 (3- to 4-lb.) beef
  brisket
3 tablespoons vegetable
  oil
2 onions, chopped
2 cups dry red wine
2 cups beef broth
3 tablespoons red-wine
  vinegar
10 peppercorns
5 whole allspice
2 whole cloves
1 thyme sprig
Salt to taste
4 carrots, cut in chunks
1 large leek, sliced

1. Trim fat from meat.
Heat oil in a large heavy
saucepan. Add meat;
brown on both sides.
Remove meat from
saucepan; set aside.

Drain off all but 2
tablespoons fat.
2. Add onions to
saucepan; cook until
transparent. Return
meat to saucepan. Add
wine, broth, vinegar,
peppercorns, allspice,
cloves, thyme and salt.
Bring to a boil. Reduce
heat; cover and simmer
2 to 2-1/2 hours or until
meat is almost tender.
3. Add carrots, leek and
additional liquid, if
necessary. Cover and
cook 40 to 60 minutes or
until vegetables are
cooked and meat is
tender.
4. Remove meat and
vegetables to a platter;
keep warm. Strain
cooking liquid; skim off
fat. Serve sauce with
meat and vegetables.
Makes 4 to 6 servings.

Pork Loin in Beer

1 (3- to 4-lb.) boneless
  pork loin roast
Salt and pepper to taste
2 tablespoons vegetable
  oil
3 medium onions, cut
  in wedges
2 garlic cloves
1-1/2 cups beer
2 bay leaves
1 rosemary sprig or 1/2
  teaspoon dried
  rosemary
3 large carrots, thickly
  sliced
Parsley sprigs

1. Season meat all over
with salt and pepper.
Heat oil in a large heavy
saucepan. Add meat;
brown on all sides.
Remove meat from
saucepan; set aside.

Drain off all but 2
tablespoons fat. Add
onions and garlic; sauté
3 to 4 minutes.
2. Preheat oven to 325F
(170C). Return meat to
saucepan. Add beer,
bay leaves and
rosemary. Cover; cook 1
hour. Add carrots; cook
40 to 60 minutes or until
internal temperature of
meat registers 170F
(75C) on meat
thermometer and carrots
are tender.
3. Remove meat and
vegetables to a serving
platter; keep warm.
Strain cooking liquid;
skim off fat. Serve pan
juices with meat or
prepare gravy, pages
258-259.
Makes 6 to 8 servings.

The Many Ways to Make Roasts Special

A large tender roast, cooked in the oven on a rack in a roasting pan, does not necessarily require much more than salt and freshly ground pepper and, in some cases, not even salt. But there are many ways even the best roast, whether cooked by dry or moist heat, can be made still more delicious by using appropriate herbs and spices, adding the flavor of alcohol or other liquids, adding fat to a lean roast or by making a well-flavored stuffing.

Herbs

Certain herbs are well-suited to each species of meats. Herbs can be sprinkled on before roasting, added to liquid in which pot roast is cooked, or added to gravy or stuffing.

Beef—Basil, chives, garlic, marjoram, oregano, rosemary, tarragon and thyme.

Veal—Basil, chervil, dill, garlic, oregano, paprika, rosemary, sage, tarragon and thyme.

Pork—Basil, chives, dill, garlic, marjoram, oregano, rosemary, sage, tarragon and thyme.

Lamb—Basil, dill, garlic, marjoram, mint, oregano, rosemary, tarragon and thyme.

Alcohol & Other Liquids

Occasional basting with a flavorful liquid can help keep meat from getting too dry and can add flavor to meat and pan drippings used to make gravy. Alcohol can also be used to flambe meat. Alcohol and other liquids can be used to braise meat and make gravies and sauces.

Dry white wine—Goes well with all meat, particularly light colored meat, such as veal.

Dry vermouth—Goes well with all meat, particularly light colored meat, such as veal.

Dry red wine—Best with beef, lamb and game. Can also be used with veal and pork.

Dry sherry—Good with veal.

Beer—Good with pork and beef.

Brandy—Good with beef and veal.

Apple juice, cider and Calvados—Good with smoked ham, fresh pork, veal and lamb.

Orange juice—Good with smoked ham and fresh prok.

Ginger ale—Good with smoked ham.

Stock—Good with all meat.

Inserting Fat or Garlic in Roasts

When meat is very lean, it can be larded with extra fat to make it moist and juicy. Buy a slab of fatback; pound it flat with a mallet. Cut off the rind, then slice into thin strips. Place in iced water until firm. Pat dry; thread into a larding needle. Use needle to insert fat into meat along the grain.

Garlic, added to lamb and beef while cooking, can be very appealing. Peel garlic cloves; cut into thin slivers. Make slits several places in roast; insert garlic.

Spices

Spices bring out the flavor of meat and gravy and add wonderful flavor of their own, but they should be used sparingly. When whole spices are used instead of ground spices, they must be removed from a sauce or gravy before serving. Four of the spices that go well with meat are shown here.

Bay leaves—In spite of the fact that some recipes still call for crumbled bay leaves, they should always be used whole so they can be removed easily. It is a simple matter to remove a whole bay leaf from a sauce or gravy, but a crumbled bay leaf cannot be removed without straining the liquid. Use sparingly in lamb stew, beef stew, pot roast and in marinades.

Whole cloves—Whole cloves look like little nails and are used effectively to stud some meat. When used to make a design in meat, they are attractive as a garnish. Use cloves to stud ham or glazed corned beef and fresh pork. Cloves can also be used to stud an onion added to a cooking liquid for flavor and can be used in marinades.

Juniper berries—Juniper berries are more popular in Europe than in the United States although they are becoming increasingly available here as interest in ethnic recipes grows. They can be crushed and rubbed into meat before cooking, used in stuffing and gravy, and to flavor pork, lamb and wild game.

Peppercorns—Peppercorns can be used to flavor any kind of meat, but should only be used whole in liquid that is going to be strained. Use freshly ground pepper in all other instances.

Stuffing

There are many cuts of meat in which it is possible to cut a pocket for stuffing. Breast of lamb or veal are good choices. When pastry is wrapped around meat, stuffing is often spread over the meat before wrapping. Stuffings can be made from a variety of ingredients including seasoned ground meat and dried-fruit mixtures. A good stuffing can be made with mushrooms.

Mushroom Stuffing
Sauté 1 pound minced mushrooms and 8 minced shallots in 1/4 cup butter until mushrooms are soft. Add 1/4 cup freshly chopped parsley, 2 tablespoons snipped chives, 3 tablespoons lemon juice, salt and pepper. Cook, stirring, until liquid has evaporated. Stir in about 3 tablespoons dry sherry.
Makes about 1-1/2 cups.

Meat Dishes from Around the World

Every country has its own special way of preparing food. Sometimes special dishes become so well known it isn't even necessary to identify the country from which they originate. Osso Buco from Italy and Sauerbraten from Germany are typical examples. Rabbit is so popular in France, it isn't difficult to guess a rabbit dish might come from France. Try these international favorites to add variety to your menus.

Osso Buco

4 lbs. veal shanks, sliced about 2-inches thick
Salt and pepper to taste
All-purpose flour
1/4 cup olive oil
3 garlic cloves, crushed
1 large onion, minced
1 cup diced carrots
1 celery stalk, minced
1 cup dry white wine
1 (16-oz.) can crushed tomatoes
1 teaspoon dried leaf oregano
1 teaspoon grated lemon peel
1/2 teaspoon grated orange peel
2 tablespoons freshly chopped parsley

1. Season veal shanks with salt and pepper. Dredge in flour; shake off excess.
2. Heat oil in a large heavy skillet. Add veal shanks, a few at a time; brown on all sides. Remove from skillet; set aside.
3. Add garlic, onion, carrot and celery to skillet; cook, stirring, 5 minutes. Add wine; cook over high heat until reduced by half. Add tomatoes, oregano, salt and pepper; stir well. Return meat to skillet; cover and simmer 1 to 1-1/2 hours or until tender, adding water or stock if sauce is too thick.
4. Combine lemon peel, orange peel and parsley. Add to sauce; stir well. Simmer 5 minutes. Makes 4 servings.

Rabbit with Prunes

1 (3-lb.) rabbit, cut in serving pieces
Salt and pepper to taste
All purpose flour
1/4 cup butter
2 tablespoons vegetable oil
1/2 cup water
1 cup dry red wine
4 shallots, minced
1 (12-oz.) box pitted prunes
Bouquet garni, page 145
2 tablespoons red-currant jelly

1. Season rabbit pieces with salt and pepper. Dredge in flour; shake off excess.
2. Heat butter and oil in a heavy skillet. Add rabbit pieces, a few at a time; brown on all sides.
3. Add water, wine, shallots, prunes, bouquet garni, salt and pepper. Bring to a boil. Reduce heat; cover and simmer 1 hour or until tender. Discard bouquet garni; place rabbit and prunes on a serving dish. Add jelly to saucepan; stir until melted. Spoon sauce over rabbit. Makes 4 servings.

Sauerbraten

1 (5-lb.) beef bottom-round roast
2 onions, chopped
1 large carrot, chopped
1 celery stalk with leaves, chopped
1 cup dry red wine
1 cup red wine vinegar
Water
3 whole cloves
2 bay leaves
10 peppercorns
2 to 3 teaspoons salt
1/2 teaspoon pepper
1/4 cup vegetable oil
10 to 12 gingersnaps, crushed
1/3 cup raisins
1 tablespoon sugar

1. Place beef in a large deep glass bowl. Add onions, carrot and celery. Combine wine, vinegar, 2-1/2 cups water, cloves, bay leaves, peppercorns, salt and pepper. Pour over meat. Cover with plastic wrap; refrigerate 3 days, turning meat several times.
2. To cook, remove meat from marinade; reserve marinade. Pat dry with paper towels.
3. Heat oil in a heavy saucepan. Add meat; brown on all sides. Drain off fat; add reserved marinade. Bring to a boil. Reduce heat; cover and simmer 2-1/2 to 3 hours or until tender.
4. Remove meat to a platter; keep warm. Strain cooking liquid; skim off fat. Return liquid to saucepan; bring to a boil. Reduce heat; add gingersnaps, raisins and sugar. Simmer 5 minutes or until slightly thickened. Spoon over sliced meat. Makes 8 to 10 servings.

Hungarian Goulash

2 lbs. beef cubes for
   stew
Salt and pepper to taste
2 tablespoons butter
1 tablespoon olive oil
2 garlic cloves, minced
2 medium tomatoes,
   peeled, coarsely
   chopped
2 tablespoons
   Hungarian paprika
4 to 6 small onions, cut
   in half
1 bay leaf
1/2 teaspoon caraway
   seeds, if desired
2 tablespoons tomato
   paste
4 cups beef broth or
   water
2 small red-bell
   peppers, seeded,
   diced
4 to 6 small red
   potatoes, peeled, cut
   in chunks

1. Season meat with salt and pepper. Heat butter and oil in a large heavy saucepan. Add meat; brown on all sides. Add garlic, tomatoes, paprika and onions; stir well. Cook over low heat 5 minutes, stirring occasionally.
2. Add bay leaf, caraway seeds, tomato paste, broth, salt and pepper; stir well. Bring to a boil over medium heat. Reduce heat; cover and simmer 1-1/2 hours. Add red peppers and potatoes; cook 30 to 40 minutes or until meat is tender and vegetables are cooked. Remove bay leaf before serving. Makes 4 to 6 servings.

Is It a Stew or a Casserole?

This is not easy to answer because the terms are used interchangeably. Casseroles and stews are usually one-dish meals that include meat, fish or poultry, a starch, a vegetable and sauce. But a casserole can also be a much simpler dish, such as baked beans. One way to distinguish between a casserole and stew is to use the cooking method as the determining factor—a casserole is generally baked and a stew is usually simmered on top of the stove. Whatever you call these dishes, they are wonderful for busy cooks because they can be prepared ahead of time and kept in the freezer or refrigerator until needed.

Pork Goulash

2 tablespoons butter
1 tablespoon vegetable
 oil
2 lbs. boneless pork
 cubes
2 large onions, sliced
1 garlic clove, minced
1 cup chicken broth
2 tablespoons tomato
 paste
1 tablespoon Hungarian
 paprika
1 (16-oz.) can
 sauerkraut, drained
Salt and pepper to taste
1 cup dairy sour cream

1. Heat butter and oil in a large heavy skillet. Add meat; brown on all sides. Add onions and garlic; cook until onions are transparent.
2. Blend chicken broth, tomato paste and paprika. Pour over meat; stir well. Bring to a boil over medium heat. Reduce heat; cover and simmer 30 minutes.
3. Add sauerkraut, salt and pepper. Simmer 30 to 45 minutes or until meat is tender. Stir in sour cream; cook until heated through. Do not allow mixture to boil. Makes 4 to 6 servings.

Goulash

The term goulash is derived from the Hungarian term *gulyas* which means "herdman's meat." Classic goulash is a stew made with meat and vegetables, seasoned with Hungarian paprika. The flavor of Hungarian paprika is stronger than most domestic paprika and should be used in order to get the full and proper flavor of a good traditional goulash. Either mild or hot Hungarian paprika can be used, depending on how spicy you want the finished dish to taste. In many instances, dairy sour cream is stirred into the gravy just before the goulash is served.

Roasting Meat

Choose large tender cuts of meat for dry-heat roasting. Preheat oven. Season meat on all sides before cooking; then place on a rack in a shallow roasting pan. Estimate the amount of time necessary to cook meat to desired doneness or, in the case of fresh pork, until thoroughly cooked. Set timer; place meat, uncovered, in oven. When a glaze is used with meat, such as smoked ham, brush glaze on meat during the last 20 minutes of cooking only. Test for doneness with a meat thermometer inserted into the center of the thickest part of the meat, being sure the point of the thermometer does not touch bone or a very fatty area. When meat has reached desired temperature, remove from oven; cover and let stand 15 to 20 minutes to firm meat before carving. The internal temperature will rise about 5 degrees during standing time. If you are going to make gravy from pan drippings, remove meat to a carving board; remove rack from roasting pan; place pan on top of range. Make the gravy directly in the pan. Although a roast surrounded by vegetables may look beautiful when it is brought to the table, the vegetables will make carving very difficult. Place vegetables in a separate serving dishes in order to give the carver room to maneuver. Be sure the carving knife is very sharp so it will slice meat neatly rather than tear it. Store leftover meat in the refrigerator. Serve cold, slice and reheat, or use diced or ground in a casserole.

Herbed Leg of Lamb

2 garlic cloves
1/4 cup freshly chopped
  mixed herbs, such as
  mint, rosemary,
  thyme, basil and
  parsley
1 (7- to 9-lb.) leg of
  lamb
Salt and pepper to taste
Juice of 1 lemon
6 to 8 medium tomatoes
Mint jelly or mint sauce

1. Preheat oven to 325F (170C).
2. Peel garlic; cut into slivers. Combine herbs in a small bowl. Cut several slits in lamb. Insert a garlic sliver and a small amount of herb mixture into each slit, reserving 2 tablespoons herb mixture to sprinkle over lamb.
3. Rub lamb with salt, pepper, reserved herb mixture and lemon juice. Place lamb on a rack in a large shallow roasting pan.
4. Cook in preheated oven 18 to 20 minutes per pound for rare, or until internal temperature registers 140F (60C) on a meat thermometer, basting lamb with pan drippings occasionally.
5. Add tomatoes to roasting pan during last 15 to 20 minutes of cooking; baste with pan drippings.
6. Place lamb on a serving platter. Remove tomatoes from pan with a slotted spoon. Make gravy with pan drippings if desired, pages 258-259, or serve with mint jelly or mint sauce.
Makes 6 to 8 servings.

Baked Ham

1 (5- to 7-lb.) shank half
  smoked ham
1 cup orange juice
2 teaspoons cornstarch
Whole cloves
Brown sugar

1. Preheat oven to 325F
(170C).
2. Place ham on a rack
in a large shallow
roasting pan; cook in
preheated oven 22 to 25
minutes per pound.
3. Stir orange juice and
cornstarch in a small
saucepan until blended
and smooth. Place
saucepan over low heat;
cook, stirring, until
mixture is thickened and
clear. Remove from
heat; set aside.
4. About 45 minutes
before ham is done,
remove ham from oven;
drain off pan drippings.
Score fat on ham in a
diamond pattern; rub
ham generously with
brown sugar. Insert a
whole clove in center of
each scored diamond.
Pour 1/2 cup orange
mixture over the ham.
Return ham to oven;
bake until internal
temperature registers
160F (70C). Pour
remaining glaze over
ham during the last 10
minutes of baking.
5. Place ham on a
carving board, remove
cloves. Cover and let
stand 20 minutes before
carving.
Makes 10 to 14 servings.

Note—For precooked
ham, cook 18 to 14
minutes per pound to
internal temperature of
140F (60C).

Roast Beef

1 (4- to 5-lb.) beef
  top-round roast
Salt and pepper to taste
Horseradish Cream,
  below

1. Preheat oven to 325F
(170C).
2. Season meat all over
with salt and pepper;
place roast, fat-side up,
on a rack in a shallow
roasting pan.
3. Cook in preheated
oven 20 to 25 minutes
per pound for rare or
until internal
temperature registers
125F (50C) on a meat
thermometer. Cook
longer if desired.
4. Remove meat to a
carving board; cover and
let stand 10 to 15
minutes before carving.
Serve with pan juices or
Horseradish Cream.
Makes 8 to 10 servings.

Horseradish Cream

1/2 cup mayonnaise
2 tablespoons prepared
  horseradish
2 tablespoons lemon
  juice
1 to 2 tablespoons
  whole-grain
  Dijon-style mustard
1 teaspoon super fine
  sugar
1/2 cup whipping cream
Salt and white pepper
  to taste
Hot-pepper sauce to
  taste

1. Place mayonnaise,
horseradish, lemon
juice, mustard and
sugar in a bowl; stir
until blended.
2. Beat cream in a
separate bowl until stiff
peaks form. Fold
whipped cream into
horseradish mixture.
Season with salt, pepper
and hot-pepper sauce.
Refrigerate 1 hour.
Makes about 1-1/2 cups.

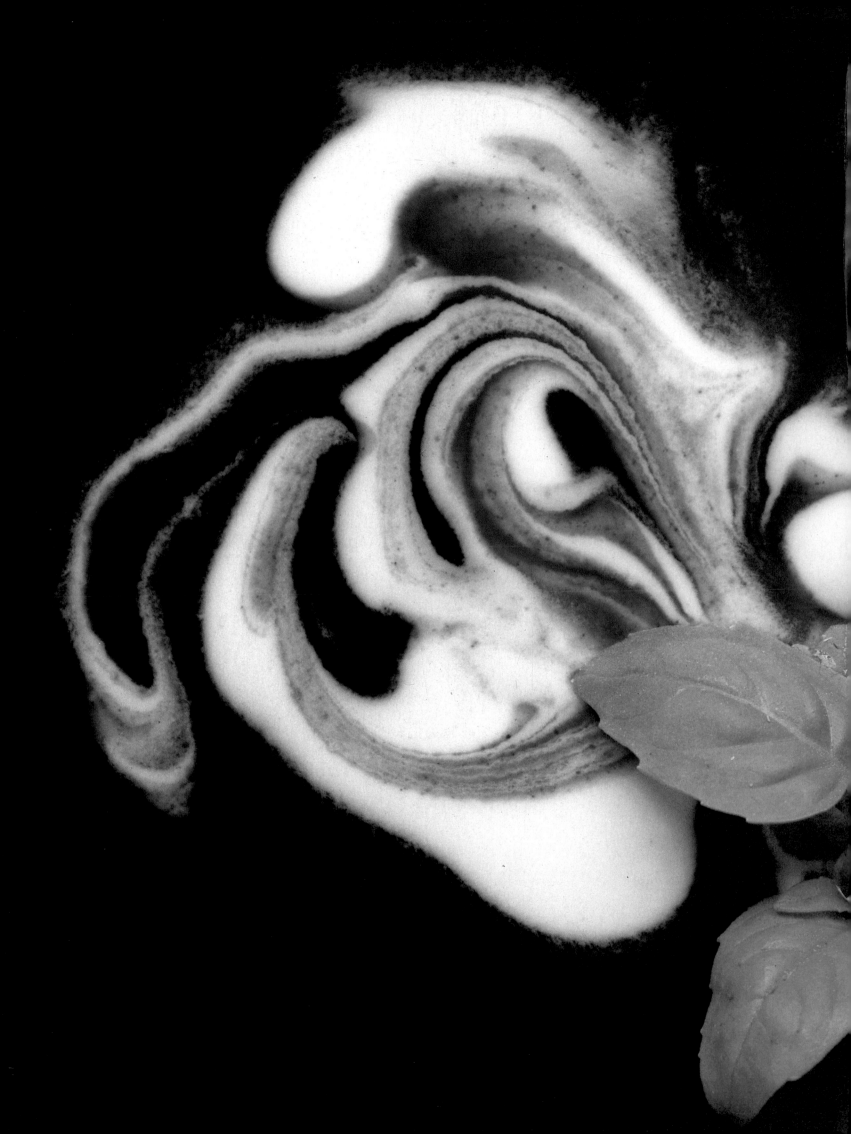

Sauces & Gravies: A Special Touch of Elegance

Most food historians believe sauces and gravies were first invented to mask the unpleasant taste of food that was slightly off as a result of lack of refrigeration. But over the years, they have moved up the scale to a point where well-made sauces and gravies have become an integral part of haute cuisine. Chefs who created sauces remain famous long after their deaths, as with Louis de Béchamel for whom Béchamel or White Sauce is named. Fine restaurants could not function without a saucier on whom they depend to provide the special touch that often separates an adequate restaurant from a superb one. Although few cooks have either the time or inclination to make the basic "mother" sauces from which a saucier makes sauces, superb sauces can be made at home, quickly and easily, and can be used to turn an ordinary meal into something very special.

Sauce Techniques

Sauces are made by different methods, depending on the type of sauce required. Each sauce can become the basis from which other sauces are made. Beurre Blanc, Cream Sauce and Cream Gravy are made by heating liquid over high heat to reduce the liquid and thicken the sauce. Hollandaise Sauce is an egg-based sauce in which the addition of butter to egg yolks causes the sauce to thicken in the same way oil added to egg yolks will make a smooth thick mayonnaise. The Béchamel or White Sauce is made by combining butter and flour to make a smooth paste or roux, then adding liquid to the roux. In each case, the thickening agent is different.

Reduction Method

Heat liquid, uncovered, over high heat. Evaporation will cause the liquid to reduce and thicken. This cooking method intensifies flavor, so seasoning should be light and adjusted after liquid is reduced.

Egg-Based Sauces

Add butter or oil to beaten egg yolks very slowly so the egg yolks can absorb the fat. Egg yolks can absorb only a limited amount of fat, so the correct ratio of egg yolk to fat must be maintained: 1 large egg yolk can handle 2 to 3 ounces fat.

Béchamel or White Sauce

Melt butter in a saucepan; add flour. Stir to make a smooth paste or roux. Cook 1 or 2 minutes to eliminate the raw-flour taste. Slowly add milk, cream, stock or wine, stirring constantly. Equal amounts of butter and flour are used. It is the amount of liquid added that determines the thickness of the sauce.

Brown Sauces

One of the easiest ways to make a Brown Sauce is to reduce seasoned dark stock or beef broth and thicken it with a beurre manie, page 153. It is also possible to make a Brown Sauce by browning a roux and then adding liquid. But this method can give the flour a slightly burnt flavor that can spoil the flavor of the finished sauce.

Beurre Blanc

4 shallots, minced
1/3 cup white wine vinegar
1/3 cup dry white wine
1 cup unsalted butter, cut in 16 pieces
Salt and white pepper to taste

1. Place shallots in a heavy skillet.

2. Add vinegar and wine to skillet; bring to a boil.

Hollandaise Sauce

1/2 cup butter
3 egg yolks
1 tablespoon cold water
1 tablespoon lemon juice
Hot-pepper sauce
Salt to taste

1. Cut butter into small pieces; set aside.

2. Place egg yolks and water in top of a double boiler.

Béchamel Sauce

2 tablespoons butter
2 tablespoons all-purpose flour
1 cup half and half or milk
Salt and white pepper to taste

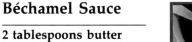
1. Melt butter in a saucepan over medium heat.

2. Add flour.

Cream Sauce

1/2 cup dry white wine
2 cups whipping cream
1 tablespoon butter
Salt and white pepper to taste

1. Pour wine into a saucepan.

2. Cook over medium heat until wine is reduced by half.

Cream Gravy

1/4 cup pan drippings
1/2 cup dry red or white wine
1 cup whipping cream
Salt and pepper to taste

1. Place pan drippings in a saucepan; add wine.

2. Cook over medium heat until reduced by one-third.

3. Boil vigorously to reduce liquid.

4. Cook until almost all liquid has evaporated.

5. Reduce heat, beat in butter quickly, 1 piece at a time.

6. Beat to make a smooth sauce. Season to taste. Makes about 1 cup.

3. Place over, not in, simmering water; beat until slightly thickened.

4. Add a few pieces of butter; beat until melted.

5. Add more butter slowly; beat until sauce is thickened.

6. Beat in lemon juice, and spices. Serve immediately. Makes about 1 cup.

3. Stir over medium heat until mixture is smooth and thick.

4. Add cream very slowly, stirring constantly.

5. Cook, stirring, until sauce thickens. Season to taste. Makes about 1 cup.

3. Slowly pour cream into saucepan.

4. Cook over medium heat, stirring, until sauce is reduced by half.

5. Beat in butter.

6. Season with salt and pepper to taste. Makes about 1-1/4 cups.

3. Slowly add cream, stirring constantly.

4. Cook over medium heat, stirring constantly, until reduced by half.

5. Remove from heat; season with salt and pepper to taste. Makes about 1 cup.

Help From the Supermarket

You can buy just about any kind of ready-made sauce in most supermarkets as easily as you can buy the ingredients necessary to make sauces at home. Some of the ready-made sauces are luxury items, expensive and not nearly as good as homemade. But some of the products are basic to good cooking, some are all but impossible to duplicate at home and some are genuinely worthy substitutions.

Convenience Products to Keep on Hand

Bouillon cubes and instant bouillon granules are superb cooking aids used to make instant substitutes for stock or to flavor liquid in which foods are cooked. Worcestershire sauce and soy sauce cannot be made at home. They are good examples of sauces that belong in a well-stocked pantry. Mayonnaise, ketchup and tartar sauce most cooks want to have on hand at all times. For those who prefer homemade, it is always possible to make it.

Oil & Vinegar

Recipes for marinades and many salad dressings and sauces often call for oil and vinegar. There are many different kinds of oil, and just about as many different kinds of vinegar. Most oils can be used almost interchangeably, depending on the flavor desired for a specific dish. Many vinegars can also be used interchangeably too, but the flavors of different vinegars are more pronounced.

Varieties of Oil

Oils used in cooking are vegetable oils that have been pressed or squeezed from seeds or fruit. Most of the oils available have minimal flavor. However, the flavor of good quality olive oil is distinguishable and should be used when flavor from oil is particularly important. The best olive oil comes from the first pressing of the olives and is called *virgin oil*. It is light and delicate in flavor. Corn oil, peanut oil, safflower oil, soy bean oil and sunflower oil are among the most popular, but bland oils. Sesame-seed oil is very flavorful and used primarily with strongly flavored foods. Special oils, such as hazelnut and walnut, are expensive and often difficult to find, but have a nice light special flavor, excellent in salad dressings. Oils made from coconut, grape seed and mustard seed are more easily available abroad and popularly used in ethnic cooking.

Varieties of Vinegar

Vinegar is a sour liquid made from the fermentation of distilled alcohol. It is effective in a marinade because it breaks down the connective tissue of meat. It also provides an acidic flavor to salad dressing and sauces. Vinegar should not be used in a metal dish because it has a corrosive effect on metal. Use glass, china or enamel instead. There are 4 categories of vinegar: white vinegar, cider vinegar, wine vinegar and herb or flavored vinegar made from one of the other 3 kinds of vinegar. The flavor and strength of different kinds of vinegars are very different and it is therefore important to be sure you know what flavor you want to achieve in a marinade, salad dressing or sauce before you decide which vinegar to use. Once you determine which vinegars you like best, you can keep a variety on your pantry shelf.

Sauces for Food Cooked on an Outdoor Grill

Food, cooking on a barbecue grill, usually means a picnic—formal or informal. No matter what kind of party it is, most barbecued food benefits from the addition of some kind of sauce either served with the food or brushed on it during cooking. Mild or hot ketchup, mustard, steak sauce and relish are standard fare on most picnic tables. If you serve lamb kabobs or a butterflied leg of lamb, don't forget the mint sauce. Meat, fish and poultry often have a sauce brushed on them during cooking to keep them from drying out. If meat has been marinated to make it tender and to provide extra flavor, the marinade can be used as a basting sauce to keep the meat moist. Clarified butter and vegetable oil can be used too. Ready-made barbecue sauces range from very mild to breath-takingly hot. They should not be brushed on food until 15 to 20 minutes before cooking is completed. If they are brushed on sooner, the sauce will burn. There are also several sweet and sour sauces available that can be brushed on poultry about 10 minutes before cooking is completed. Be sure to brush sauce on all sides of the food and watch the grill carefully to prevent flare-ups if sauce drips into the fire.

Special Mixed Seasonings

Various kinds of mixed seasonings are available at the supermarket. Some mixtures are made for specific purposes, such as poultry seasoning or seafood seasoning. Some have more general use. Two of the most popular are given here.

Italian Seasoning— Usually made from a mixture of thyme, oregano, savory, marjoram, basil, rosemary and sage. This seasoning is particularly good with tomato and can be used successfully in a spaghetti or marinara sauce. It is also an excellent seasoning to add to a marinade or salad dressing.

Herbes de Provence—A mixture of lavender, thyme, basil, summer savory and fennel seeds made in southern France and packaged in clay crocks jars. Excellent as a seasoning in sauces and salad dressings, sautéed vegetables or meats and poultry.

Liquid Seasonings

Liquid seasoning, usually used in small amounts, often provides a final special flavor and color to a finished sauce. These are not sauces that can be made at home.

Worcestershire Sauce—The ingredients in Worcestershire sauce have been a secret for a long time. However, since this sauce is no longer made by just one company, the secret must have been leaked. At a guess, it probably includes such things as soy sauce, garlic, onion, molasses, anchovies and much much more. It can be used as a sauce directly on meat, fish or poultry, but more often it is used as a flavoring agent in sauces, gravies and marinades.

Soy Sauce—Oriental in origin, soy sauce is made from fermented soy beans and is very salty unless you purchase the reduced salt version. Both light and dark soy sauce are available and are used as a dipping sauce as well as seasoning for other sauces.

Hot-Pepper Sauce—This sauce is made from chili peppers and even the so-called mild version can be very hot indeed. Use only a very few drops at a time to season sauces.

Browning Sauce—A mixture of caramelized sugar, salt, vegetable protein, vinegar, onion, parsley and garlic that adds both flavor and dark brown color to gravies and other sauces.

Liquid Smoke—Made from nothing more than water and natural liquid smoke, it can be used directly on meat, fish and poultry or added to barbecue sauces.

247

Additional Ways to Thicken Sauces

If desired, sauces can be thickened with cornstarch, arrowroot or potato starch instead of flour. All these thickeners have twice the thickening power of flour; 1 tablespoon equals 2 tablespoons of flour so amounts must be cut in half. Cornstarch will add a slightly translucent look to sauce, and sauces made with arrowroot or potato starch cannot be heated higher than 175F (80C). If they are heated beyond that temperature, the sauce will begin to thin out. Dissolve the thickening agent in liquid; stir it to a smooth thin paste that can be poured into the sauce. Never add flour, cornstarch, arrowroot or potato starch directly to a sauce. If you do, you will have lots of lumps and they will have to be strained out or smoothed in a blender or food processor, and the sauce will never thicken properly. Sauces can also be thickened by the addition of potato flakes or pureed vegetables.

Beurre Blanc & Beurre Rouge

These sauces, made with either white or red wine, are very popular with proponents of nouvelle cuisine because they are lighter than sauces thickened with egg yolks or flour, and can be made very quickly. Actually neither Beurre Blanc nor Beurre Rouge are new or modern sauces, as nouvelle cuisine chefs might have us believe. They are in fact old favorites of French housewives who have used them for many years. Chefs, interested in serving food with light sauces that can be made quickly, particularly with food that does not produce any sauce of its own during cooking, have adopted them and made them an important part of the nouvelle cuisine repertoire.

Beurre Blanc

Follow directions on pages 244-245. Use a good quality dry white wine and add additional seasoning to compliment the dish for which the sauce is made. Although the literal translation of Beurre Blanc is "white butter," the sauce will, in all likelihood, be yellow because our butter is yellow. Serve with poached fish, poultry with light meat, veal, pork and vegetables.

Beurre Rouge

Follow directions on pages 244-245 for Beurre Blanc. Substitute good quality dry red wine for white wine. Season as desired. Serve with beef, lamb, poultry with dark meat and game.

Tips:

● Serve immediately. Sauce made ahead of time will separate.
● Do not reheat sauce. Reheating will make sauce thin.
● Sauce should not be made in large quantities. About the most that can be made at one time is double the recipe on pages 244-245.
● If desired, substitute the white part of green onions for shallots.

Hot Butters: Full of Flavor

Hot melted butter, seasoned with fresh herbs and lemon juice, is a quick and easy way to sauce broiled meat, fish, poultry and vegetables. When the only thing required is hot seasoned butter, it usually is not necessary to clarify the butter. However, when nuts or other food are browned in butter, the butter will burn easily if it is not clarified. Clarified butter is also used as a dipping sauce for such foods as lobster and artichokes.

Clarified Butter

Melt 1/2 cup butter in a saucepan over medium heat. Remove from heat; let stand a few minutes to allow milk solids to settle on bottom of pan. Strain clear yellow liquid into a container, leaving milky residue in bottom of pan. Refrigerate until ready to use.
Makes 1/4 to 1/3 cup.

Variations
● Add finely chopped hard-cooked eggs, chopped walnuts or finely chopped anchovy fillets to clarified butter.
● To make Brown Butter, heat clarified butter over medium heat until golden brown.
● To make Black Butter, heat clarified butter over medium heat until dark brown. Stir 1-1/4 teaspoons lemon juice or vinegar into butter. Add chopped capers and freshly chopped parsley, if desired.

Tarragon Butter
Add 1 to 2 tablespoons freshly chopped tarragon to 1/3 cup melted or clarified butter. Serve over poached fish.

Herb & Wine Butter
Add 1 to 2 tablespoons freshly chopped herbs, such as parsley, chives, basil or thyme, and 2 tablespoons dry white wine to 1/3 cup melted or clarified butter. Stir until blended. Serve over broiled meat.

Hazelnut Butter
Sauté 2 to 3 tablespoons chopped hazelnuts in 1/3 cup clarified butter until golden brown. Serve over broccoli.

Bread-Crumb Butter
Brown about 5 tablespoons plain or seasoned dry bread crumbs in 1/3 cup melted, clarified or Brown Butter. Spoon over cauliflower.

Garlic Butter

Thinly slice 1 or 2 garlic cloves or press through a garlic press; add to 1/3 cup melted or clarified butter. Cook 1 minute to release garlic flavor. Serve over shrimp.

Simple Butter Sauce

Season hot melted butter with lemon juice, salt and pepper. Serve over asparagus.

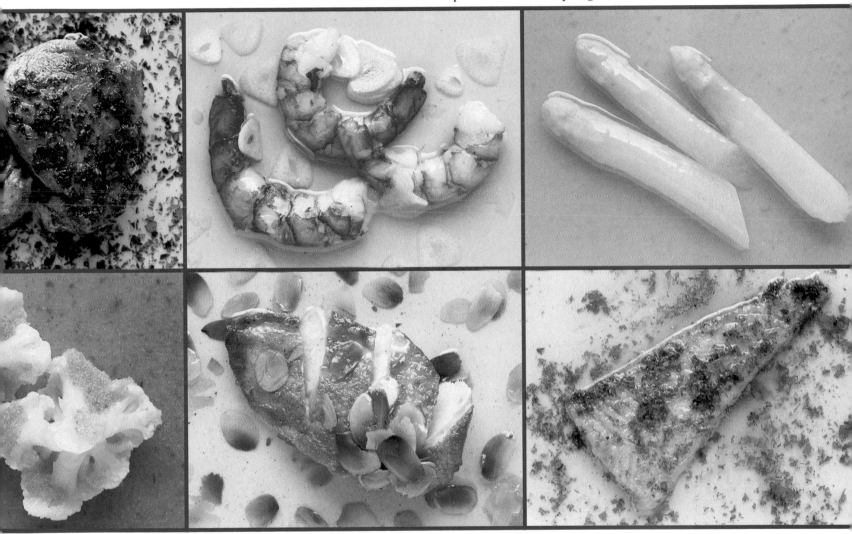

Almond Butter

Sauté 2 to 3 tablespoons sliced almonds in 1/3 cup clarified butter until almonds are golden brown. Serve over poultry.

Maitre d'Hotel Butter

Add 1 to 2 tablespoons freshly chopped parsley, 1 tablespoon lemon juice, salt and pepper to 1/3 cup melted, clarified or Brown Butter; stir until blended. Serve over broiled fish.

Hollandaise Sauce: Always Special

The thought of making Hollandaise Sauce can turn some cooks pale with terror. It's a shame this sauce has such a formidable reputation because it can be made without difficulty once the principles behind the methods are understood. The most important thing to remember is that directions must be followed carefully.

The classical method for Hollandaise is to heat egg yolks slowly and gently over simmering water; then add butter, a little at a time. Stir the sauce after each small addition of butter until the butter is completely melted to enable the egg yolks to absorb the fat. Contrary to rumor, this procedure doesn't take a great deal of talent, but it does take time and patience. Even that problem can be solved by making Hollandaise in a food processor or blender, an almost foolproof method. Place the egg yolks in a completely dry container of a blender or food processor and process briefly. With the motor running, slowly pour in melted butter until the sauce thickens. This is a quicker and easier method than the classical method, and the sauce is just as good when it is made this way. Hollandaise made in a blender or food processor is such a quick method, you can make it just before you are ready to serve it, and eliminate the biggest problem—how to keep the sauce warm without having it separate or curdle. Hollandaise is not supposed to be served hot, but it isn't supposed to be served cold either. If necessary, it can be kept warm for a short period of time over simmering water, but never over high heat. If you have to hold the sauce for a long period of time, and don't want it to curdle, add 1 or 2 tablespoons Béchamel Sauce to stabilize it.

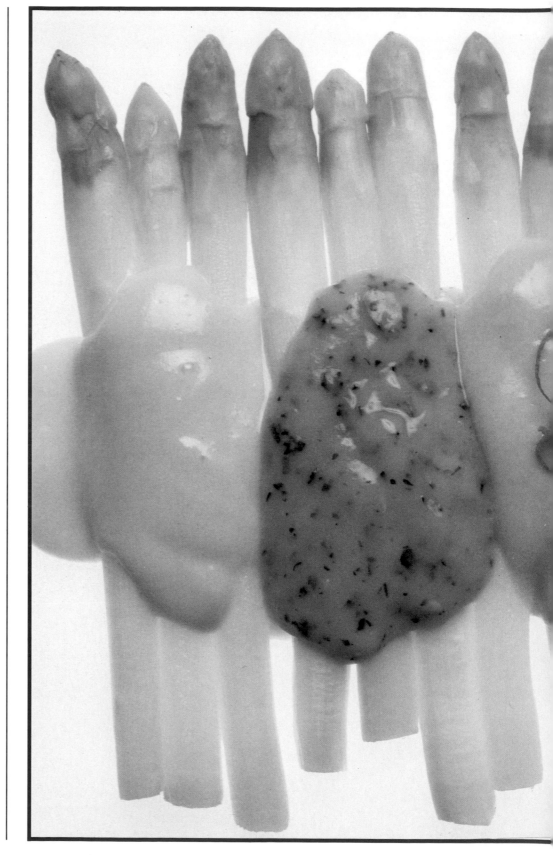

Hollandaise Sauce

Prepare Hollandaise Sauce according to step-by-step directions on pages 244-245.

Béarnaise Sauce—Blender or Food Processor Method

Place 2 tablespoons tarragon vinegar, 2 tablespoons dry white wine or dry vermouth, 2 teaspoons chopped shallots, 2 teaspoons finely chopped tarragon and 1 teaspoon finely chopped chervil in saucepan. Cook, uncovered, until reduced to about 2 tablespoons liquid. Set aside. Melt 1/2 cup butter; set aside. Place 3 egg yolks in a very dry container of a blender or food processor. Add salt and cayenne pepper to taste; process 30 seconds. With motor running, slowly pour in melted butter. Add reserved herb mixture; process 5 seconds. Makes about 1 cup.

Maltese Sauce

Prepare Hollandaise Sauce according to step-by-step directions on pages 244-245. After butter has been incorporated, add 2 to 3 tablespoons orange juice and 1 teaspoon grated orange peel, omitting lemon juice. Beat until throughly blended.

Mousseline Sauce

Prepare Hollandaise Sauce according to step-by-step directions on pages 244-245. Fold in 1/2 cup whipped cream just before serving.

Choron Sauce

Prepare Béarnaise Sauce following directions above. Beat 2 tablespoons tomato paste with 2 tablespoons warm whipping cream until blended. Add to sauce; beat until blended.

Tips:

● If the water in the double boiler is too hot, sauce will curdle.
● If butter is added quickly, sauce will curdle and will not thicken.
● If sauce separates, add 1 tablespoon cold water; beat vigorously with wire whisk.
● If sauce is too thick, beat in 1 to 2 tablespoons hot water or add a little lemon juice.
● Sauce can be kept warm over a pan of hot water for a limited time.

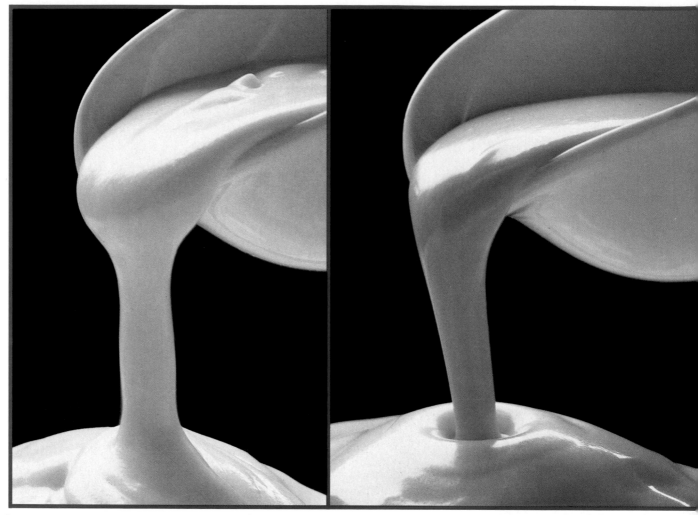

Béchamel Sauce: A Favorite

There really is no mystic to making a smooth creamy Béchamel Sauce. Slow careful combining of top quality ingredients is almost all that is required. Once the butter and flour have been combined and stirred to a smooth paste, if the liquid is added slowly, and the sauce is stirred constantly while the liquid is being added, there should be no problem. The easiest way to make this sauce is to add a small amount of cold liquid at a time and stir over low heat, until the sauce thickens. Then add a little more liquid and stir some more. The result should be smooth, creamy and, most important, lump free.

Mornay Sauce (Cheese Sauce)

Prepare Béchamel Sauce following step-by-step directions on pages 244-245. When sauce thickens, remove from heat. Add 1/2 cup grated Parmesan cheese; stir until cheese is melted. Season to taste with nutmeg, hot-pepper sauce and salt.

Variations
• Use 1/4 cup grated Parmesan cheese and 1/4 cup grated Swiss or Gruyère cheese.
• Use 1 cup grated extra-sharp cheddar cheese and paprika to taste. Serve with pasta or vegetables.

Mustard Sauce

Prepare Béchamel Sauce following step-by-step directions on pages 244-245. When sauce thickens, remove from heat and add 1 tablespoon Dijon-style mustard. Beat until blended.

Variation
• Combine 1 teaspoon dry mustard with 2 tablespoons all-purpose flour in step 2; add to melted butter. Cook as directed above. Serve with fish or eggs.

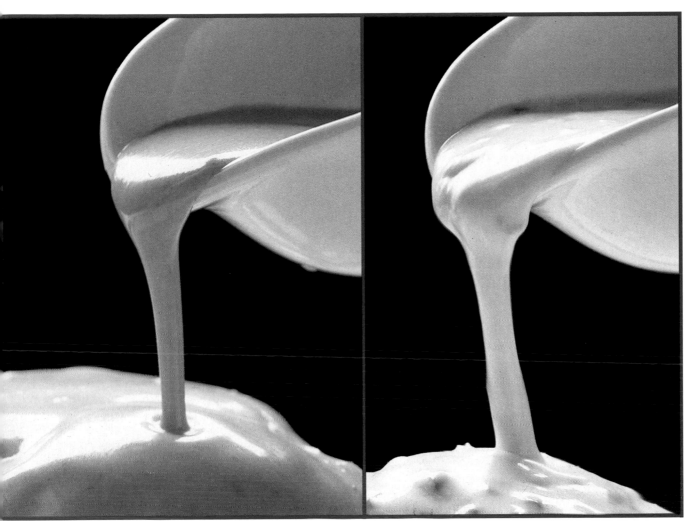

Curry Sauce

Prepare Béchamel Sauce
following step-by-step
directions on pages
244-245. Combine 1 to 2
tablespoons curry
powder with 2
tablespoons flour in step
2; add to melted butter.
Cook as directed above.
When sauce thickens,
remove from heat; add 2
tablespoons sweetened
applesauce. Stir until
blended. For variety,
add chopped fresh
ginger or chutney. Serve
with poultry, fish, rice
or eggs.

Chive Sauce

Prepare Béchamel Sauce
following step-by-step
directions on pages
244-245. When sauce
thickens, remove from
heat; add 2 tablespoons
snipped chives, 1
tablespoon lemon juice
and 1 tablespoon dairy
sour cream. Beat until
blended. Serve with
fish, meat or pasta.

Tips:
• To make Veloute Sauce, substitute
meat, fish or vegetable stock for milk or
cream.
• Sauce can be enriched and thickened
by the addition of egg yolk to make
Allemande Sauce. Use 1 beaten egg yolk
for each cup of sauce. Add 2 to 3 tablespoons hot sauce to egg yolk; stir until
blended. Return egg-yolk mixture to
sauce and cook, stirring constantly, 1
minute over low heat or until sauce
thickens.
• To prevent lumps, add liquid gradually, beating constantly.
• Béchamel Sauce can be made in advance, refrigerated and reheated gently
when ready to serve.

Cream Sauce Variations

If you want a sauce that is lighter than a Béchamel and can be made more quickly, Cream Sauce is the answer. The simple reduction of wine and cream provides a lovely sauce that can be seasoned in many ways. When wine is reduced, it loses its alcoholic content but the flavor of the wine is intensified. Therefore, it is important, as always, to use a good quality wine with a pleasing flavor.

Herb Cream Sauce

Prepare Cream Sauce following step-by-step directions on pages 244-245. Add 2 tablespoons freshly chopped herbs, such as parsley, chervil, basil, thyme or chives; season to taste. Serve with fish, pasta, poached eggs or poultry.

Tomato Cream Sauce

Prepare Cream Sauce following step-by-step directions on pages 244-245. Add 2 tablespoons tomato paste and 1 tablespoon brandy. Beat until blended. Stir in 1 to 2 teaspoons chopped basil, if desired. Serve with pasta, veal or pork.

Roquefort or Blue-Cheese Cream Sauce

Prepare Cream Sauce following step-by-step directions on pages 244-245. Add 1/2 cup crumbled Roquefort or Blue cheese; beat until cheese is melted. Serve with pasta or broiled meat.

Saffron Cream Sauce

Prepare Cream Sauce following step-by-step directions on pages 244-245. Add 1/2 teaspoon ground saffron or a generous pinch of saffron threads to white wine; reduce as directed in step 2. Serve with fish or rice.

Sorrel Cream Sauce

Cook 1 cup rinsed sorrel leaves until just wilted. Drain well; puree in a food processor or blender. Prepare Cream Sauce following step-by-step directions on pages 244-245. Add pureed sorrel leaves and 2 to 3 teaspoons lemon juice; beat until blended. Serve with eggs, shrimp or veal.

Variations

- Use 1 cup whipping cream and 1 cup dairy sour cream instead of 2 cups whipping cream for a slightly tart sauce.
- Add 1/2 cup whipped cream to sauce just before serving for a very light airy sauce.
- Substitute 1 cup dry vermouth for white wine.
- Substitute 1 cup orange juice for white wine.
- Stir in 2 tablespoons minced chanterelles, morels or other mushrooms.
- Stir in 2 tablespoons dry red wine.
- Stir in 2 to 3 tablespoons grated Gruyère, Swiss or Parmesan cheese.

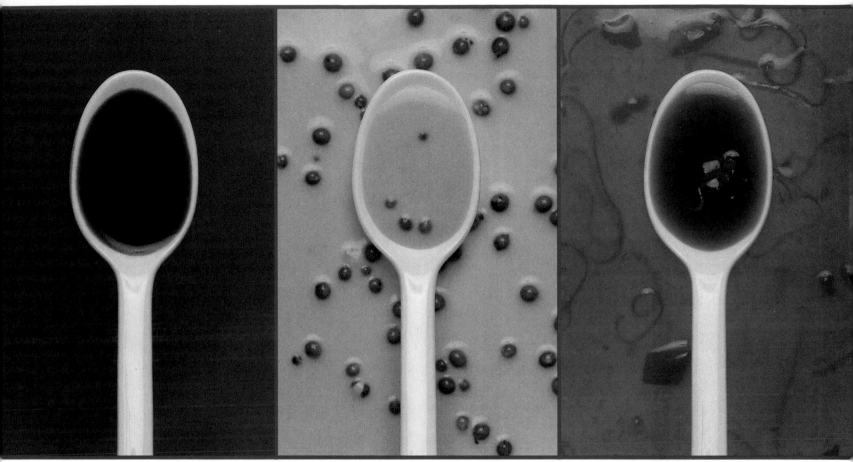

Perfect Gravy

The flavor of most meat or poultry is enhanced by gravy made from pan drippings. Gravy can be made by the reduction method, see Cream Gravy, pages 244-245, or it can be made in the same way a Béchamel Sauce is made, pages 244-245. It can also be made by using a beurre manie, page 153, as a thickener.

There are two major components to pan drippings—fat and meat juices. All of the meat juices can be used to make a flavorful gravy, but in most cases only a portion of the fat should be used.

The first step in making gravy is to pour off the fat and set it aside. When you make Cream Gravy, you can substitute fat for butter. If you make gravy as you would make Béchamel Sauce, substitute fat for butter using equal amounts of fat and flour so the flour can absorb all the fat. If too much fat is used, the gravy will be greasy and unpleasant to eat. Whichever way you make gravy, you can add interesting flavor by using some of the suggestions on the right.

Deglazing a Roasting Pan

Pan drippings usually contain bits of solidified drippings that should be scraped off the bottom of the roasting pan. They add wonderful flavor to gravy. The procedure for doing this is called *deglazing*. Drain fat from roasting pan; place pan on top of range over medium-high heat. Pour in 1/4 to 1/3 cup liquid, such as dry wine, dry vermouth, stock or water. Stir briskly with a wooden spoon, scraping bottom of pan to loosen browned particles. Add additional liquid, if necessary; stir until liquid has been incorporated into drippings.

To Thicken Gravy with Flour

Drain fat from roasting pan; deglaze pan drippings. Return 2 tablespoons fat or butter to roasting pan; stir into drippings. Add 2 tablespoons flour; stir to make a smooth paste. Cook over medium heat 1 to 2 minutes to eliminate the raw-flour taste. Slowly add 2 cups liquid, stirring constantly, until gravy begins to thicken. Adjust seasoning and add browning sauce, if desired.

Red-Wine Gravy

Use dry red wine instead of cream or milk. Serve with beef.

Green-Peppercorn Gravy

Add 1/4 cup Calvados to pan drippings. Stir 1 to 2 tablespoons green peppercorns into gravy just before serving. Serve with pork.

Orange Gravy

Use orange juice instead of cream or milk. Stir 1 tablespoon orange marmalade into gravy just before serving; cook until dissolved. Serve with poultry.

White-Wine Gravy

Use dry white wine instead of cream or milk. Stir 2 to 3 tablespoons dairy sour cream into gravy just before serving. Serve with veal.

Cranberry Gravy

Use chicken stock instead of cream or milk. Stir 1/4 cup port and 1/3 cup whole berry cranberry sauce into gravy just before serving. Cook until cranberry sauce is dissolved. Serve with poultry or game.

Sherry & Mint Gravy

Use chicken stock instead of cream or milk. Add 1/2 cup dry sherry, 1 minced garlic clove, 1 tablespoon chopped mint and 1 small tomato, peeled, seeded and diced. Serve with lamb.

Pointers for Making Gravy

● Liquid added to gravy can be dry red or white wine, dry vermouth, stock or broth, milk, cream, water or a combination of liquids, such as 1-1/2 cups stock and 1/2 cup dry wine.

● If you want to make gravy a dark rich color, add about 1 teaspoon browning sauce; stir. If color is not dark enough, add a little more.

● Don't add any seasoning to gravy without tasting it first. Seasoning that has been sprinkled on a roast will flavor pan drippings and will intensify with cooking. If you add salt without tasting first, for example, you may make the gravy too salty.

● Leftover gravy can be stored in the refrigerator and reheated. If reheated gravy is too thick, add additional liquid.

Desserts: Endings with Finesse

With guests sitting around the table feeling well-fed and content, the time is right to present the grand finale—dessert. Dessert should be the perfect conclusion to a meal, a dish that compliments the food that has come before and appeal to three senses—sight, smell and taste. A light, sweet dessert after a heavy meal is ideal. It can be served simply, with just a touch of decoration, or it can be a molded, elegantly decorated, work of art. Serve dessert with freshly brewed coffee or tea, and relax with your guests. Your work is finished and nothing remains to be done except ... Oh, well, perhaps when you return to the kitchen, the dishes will have miraculously vanished.

5 Special Desserts

To think of dessert is, more often than not, to think in terms of cakes and pastries. But for those who do not want to bake, but want to make their own desserts, there are many other options. Fresh fruit can be served in many ways, sorbets are easy to make, and mousses and creams are not nearly as difficult to make as many think. Excellent ice cream or cookies can be bought to go with a special dessert you have made. Providing the perfect conclusion to a family or company meal can be a delightful and rewarding challenge.

Hints for Handling Gelatin

One envelope of unflavored gelatin is equal to 1 tablespoon. It will set 2 cups of liquid. Gelatin must be softened in a small amount of cold water about 10 minutes, then dissolved in hot liquid before it is combined with other ingredients. It can be dissolved over direct heat or by the addition of hot liquid. Some fresh or frozen fruits and their juices have enzymes that will prevent gelatin from setting, although they are safe to use in canned form. Don't use fresh or frozen pineapple, figs, mangoes or papayas in a gelatin mold.

Hints for Handling Chocolate

Coarsely chop chocolate, then melt it in a heavy saucepan over very low heat or in the top of a double boiler. Don't cover chocolate that is being melted because moisture will collect under the cover and drop onto the chocolate. This will cause the chocolate to stiffen. Remove chocolate from the heat as soon as it is melted. Overcooking will cause chocolate to burn which will give it an unpleasant bitter taste. There is nothing you can do with burned chocolate except throw it away!

Fruit Compote

1 lb. apricots, other fruit or combination of fruits
1/2 cup sweet white wine
1/2 cup water
1 (3-inch) cinnamon stick
3 to 4 tablespoons sugar

1. Plunge apricots into boiling water 2 to 3 minutes to blanch.

2. Remove with a slotted spoon; cool. Peel with a small knife.

Fruit Puree

1 pint strawberries or other fruit, about 3/4 lb.
1 to 2 tablespoons powdered sugar

1. Wash and hull strawberries.

2. Place in a strainer set over a bowl; press through strainer with a spoon.

Sorbet

8 to 10 oranges or 4 cups fruit juice
About 1/2 cup sifted powdered sugar

1. Cut oranges in half; squeeze to make 4 cups juice.

2. Stir in sugar until dissolved. Freeze 3 hours, stirring 3 times during freezing.

Chocolate Mousse

6 oz. semisweet chocolate
3 eggs
2 to 3 tablespoons liqueur or dark rum
2 cups whipping cream

1. Coarsely chop chocolate; melt in top of a double boiler.

2. Beat eggs over hot water until frothy; beat in liqueur.

Bavarian Cream

1 vanilla bean, split
2 cups milk
4 egg yolks
3/4 cup sugar
1-1/2 envelopes unflavored gelatin, softened in 1/4 cup cold water
2 cups whipping cream

1. Place vanilla bean in saucepan; add milk. Cook until bubbles form around edge; set aside.

2. Beat egg yolks and sugar in a large bowl until blended. Remove vanilla bean from milk.

3. Cut apricots in half; remove pits.

4. Place apricots in a saucepan; add wine, water and cinnamon.

5. Sprinkle sugar over apricots. Bring to a boil over medium heat.

6. Simmer, uncovered, about 5 minutes or until tender.

3. Sift powdered sugar over mashed berries.

4. Stir thoroughly. Taste and adjust seasoning.

3. If solidly frozen, break up mixture with a flat-bladed knife.

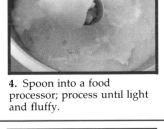

4. Spoon into a food processor; process until light and fluffy.

3. Remove bowl from water; stir in melted chocolate until thoroughly combined.

4. Beat cream in a separate bowl until stiff peaks form.

5. Stir one-third whipped cream into mixture; fold in remaining cream.

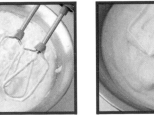

3. Gradually add hot milk to egg-yolk mixture, beating constantly. Add softened gelatin; heat until dissolved.

4. Cool and refrigerate until almost set. Beat cream until stiff peaks form.

5. Fold whipped cream into chilled mixture. Refrigerate 3 to 4 hours or until firm.

Apricot Compote

Cook according to step-by-step directions, pages 262-263. Add 1 to 2 teaspoons apricot jam, if desired.

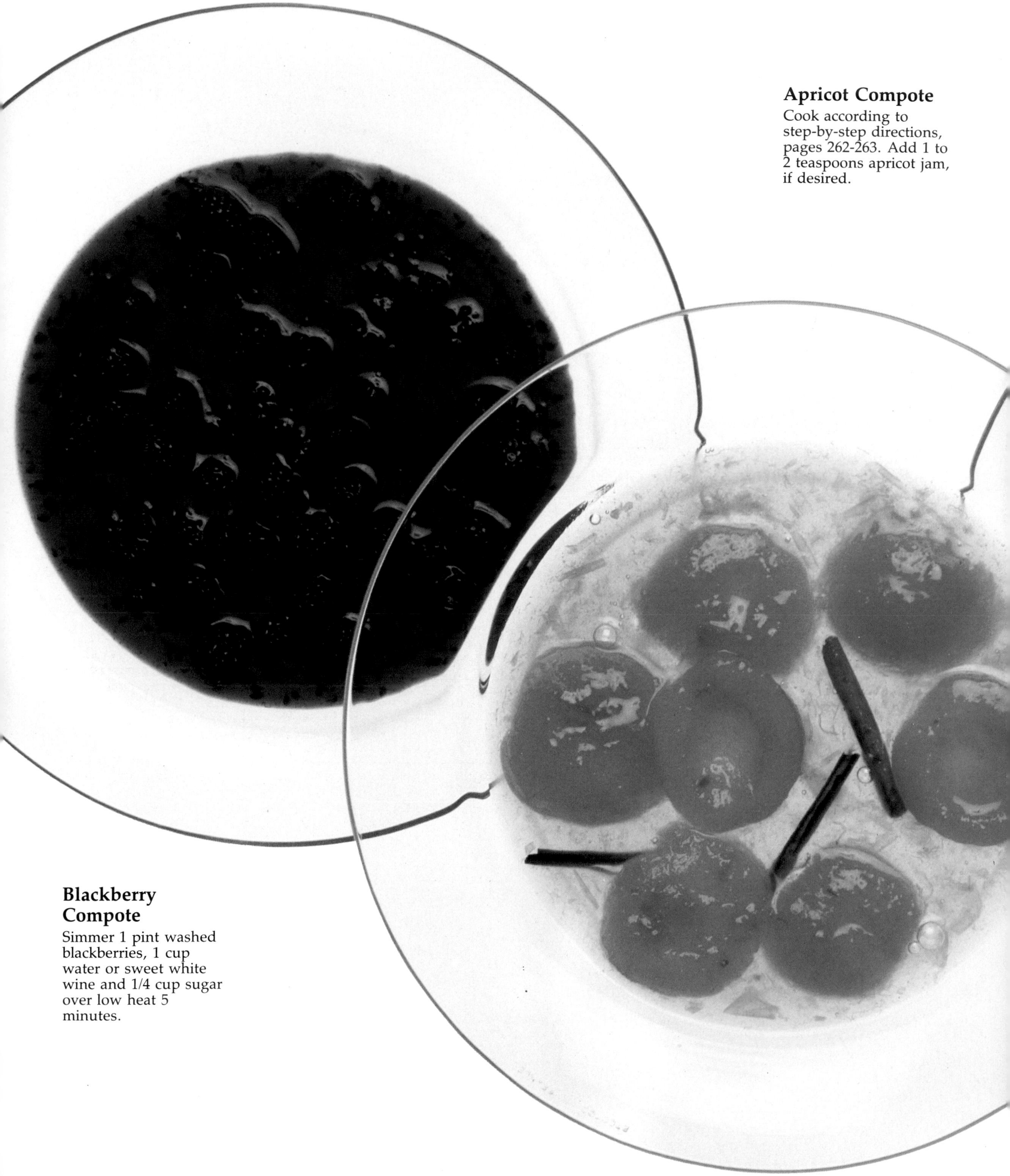

Blackberry Compote

Simmer 1 pint washed blackberries, 1 cup water or sweet white wine and 1/4 cup sugar over low heat 5 minutes.

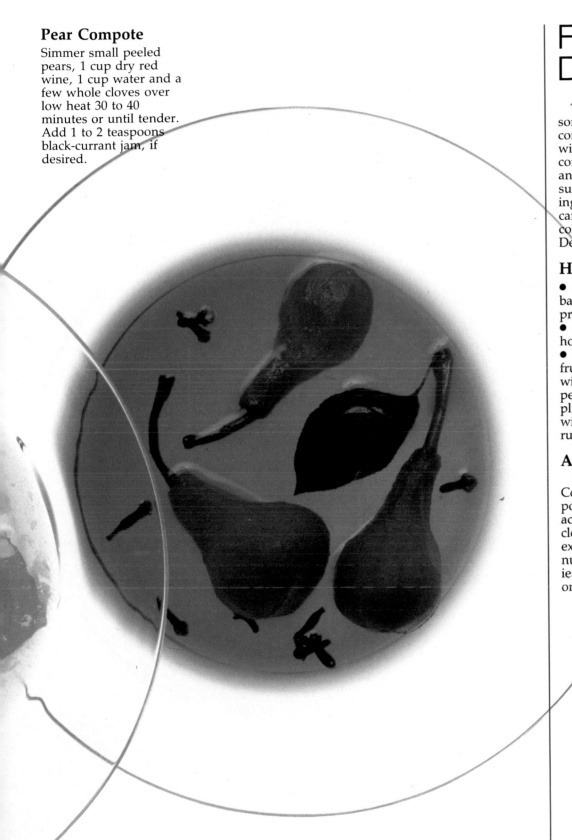

Pear Compote

Simmer small peeled pears, 1 cup dry red wine, 1 cup water and a few whole cloves over low heat 30 to 40 minutes or until tender. Add 1 to 2 teaspoons black-currant jam, if desired.

Fruit Desserts

Take advantage of fresh fruit in season or use dried fruit to make delicious compotes. You can make a compote with just one kind of fruit or with a combination of different fruits. Almost any fruit can be used. Simmer gently in sugar and water with additional flavoring, as desired. Fruit should be cooked carefully so it will retain its shape. Serve cold or heat gently before serving. Decorate with fresh mint sprigs.

Hints for Making Compotes

● Sprinkle peeled apples, peaches, bananas and pears with lemon juice to prevent them from browning.
● Soak dried fruit in warm water 2 to 3 hours before cooking.
● Create interesting combinations of fruit and liqueur, such as purple plums with Armagnac, apples with Calvados, pears with pear liqueur, yellow or green plums with apricot brandy, peaches with Cointreau, or raisins with dark rum.

Adding Flavor to Compotes

See Fruit Compote, pages 262-263. Cook fruit in red or white sweet wine, port, sweet sherry, fruit juice or water according to taste. Add cinnamon, cloves, ground ginger or citrus peel for extra flavor. Sprinkle with flaked coconut or serve with ice cream, cake, cookies, Bavarian Cream, dairy sour cream or yogurt.

Colorful Fruit Purees

If you want to maintain the full flavor of the fruit, don't add additional liquid to the puree. Use fruit purees to add color and flavor to desserts or use as a sauce. Swirl 2 or 3 different fruit purees together and serve over ice cream or frozen yogurt. Use fruit purees as a base on which to build other dishes.

Basic Rules

Strain fruit into a bowl through a fine mesh sieve to remove seeds and fiber; this makes a very smooth puree. You can also puree fruit in a food processor or blender; then strain pureed mixture to remove seeds. Remember to scrape fruit off bottom of strainer.

Fruit Soup

See Fruit Puree, pages 262-263, and Fruit Soup, page 155.

It is easy to turn a fruit puree into a fruit soup by adding milk, yogurt, fruit juice, sweet or dry wine, whipping cream or dairy sour cream. Decorate fruit soup with mint sprigs or lemon balm.

Garnishes for Fruit Purees

- Mint sprigs
- Finely chopped or coarsely ground nuts
- Sweetened whipped cream
- Dairy sour cream
- Plain yogurt
- Crushed cookie crumbs
- Crushed candy

Serving Ideas for Fruit Purees

(top right)
Chocolate mousse on kiwi puree, decorated with fresh raspberries and shaved chocolate.

(center right)
Vanilla ice cream on apricot puree, sprinkled with crushed praline.

(lower right)
Sliced kiwi and strawberries on blackberry puree, decorated with mint leaves.

(right)
Medley of fruit purees, including raspberry, strawberry, mango and kiwi.

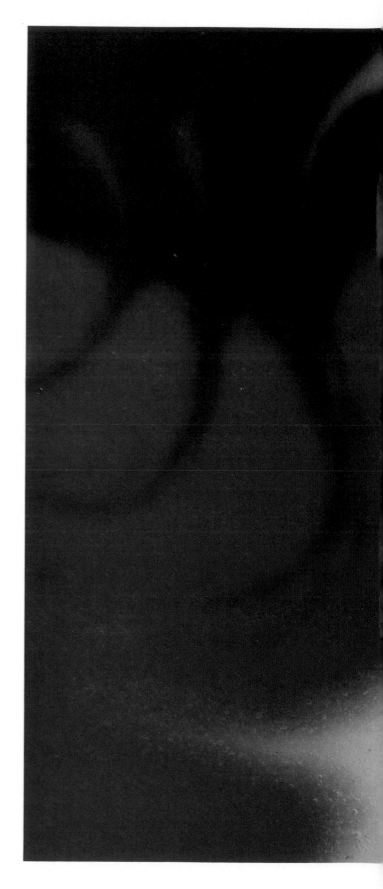

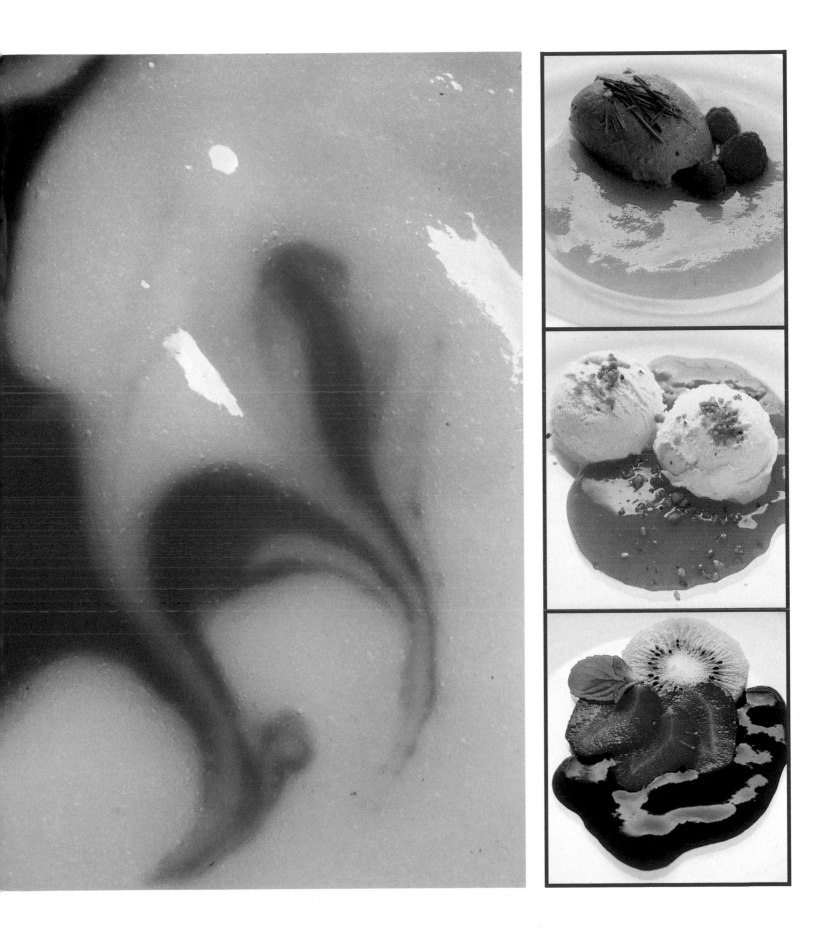

Sorbets— Sherbets with Elegance

Sorbet is the French name for sherbet, long popular as a cooling sweet made from fruit juice, liqueur or wine. Many fine restaurants have adopted the lovely and elegant European custom of serving a small portion of sorbet before the main course to *clear the palate*. Although sorbet served in this way can be made with lemons, oranges or limes, it is more likely to have been made with champagne, wine or a liqueur. Sorbets are so versatile, they can be served as a first course, between courses or as dessert. They are easy to make, and they are cool, light and satisfying to eat.

Basic Rules for Making Sorbets

Freeze sweetened or unsweetened fruit juice or fruit puree about 3 hours. One pound of fruit or 2 cups of fruit juice will make enough sorbet to serve 4 people. Basic recipe and step-by-step photos are on pages 262-263. A well-made sorbet will have a soft, smooth consistency.

Adding Flavor to Sorbets

You can add champagne, sparkling red or white wine or liqueur to a fruit puree before freezing to create an interestingly flavored sorbet. Use about 1 cup alcohol to 1 pound of fruit or 2 cups of fruit juice. Don't add too much alcohol to fruit because it will mask the fruit flavor.

More About Sorbets

Sorbet is a French word, but the origin of the word *sherbet* is Arabic. Originally it meant an iced drink made with fruit juice. The French turned this drink into a water ice, different from ice cream because it is not made with milk or cream. Early sorbets were made with either fruit or vegetable concentrates and usually flavored with alcohol. Ultimately the inventive French developed ways to make sorbet without fruit or vegetables, just with alcohol. Sorbets should not be frozen hard, but instead should be the consistency of snow that melts slowly. If sorbet is too hard, it can be crushed and served as *granita*.

Lime Sorbet

Sweeten lime juice with sugar to taste. Add 2 to 3 tablespoons Midori or melon-flavored liqueur to enhance color and flavor. Freeze, then decorate with mint leaves.

Strawberry Sorbet

Puree 1 pint strawberries, about 1/2 cup sifted powdered sugar and 1 cup sparkling white wine. Or add 2 to 3 tablespoons Grand Marnier instead of wine to pureed strawberries. Freeze, then decorate with strawberry leaves.

Apricot Sorbet

Puree 1 pound apricots, about 1/2 cup sifted powdered sugar and 1 cup champagne or sparkling white wine. Freeze, then decorate with lemon-balm leaves.

Red-Currant Sorbet

Puree 1 pint red currants, about 3/4 cup sifted powdered sugar and 1 cup champagne or sparkling white wine. Freeze, then serve in tall frosted glasses decorated with whole red currants.

Tips:

• Use fresh, ripe, unblemished fruit.
• Stir sorbet 2 or 3 times during freezing to break up ice crystals and insure a smooth sorbet.
• Serve sorbet in small hollowed-out orange or lemon baskets. Place baskets in freezer 1 hour before serving to be sure temperature of baskets does not cause sorbet to melt.

Coffee Granita

Sweeten strong black coffee with powdered sugar to taste. Pour into an ice-cube tray; freeze 2 to 3 hours or until solid. Scrape into fine shavings with a grapefruit spoon. Granita can also be made with tea or fruit juice.

The Crème de la Crème

Despite its name, Bavarian Crème is not from Bavaria. It is a French invention, similar to a cold soufflé, made with a custard base, gelatin, flavoring and whipped cream. Sometimes beaten egg whites are folded into the cream mixture to add additional lightness. Bavarian Creams can be served as molds or in individual dessert dishes. When they are spooned into a mold that has been rinsed in cold water, they should be refrigerated about 12 hours, then unmolded onto a serving plate. They can also be spooned into a bowl, refrigerated about 4 hours and then spooned into individual dessert dishes. If desired, Bavarian Creams can also be spooned directly into dessert dishes and refrigerated about 4 hours. Which ever way Bavarian Creams are presented, they can be decorated before serving.

Blueberry Bavarian

(below left)
Prepare Bavarian Cream according to directions on pages 262-263 using 1 cup milk and 1 cup blueberry puree; fold in whipped cream. Refrigerate 4 hours or until ready to serve. Spoon into dessert dishes. Decorate with whole blueberries and lemon-balm leaves.

Mocha Bavarian

(below center)
Melt 6 ounces semisweet chocolate. Prepare Bavarian Cream according to directions on pages 262-263, using 1 cup milk and 1 cup strong black coffee. Stir melted chocolate into custard mixture; fold in whipped cream. Refrigerate 4 hours or until ready to serve. Spoon into dessert dishes. Decorate with shaved chocolate.

Pistachio Bavarian

(opposite right)
Prepare Bavarian Cream according to directions on pages 262-263. Add 1 teaspoon almond extract, 3/4 cup ground pistachios and a few drops of green food coloring, if desired, to custard mixture; fold in whipped cream. Refrigerate 4 hours or until ready to serve. Spoon into dessert dishes. Decorate with whipped cream, thin strips of orange peel, maraschino cherries, chopped pistachios and cookies.

Raspberry Bavarian

(below left)
Prepare Bavarian Cream according to directions on pages 262-263, using 1 cup milk and 1 cup raspberry puree. Add a few drops of red food coloring, if desired. Fold 2 tablespoons Chambrod or black-raspberry-flavored liqueur into custard mixture; fold in whipped cream. Refrigerate 4 hours or until ready to serve. Spoon into dessert dishes. Decorate with raspberry puree and whole raspberries.

Mango Bavarian

(below right)
Prepare Bavarian Cream according to directions on pages 262-263, using 1 cup milk and 1 cup mango puree; fold in whipped cream. Refrigerate 4 hours or until ready to serve. Spoon into dessert dishes. Decorate with mango slices and crushed praline.

Adding Other Flavors to Bavarian Cream

Prepare Bavarian Cream according to directions on pages 262-263. Add 1/2 to 1 cup chopped hazelnuts, almonds, walnuts or candied fruit, or 2 to 3 tablespoons liqueur to custard mixture before folding in whipped cream. Decorate with fresh fruit, whipped cream, flaked coconut or chopped nuts.

30 Ways to Decorate Desserts

Eye appeal is always important to the presentation of food, and never more so than for dessert. There are many ways to give dessert a festive air—fresh fruit, nuts, whipped cream, chocolate, candies, bright green leaves and even fresh flowers can all be used. However, if you decorate any food with fresh flowers, be sure the flowers are not poisonous. Several species of flowers, particularly those grown from bulbs, are poisonous and should never be used to decorate food. Use some of the suggestions on the right to dress up anything from a simple chocolate pudding to an elegantly molded Bavarian Cream.

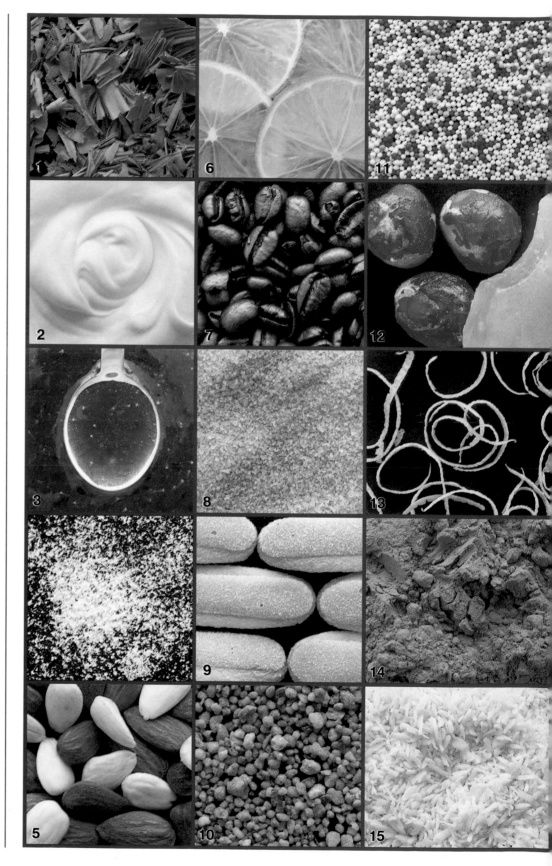

1. Shaved or grated chocolate
2. Flavored and sweetened whipped cream
3. Strawberry or raspberry jam
4. Sifted powdered sugar
5. Whole almonds, blanched or unblanched
6. Thin lime slices
7. Candied coffee beans
8. Crystalized light brown sugar or raw sugar
9. Lady fingers
10. Crushed praline
11. Multi-colored sprinkles
12. Candied cherries and pineapple
13. Julienne strips of lemon or orange peel
14. Cocoa powder
15. Flaked or shredded coconut
16. Small almond macaroons
17. Slivered almonds
18. Walnut halves
19. Sliced almonds
20. Strawberry slices
21. Chocolate sprinkles
22. Candy flower petals
23. Thin chocolate after-dinner mints
24. Pistachios, whole or ground
25. Crystal sugar, crushed sugar cubes or pearl sugar
26. Lemon balm, mint or spearmint leaves
27. Candied or stem ginger
28. Small rosettes of whipped cream or meringue
29. Dark brown sugar
30. Whole pitted dates

Tirami Su

1/4 cup coffee-flavored liqueur
1/4 cup strong black coffee
15 lady fingers or Champagne Egg Biscuits
5 egg yolks
2 to 3 tablespoons dark rum
1 cup granulated sugar
1 lb. mascarpone cheese
3/4 cup whipping cream
4 egg whites
6 to 8 tablespoons super fine sugar

1. Line an 11'' x 7'' pan with foil, extending foil at least 2 inches above rim of pan all around; set aside.
2. Combine liqueur and black coffee in a small bowl. Sprinkle over lady fingers; set aside.
3. Beat egg yolks and rum in a large bowl until thickened. Gradually add granulated sugar; beat until mixture is lemon-colored and fluffy. Add mascarpone cheese; beat until blended.
4. Beat cream in a separate bowl until stiff. Fold whipped cream into cheese mixture.
5. Pour half the cheese mixture into foil-lined pan; smooth the top. Arrange lady fingers in a single layer on top of cheese mixture, cutting last row of lady fingers to fit. Pour remaining cheese mixture over lady fingers; smooth top.
6. Place in freezer 3 to 4 hours or until firm. Invert pan onto a serving dish. Remove pan; peel off foil.
7. Beat egg whites in a bowl until soft peaks form. Add super fine sugar, 2 tablespoons at a time, beating well after each addition. Continue beating until meringue stands in stiff peaks. Spread meringue over top and sides of Tirami Su. Serve semi-frozen. Makes 12 to 16 servings.

Crème Caramel

Sugar
3 whole eggs
3 egg yolks
2-1/2 cups milk
1-1/2 teaspoons vanilla extract

1. Butter 6 (6-ounce) custard cups; place in a shallow baking pan. Preheat oven to 325F (170C).
2. Heat 1/2 cup sugar in a small skillet until syrupy and light brown in color. Pour syrup evenly into prepared custard cups.
3. Beat eggs, egg yolks and 1/3 cup sugar in a large bowl until thick and lemon-colored. Gradually add milk and vanilla; beat until blended.
4. Pour egg mixture into custard cups. Pour enough hot water into baking pan to come halfway up sides of custard cups. Bake 50 to 60 minutes or until the tip of a knife inserted in center of custard comes out clean.
5. Remove from pan; cool completely on a wire rack. Refrigerate until ready to serve. Invert custards onto individual serving dishes, letting syrup run down sides of custard. Makes 6 servings.

Berry Compote

2 lbs. mixed berries, such as raspberries, blackberries, red currants, cherries, strawberries, blueberries or cranberries
1-1/4 cups orange juice
About 1 cup sugar
2 tablespoons quick-cooking tapioca
Powdered sugar
Half and half

1. Rinse and pit fruit, if necessary.
2. Place fruit, orange juice and sugar in a medium saucepan; bring to a boil over medium heat. Reduce heat and simmer 3 to 5 minutes.
3. Drain fruit in strainer set over bowl. Set fruit aside. Pour juice into saucepan and bring to a boil. Stir in tapioca. Reduce heat and simmer 6 to 8 minutes, stirring occasionally.
4. Add reserved fruit to tapioca; let stand 20 minutes.
5. Pour into a serving bowl. Sprinkle with sifted powdered sugar. Let cool. Serve with half and half.
Makes 6 servings.

English Trifle

1 (8-inch) round sponge
   cake
1/3 cup raspberry jam
1/3 cup sliced almonds
3 tablespoons brandy
1/3 cup cream sherry or
   Marsala
1 pint raspberries
2 cups whipping cream
2 tablespoons powdered
   sugar
1 teaspoon vanilla
   extract

1. Split cake into 2
layers. Spread jam over
1 layer. Cut remaining
layer into strips. Line
bottom of a glass
serving bowl or soufflé
dish with cake strips.
2. Cut jam covered
layer into small cubes;
arrange over cake strips.
Scatter almonds over
top; sprinkle with
brandy and sherry.
3. Set 12 to 14
raspberries aside for
decoration. Scatter
remaining raspberries
over cake.
4. Beat cream in a
medium bowl until soft
peaks form. Add
powdered sugar; beat
until stiff peaks form.
5. Spoon 1 cup
whipped cream into
pastry bag fitted with an
open-star tip; set aside.
Spread remaining
whipped cream over
raspberries.
6. Pipe reserved
whipped cream
decoratively on top of
trifle. Decorate with
reserved raspberries.
Refrigerate until ready
to serve.
Makes 6 to 8 servings.

Cranberry Ice Cream

2 cups cranberries
1-1/2 cups sugar
3 eggs, separated
2 cups whipping cream

1. Place cranberries and
1/2 cup sugar in a
medium saucepan.
Bring to a boil over
medium heat. Skim
surface to remove any
foam. Reduce heat and
simmer 3 to 5 minutes
or until skins begin to
pop. Remove from heat;
set aside to cool
completely.
2. Beat egg yolks in a
large bowl until thick
and lemon-colored. Beat
in remaining 1 cup
sugar and cream until
thickened. Stir
two-thirds of cooled
cranberries into egg-yolk
mixture until blended.
3. Beat egg whites in a
separate bowl until stiff
peaks form. Fold beaten
egg whites into
cranberry mixture.
4. Pour mixture into a
foil-lined 9″ x 5″ loaf
pan. Cover and freeze 4
to 6 hours or until firm.
5. To serve, invert ice
cream onto serving
plate; peel off foil. Slice
and serve with
remaining cranberries
spooned over each slice.
Makes 8 to 10 servings.

Zabaglione

4 egg yolks
1/4 cup sugar
1/2 cup Marsala wine
Cocoa powder

1. Beat egg yolks in top
of a double boiler until
thick and pale yellow in
color.
2. Gradually add sugar;
beat until sugar is
thoroughly blended in.
3. Place top of double
boiler over, not in,
simmering water.
Slowly add wine,
beating with a wire
whisk 5 to 7 minutes or
until mixture is thick
and foamy. Mixture
should triple in volume.
4. Remove top of
double boiler from heat.
Beat 2 to 3 minutes.
Mixture should be
barely warm.
5. Spoon into individual
serving dishes. Sprinkle
with sifted cocoa
powder. Serve
immediately.
Makes 4 servings.

INDEX